QUICK SPRINGS OF SENSE

For

Lodwick Hartley

—scholar and gentleman—
who for more than forty years
as teacher and administrator
has promoted the cause of the humanities

QUICK SPRINGS OF SENSE

Studies in the Eighteenth Century

Edited by Larry S. Champion

"To ask, to guess, to know . . .
As Fancy opens the quick springs of sense."
    —*The New Dunciad*, IV, 155–156

University of Georgia Press, Athens

Library of Congress Catalog Card Number: 72–86783
International Standard Book Number: 0–8203–0313–5

The University of Georgia Press, Athens 30602

Printed in the United States of America

Contents

Preface

THIS volume brings together original essays by eighteenth-century scholars, American and European. The scope of the collection is intentionally broad both in topic and in method of analysis. The result, in turn, is a group of essays ranging in material from the principle of unity in *The Dunciad* to the education of the man of feeling who, in Smollett's *Ferdinand Count Fathom*, is forced to realize that the world is a place of fraud and deceit calculated to destroy virtuous men; from Cambridge University's difficulties in obtaining copies of new books, as stipulated by the Licensing Act during Queen Anne's reign, to sentimentalism in the drama; from periodical rivalry in the wake of Addison's and Steele's success to the complexities of Defoe's pamphlets. Swift is the subject of two essays, one tracing the divergent trends of interpretation of *Gulliver's Travels* and the other concerned with placing Swift's scatological poems in proper perspective. So also is Sterne treated in two pieces, one biographical in nature and the other focusing on the function of time in *Tristram Shandy*.

The volume is admittedly weighted toward the fiction of the period. Ironic, indeed, is the observation by the present under-librarian of Cambridge that, by 1740, "the library's authorities seem to have decided that there was no future for the English novel. They did not keep, or did not claim, as far as I can discover, any registered novel published during the next forty years except *Sir Charles Grandison*." So acclaimed are these novels today that one essay emphasizes the need to maintain a balanced perspective in evaluating them as art, while others are concerned with such matters as unity, style, authorial voice, and theme.

The essays, in short, provide perceptive insights into a wide variety of the literary activities and interests of eighteenth-century England. They provide also an opportunity for an acknowledgment in which all concerned with this project take a great pleasure—a dedication to Lodwick Hartley, a friend and colleague whose contributions to eighteenth-century scholarship, especially in Sterne and Cowper, are significant and varied.

Abbreviations

ECS	*Eighteenth-Century Studies*
ELH	*ELH: A Journal of English Literary History*
ELN	*English Language Notes*
JEGP	*Journal of English and Germanic Philology*
JHI	*Journal of the History of Ideas*
MLN	*Modern Language Notes*
MLQ	*Modern Language Quarterly*
MP	*Modern Philology*
N&Q	*Notes & Queries*
PMASAL	*Papers of the Michigan Academy of Science, Arts, and Letters*
PMLA	*PMLA: Publications of the Modern Language Association*
PQ	*Philological Quarterly*
REL	*Review of English Literature*
SEL	*Studies in English Literature*
SP	*Studies in Philology*
TLS	*Times Literary Supplement*
TSL	*Tennessee Studies in Literature*
UTQ	*University of Toronto Quarterly*

THE SHORTEST WAY
Characteristic Defoe Fiction

Benjamin Boyce

> 'Tis a little Mysterious, Sir, that the Church Men are
> affronted because 'twas Writ against them, and the
> Dissenters are affronted because 'tis Wrote against
> them too. I don't well understand it, one sort must be
> Fools, that's certain.
>
> *A Dialogue between a Dissenter and
> The Observator*, 1703

ONE of the best-known episodes in the life of Daniel Defoe,
and indeed in early eighteenth-century political history, resulted
from the publication in December 1702 of his pamphlet *The
Shortest Way with the Dissenters*. The traditional view has been
that the pamphlet failed because it was a "too faithful copy"[1]
of current High Church effusions, an "astute and skillful imitation"[2] of the High Fliers, written with "perfectly controlled
irony"[3] but without enough exaggeration to make it
immediately recognizable as satire. This view has been modified
by John Robert Moore, who has sketched the complexity
of the political background,[4] and by Maximillian E. Novak,
who has found in the pamphlet an "extraordinarily clever"
but complex rhetoric.[5] My purpose is to carry the discussion
a little farther in order to show that *The Shortest Way* was not
in all respects clever as an ironic satire and that the figure im-
personated was not quite the sort of High Churchman readers
of either party would be likely to expect. Defoe's High
Churchman, like many other of the fictional characters he
created, is not a consistent, entirely familiar type, nor need we
accuse the Dissenters of obtuseness in being puzzled and alarmed
by *The Shortest Way*.

Why the High Church partisans should have taken the
pamphlet as the work of one of their own group is easy to see.[6]
Its argument from past history, running back as far as the reign
of injudicious James I, makes much of the "clemency" of the

I

Stuart monarchs and the horrors of the Puritan revolt—mistreatment of the clergy, appropriation of Church property, outrageous taxing of the gentry, and bloody regicide. The alleged cruelty of the Scots to their Episcopal clergymen is excitedly reviewed and the Rye-House plot recalled. The Declarations of Indulgence of James II receive praise; the nation's abandonment in 1688 of God's anointed ruler and the coolness of the "Dutch Monarch" William to High Church hopes are lamented. The enmity of France is spoken of as unnecessary, something created only by the Dissenters. True history and distorted history are interwoven: one reads that after 1660 the bloody doings of the Puritan period were treated with "Lenity and Mercy, except the barbarous Regicides of the Pretended Court of Justice; not a Soul suffer'd" otherwise; and Charles cherished and employed those nonconformists. But the author neglects to mention the Clarendon Code, the exclusion of some two thousand clergymen who would not accept the full scheme of reestablished Episcopacy, and the excesses of the Bloody Assizes of 1685.

The weaving together of true history and false history leads to alarmist references to the allegedly large number of Dissenters and the danger of their repeating what happened in 1642–1660; it leads also to a declaration that it is the Queen's duty to cease toleration of a party that threatens the existence of true religion. A rather long attack upon the dangerous allowance of Occasional Conformity is followed by an open cry (a culmination of previous broad hints) for rooting out and destroying the Dissenters.

Not only would these arguments seem in themselves meaningful and persuasive to any High Church zealot. They also had the advantage of familiarity from previous utterance in the sermons, spoken and printed, of Henry Sacheverell and Philip Stubbs, the publications of the non-juror Charles Leslie, and others of their sort. As Mr. Novak notices in reviewing these latter works,[7] Defoe picks up ideas from them for various parts of his own strategy—the biased resort to history, the bitter chiding and sarcasm, references to the number and wealth of the Dissenters, the strong demand to close up the Church in strict union, the biblical allusions that seem to justify treating Dissent as Moses did the Amalakites and that make the Dissenters seem like worshipers of Baal. These features of Defoe's piece would win High Church readers to some degree of sympathetic response and to accepting the piece as seriously intended.

Likewise there are cogent reasons for the alarm of Dissenting readers and their supposition that the attitude in the pamphlet was genuine. It was now six months since the newly crowned Queen had made her unfortunate declaration to Parliament of her allegiance to "the interests and religion of the Church of England," and during that time the High Church and High Tory partisans had been using every opportunity to try to regain control of the government and the Church. People of mature years in 1702 were too close to past violences caused by religious and political opinion to doubt that such things could happen again, and extremist writers sometimes hinted and sometimes plainly stated that Dissenters constituted a destructive influence in religion and society and should be subjugated and severely controlled if indeed they could not be totally eradicated. What Defoe's High Church speaker does (if we may believe what Defoe said in self-defense soon afterward) is to express ideas which had already appeared in the books of "Virulent" authors, "though not in words so plain."[8] James Sutherland in his biography of Defoe speaks of *The Shortest Way* as "not much more extravagant than the sermons of several High Church divines,"[9] but Mr. Novak insists that Defoe (and Mr. Sutherland) minimize an important difference: Defoe's fictitious pamphleteer makes a literal demand for the extermination of the Dissenters whereas the High Church writers had only implied such a wish by means of metaphor and biblical analogy.[10]

One does not need to read all the tracts of the day to discover some pretty clear curses and threats. In *A New Test of the Church of England's Loyalty* (June 1702) Defoe printed a sampling of quotations from High Flier authors. All Englishmen, including of course nonconformists, should regard it as their duty to submit to "the greatest Violence upon either [their] Person or Estate" executed by God's anointed agent, the monarch. Dissenters are "Incendiaries, Phanaticks, and Bloody Peace-breaking Whigs" and nourish the "Vip'rous Principles of Treason and Rebellion"; they should be given their due reward by a troubled nation. They "drink in Rebellion as Water."[11] Henry Sacheverell in his Oxford sermon *Political Union* (2 June 1702)[12] attacked the Dissenters with uncontrolled ferocity for their being atheists and, consequently, a destructive counterforce to government as well as religion. "Presbytery and Republicanism go hand in hand." "Boar," "beast," and "viper" are proper labels for the nonconformists, who agree "in Nothing but the utter

Extirpation of the Establish'd Government," and those Anglicans in the government or the Church who advocate friendliness towards them are "Infatuated Sots, and Bigots," traitors to their "Trusts and Offices." Against such desperate enemies of the Church all well-wishers of the proper communion "ought to Hang out the Bloody Flag, and Banner of Defiance."[13] In Sacheverell's Oxford sermon of June 10, *A Defence of Her Majesty's Title to the Crown*, the attack on Dissent develops more slowly and more quietly, but what the "Bloody Flag" implies is suggested by allusions to the murderous effectiveness of Moses, Joshua, Samson, Jephthah, et al., in their treatment of God's various enemies. One can expect that God will punish England, probably with a flow of blood, if by indulging in "Divisions and Unnatural Breaches" it departs from "the Good Old Principles of Our English Church, and Our English Government."[14] In another of the pamphlets that Defoe said he was trying to combat, Charles Leslie argued that Sacheverell was correct in calling Dissenters "Sharers in Villany and Rebellion," for their "Mouths were Flaming Ovens, and Breath'd forth nothing but Fire and Sword"; we loyal Englishmen should "look to our selves, before it be too late."[15] According to the Rev. Philip Stubbs, the man who wavers between God and Baal (the true Church and Dissent are so plainly meant that Stubbs inserts an absurd denial of that intention) is fit for Bedlam and "ought to be beaten with most Stripes."[16] Defoe's High Churchman does indeed speak more precisely than these others in advocating the gallows for Dissenting preachers and the galleys for worshipers at conventicles. But what else, one might have asked, could the High Fliers mean by urging their friends to "Hang out the Bloody Flag"?

There are additional features of Defoe's pamphlet that would strike confusion if not fear into the hearts and minds of numerous Dissenters. In the latter part of *The Shortest Way* the attack upon Occasional Conformity would give the pamphlet a distinctly hostile look because of the clear, logical exposure of what Defoe in his first *Enquiry into the Occasional Conformity* (1697) had called "Playing Bo-peep with God Almighty." And even those conscientious Dissenters who agreed with the High Church author (and with Defoe) that occasional conforming was wrong might still be disturbed on another score, the pamphleteer's unexpected chiding of the Dissenters for making "a mock King," a "meer King of Cl[ub]s," of their own William and for "pitiful" management of the government while they were in power.[17] Though Defoe may have meant his High Church speaker to be alluding to the peculation just recently—and falsely—charged by the Tories against William's ministers, Somers and Halifax, the thoughts of many Dissenters probably would be turned rather to the unpleasant fact that during the 1690s a number of Whigs and nonconformists in the ministry and in Parliament had gone over to the Tories (put off by William's favoritism to his Dutch friends as well as by certain of his military policies and his secret treaties).[18] To be reminded at this point of flagrant disloyalty within their own party would pain and offend the serious Dissenters.

One asks now, as the more enlightened readers doubtless did then, what precisely was the author trying to do in his pamphlet? About two months after it was published Defoe issued *A Brief Explanation Of a Late Pamphlet, Entituled, The Shortest Way with the Dissenters* in which the "Author" declares that work to have been a mere "Banter" or "Irony" upon the "High-flying Church-Men"[19] without any seditious intention of stirring up rebellion among Dissenters. It had, he affirms, no connection with the bill against Occasional Conformity (which, having been passed in the Commons a week or two before *The Shortest Way* appeared, was, on the next day, to be debated in the Lords). The author declares that *The Shortest Way* meant to put into plain words the hopes for "Persecution and Destruction of the Dissenters" which had been expressed in terms very little darker in Sacheverell's Oxford sermon and Leslie's *New Association;* thus it would expose the brutal and un-English designs of the High Church party.

But when Defoe issued that *Explanation* he had already been questioned, indicted, and his pamphlet condemned to be burned by the common hangman, and he, in hiding, was of course putting the best face on the affair. It was, indeed, the same face that he put upon it in his numerous later references to the affair. In April 1703 he wrote in aggrieved fashion that he had intended to benefit the Dissenters but they had lifted a dagger against him.[20] Yet the majority of Dissenters, as he must have known, would regard an attack on Occasional Conformity as of no benefit to them. In fact they might suspect the anonymous author of trying to encourage the passage of the bill in the Lords. But as Mr. Moore has pointed out, one contemporary declared *The Shortest Way* to have been instigated by Harley, who wanted the bill defeated but dared not say so publicly. Some thought Defoe was trying to forestall attacks on Somers and Halifax.[21]

When the Whigs and moderate Tories in the House of Lords had managed to attach a number of amendments to the bill which they knew would sink it in the Commons, they published the bill and these amendments along with a strikingly mild explanation that, though they did not excuse or defend Occasional Conformity, they found that in time of war the original bill might create "Divisions amongst Protestants at home" and that the "Alterations" required by the bill would be "unnecessary, and dangerous"; they did not wish at this time to give the Dissenters "any cause of Jealousies or Fears."[22] But the argument against Occasional Conformity in *The Shortest Way* is so acute and fervent that it would seem to operate in direct opposition to the mild tone and conciliatory statements in the Lords' publication. If Harley and Godolphin were behind the Lords' strategy, as undoubtedly they were, Defoe was undoing their work. Their eagerness to identify and silence the troublesome author of *The Shortest Way* is understandable.[23] Not only they but many other people in both political parties wanted quiet tolerance of Occasional Conformity. The attack on it in Defoe's pamphlet could not be regarded as moderate or as ironic.

We have come, then, to another question: should we call this "banter" a failure or a success? In exposing the extremist High Churchmen—if that was its purpose—it was demonstrably successful. But it seems to have stirred up hostility both among the Dissenters and toward them, and Defoe denied that he meant to do either. Whether the pamphlet helped to defeat the bill in the House of Lords and thus permit Occasional Conformity to continue, or, on the other hand, whether it caused many previously thoughtless practicers to give up that wicked course, we have no way of knowing. The pamphlet ruined Defoe's life and business for the time-being; it also led to his long career as secret agent, adviser, and journalist for Harley and his successors. A perfect satire, a truly successful satire on the High Church extremists would not, one may suppose, have been so puzzling, so offensive to the Dissenters or so unsympathetic to the efforts of a conciliatory ministry. Was Defoe indeed "extraordinarily clever"? Must the mistaken readers have been "Fools"?

Anyone wishing to clarify a problem in technique in a piece of Augustan satire can usually get help by turning to Jonathan Swift. A comparison of *The Shortest Way* and Swift's *Modest Proposal* is immediately helpful. In Swift's ironic pamphlet all the foolish and shocking proposals for helping the poor Irish (by selling their children to be eaten) are presented in a serious mien, and the appalling brutality of the speaker grows increasingly oppressive as his logical argument proceeds. Swift's own humane, sensible proposals are lumped together as impractical and negligible in a late paragraph of bitter and obvious irony; the rejection of good sense explodes into clear satire. What the speaker recommends is at last transparently bad; what he rejects is transparently good.

Defoe was an incorrigible preacher and projector, an habitual dispenser of practical good advice, and only intermittently an artist. In *The Shortest Way* he imitates, most of the time, the biased, angry tracts of the High Church zealots very well; as he later insisted, he merely brought into full daylight the malicious and extreme measures recommended by those zealots. So far so good. The mingling of true history and false history may for such a purpose be a proper procedure; but one imagines that if Swift were writing to help the Dissenters (impossible thought!) he would play down those episodes in actual history which would embarrass his own party.

But not so Defoe. It was not only in his High Churchman's diatribe that Defoe revealed regret for the execution of Charles I, and there is no minimizing of that episode here. A notion that became an *idée fixe* of Defoe's was that William III, a very great man, had been shamefully unappreciated by his English subjects. But a High Flier seems hardly likely to scold Dissenters for making a "mock King" of William. Another of Defoe's most earnest beliefs was that the practice of Occasional Conformity could only mean either that Dissent is unlawful or that occasional conforming is sinful.[24] Before and after 1702, in one work after another, he assailed that practice. His famous *True Born Englishman* (1700) had anticipated the rebukes in *The Shortest Way* to those who had failed to honor King William. Swift, one imagines, would have omitted all mention of such weaknesses in his own group; in his *Tale of a Tub* he acknowledges only one fault in Martin (the Church of England), his early mistake of decorating his coat, and this mistake Martin soon carefully corrected. But Defoe allows his High Churchman to ridicule

Occasional Conformity with an excellent complaint: fines
of five shillings a month for not coming to the Sacrament are
an absurdity, a selling cheaply the liberty to sin against God
and the government. Defoe clinches the point with a characteristic piece of his own enlightened social criticism: we *hang*
men for trifles and *banish* them for small reasons but offer this
easy escape from a fundamental sin or crime.[25] Defoe confuses
the reader further by quoting John How, one of his Dissenting
opponents, on the subject of Occasional Conformity and agree-
ing, with an almost undetectable irony, that the differences in
Church doctrine between the two parties are limited to three
minor points. A reference in passing to the wealth of the
Dissenters and an argument for the immediate suppression of
faction because the next monarch will probably be a foreigner,
perhaps of a "Dutch Turn," are, as they stand, of ambiguous
import; both parties could make something of them for their
own use.

Defoe's fictional speaker, one sees, can be as bloody and
ruthless as the wildest High Churchman but as clear-headed
and sensible as Defoe on the subject of Occasional Conformity
and the penal laws and, like a good Whig, loyal to the Dissenters'
King William. While he is eloquent and convincing as he rushes
ahead, for the Dissenting reader he would be fearfully wrong
most of the time, yet at moments shrewdly, sadly right; though
in general position clear, yet on two or three topics he is, for a
High Churchman, surprising and puzzling. Swift in his satire
made his "villains" seem entirely villainous, but Defoe gives
to his villain a direct expression of two of his own most cherished
beliefs.[26] As a satiric invention Defoe's speaker is imperfect
even if as an invented human being he might perhaps seem
plausible though inconsistent. He is not so simple and obvious
a type as modern commentators have taken him to be. And in
his lack of conformity to an expected pattern he is a characteristic
Defoe creation.

In the romances (or "novels") that Defoe began producing
about seventeen years after *The Shortest Way* one notices that
the major characters are usually designed in a comparable way:
Defoe chooses a recognizable category or label or type (a cavalier,
a moll, a pirate) but qualifies and modifies it by features that
depart from or even contradict the traditional outline. At a
time when in both literary theory and actual practice—in plays,
in periodical essays, and, with some important exceptions, in

prose fiction—the preference was for the depiction of universal types of human beings, this aspect of Defoe's fiction deserves notice.

In *Memoirs of a Cavalier* (1720) the speaker-narrator is a brave and eventually expert soldier who learned the art of war by observing campaigns in Savoy and Germany[27] and by serving as an officer in the army of Gustavus Adolphus, whom he adores. He is a gallant eager fighter, both abroad and after his return to England in 1635, when he offers his services freely to Charles. But though a royalist, he remarks that Charles had exceeded his legal prerogatives before the revolution broke out, and he observes repeatedly that Charles was incompetent in politics, incompetent in government, incompetent in war, and that he foolishly allowed himself to be guided by clerics. Our cavalier is inattentive to questions of justice in the causes and conduct of the war. He confesses "I was not very religious myself" and has, for a long time, no opinion about the religious issues in the upheaval. He is far from being the familiar image of the seventeenth-century cavalier: he is not interested in poetry or art or music or drinking or women. Of all the soldiers of his day, after the Protestant champion Gustavus he most admires the Puritan general, Lord Fairfax. Defoe's cavalier, compact of expected and unexpected features, is plausible and lifelike but not a well-established type among cavaliers. Defoe doubtless deliberately created him thus for his own purposes in this early example of thesis-novel. But the non-typical character was intended to expose certain weaknesses of his own party consciously, not in satiric, unconscious parody.

In *Captain Singleton* (1720) one again encounters a character who breaks out of a familiar mold in surprising ways. The pirate William Walters is one of Defoe's most striking creations. A Quaker, a "very merry" surgeon of "good solid sense," he as a Quaker refuses to take part in the fighting on board the ship of his "captor," Bob Singleton; yet he lashes the bowsprit of a Portuguese warship to the mainmast of Singleton's ship so that a fight must occur. Perpetually eager for money, he either helps kill the natives whom his pirate-colleagues meet on land or he urges that they be spared, ostensibly according to proper moral principles but actually depending upon the likelihood of financial gain. Inventive and even intellectual, we expect him to offer unfailingly practical suggestions. His advice to Bob Singleton, when at last Bob comes to repentance and shame

for his ill-gotten wealth, is both superficially Christian and
shrewdly selfish. Neither mere pirate nor true Christian nor
real pacifist Friend nor mere hypocrite and certainly not a
thoroughly evil man, he defies all simple categories. But the
amusing set of complexities in this fictional creation could
not have been unintentional on Defoe's part.

Moll Flanders is well known, a warm-hearted whore and
likable pickpocket, who blames her upbringing (really very
good) and the devil poverty (who isn't always there) for her
sins as she continues to steal and cheat and disobey the laws of
religion and society. Eventually she turns repentant and respect-
able, though at last view, says the editor in his Preface, she "was
not so extraordinary a penitent as she was at first." Surprises
and contradictions are basic and captivating in this well-developed
characterization.

Roxana, in *The Fortunate Mistress* (1724), is a more sophisticated adventuress; her peculiar capacity to weep over certain
of her children on occasion and also to ignore them altogether
seems to be explainable sometimes on grounds of social ambition
(she weeps that the magnificent prince's child must bear a bar
sinister), sometimes on grounds of brazen heartlessness, and
sometimes on grounds of momentary shame (her sending Amy
to find her first offspring "had the face of doing good"). Avarice,
ambition, and pride and delight in her own physical beauty
are, she often declares, what kept her in the sexual business,
though we can see other ways of putting the matter. Her
emotional vagaries—"love," fierce anxiety, joy, shame, hate—
are unpredictable and intense. The shallowness of her declared
repentance is dramatically exposed in the memorable latter
part of the book as her discarded, clever daughter pursues her
in order to establish their true relationship. The volume presents
also an "honest," decent, rather tricky Dutch merchant who
lies with a woman not for the usual purpose of debauchery but
rather in order to gain her as a wife. A third unusual character
is Roxana's friend, her Quaker landlady, who serves her with
loyalty, delicacy, and intelligence, who will never speak a lie
but will conceal or ignore almost anything. This latter sort of
moral inconsistency or complexity is, of course, part of the
contemporary hostile view of the Quakers, but the landlady
is not an ordinary example.

Perhaps Robinson Crusoe is the only one of Defoe's major
characterizations in which unexpected or inconsistent features

are not outstanding. Yet Crusoe's prolonged neuroticism after his discovery of the footprint in the sand may seem odd in a man who passes through many grave crises with stolid control. Though a representative of universal man, as Coleridge said,[28] one would be at a loss to identify the specific type in literature or life that, in the entire story, he portrays.

Critics have often noticed Defoe's habit of intruding in his fictions, his way of suddenly speaking in his own voice rather than in Moll's or Roxana's or Crusoe's or the cavalier's (whose list, at the end of his *Memoirs*, of providential anniversaries of King Charles's errors and sins can be credited not to his own habits of mind but to his Dissenting creator's). An uncontrollable impulse in Defoe to project a good, constructive idea wherever and whenever he can accounts for the sociological excuses of Moll, Roxana's exposition of the faults in matrimonial law in respect to the wife, Crusoe's revelation to Friday of the fraud of priestcraft, and many of the cavalier's annotations on seventeenth-century history. These interjections stamp much of Defoe's work as that of a journalist and social theorist. In *The Shortest Way* the intrusive rebukes to Dissenters for their mistreatment of King William and for the practice of Occasional Conformity as well as the brief but sharp objection to harsh penal laws spoil the characterization of the speaker as an absurd, virulent High Churchman. Defoe had not yet learned how far one can go and how far one cannot with such didactic interjections. But the inconsistency of the speaker's utterance in that pamphlet is in line with the open and interesting complexities that Defoe more successfully built into characters in his later volumes of prose fiction.

Notes

1. Bonamy Dobrée, *English Literature in the Early Eighteenth Century, 1700–1740* (Oxford, 1959), p. 46.   2. Richard I. Cook, "Defoe and Swift: Contrast in Satire," *Dalhousie Review*, XLIII (1963), 33.   3. *Eighteenth-Century Prose*, ed. L. I. Bredvold, R. K. Root, and George Sherburn (New York, 1932), p. 1.   4. *Defoe in the Pillory and Other Studies* (Bloomington, Ind., 1939), chap. 1; *Daniel Defoe: Citizen of the Modern World* (Chicago, 1958), pp. 104–144.   5. "Defoe's *Shortest Way* . . . Hoax, Parody, Paradox, Fiction, Irony, and Satire," *MLQ*, XXVII (1966), 402–417.   6. The readers'

supposition that the pamphlet offered a serious defense of an extreme position would have been encouraged by recollection of works with similar titles: cf. *A Short and Easy Method for the Extirpation of Popery* (1690) and Charles Leslie's *Short and Easy Method with the Deists* (1698).   7. Novak, pp. 404, 408–410.   8. *A Brief Explanation Of a Late Pamphlet, Entituled, The Shortest Way with the Dissenters* (1703), p. 2.   9. *Defoe* (Philadelphia, 1938), p. 86.

10. Novak, p. 404.   11. *A New Test of the Church of England's Loyalty* (1702), pp. 2, 5.   12. For the date, see Walter Wilson, *Memoirs of the Life and Times of Daniel De Foe* (1830), II, 27.   13. *The Political Union. A Discourse Shewing the Dependance of Government on Religion in General: And of the English Monarchy on the Church of England in Particular. By Henry Sacheverell* (1702), pp. 48–50, 52, 57–59. Defoe in his *Brief Explanation of . . . The Shortest Way* (1703), p. 2, mentions Sacheverell's "Sermon preach'd at Oxford" (as well as Leslie's *New Association* and the *Poetical Observator*) as examples of the malicious, dangerous publications of the High Church party. But there were in print two Sacheverell sermons delivered at Oxford in June 1702. The reference in Defoe's *Enquiry into Occasional Conformity* (1702) to the Oxford sermon of Sacheverell's that "Dooms all the Dissenters to Destruction" (p. 7) would seem to be to *Political Union*. In *A New Test of the Church of England's Honesty* (1704), pp. 2–3, Defoe remarked that when in 1703 he was charged with sedition he should have produced, to exonerate himself with the jury, a copy of *Political Union* as an example of "Church of England Sedition," licensed and approved by the University.   14. Pages 21–23.   15. *The New Association of those Called, Moderate-Church-Men, with the Modern-Whigs and Fanaticks, to Under-Mine and Blow-up the Present Church and Government* (1702; 4th ed., 1705), pp. 4–5.   16. *For God or for Baal; or, No Neutrality in Religion. A Sermon against Occasional Communion, Preach'd on Sunday Oct. 4th 1702* (1702), pp. 16–17.   17. *The Shortest Way with the Dissenters,* pp. 4, 9.   18. Stephen B. Baxter, *William III* (London, 1966), pp. 386–387; David Ogg, *England in the Reigns of James II and William III* (Oxford, 1955), pp. 442–444, 450.   19. The *Brief Explanation,* a four-page affair in its original form, used the word "Irony"; but in the reprint in the authorized *True Collection of the Writings of the Author of the True Born English-man. Corrected by himself* (1703) the word "Banter" replaces "Irony" (p. 435).

20. See the letter to William Patterson, probably intended to be shown to Harley, in *The Letters of Daniel Defoe,* ed. George H. Healey (Oxford, 1955), pp. 4–5.   21. *Daniel Defoe: Citizen of the Modern World,* pp. 110–112.   22. See the "Bill, Intituled, An Act for Preventing Occasional Conformity, and the Proceedings thereupon," in *Select Documents for Queen Anne's Reign,* ed. G. M. Trevelyan (Cambridge, 1929), p. 38.   23. See Keith G. Feiling, *History of the Tory Party, 1640–1714* (Oxford, 1924), p. 369. The reasons for Defoe's arrest were probably several. An important one is thought to have been his part in the presentation of the Kentish Petition and in the writing of *Legion's Address* in 1701.   24. *Enquiry into the Occasional Conformity of Dissenters* (1697), p. 13.   25. *The Shortest Way,* p. 22. "Capital punishment was prescribed for more than 100 crimes in Defoe's England. Theft of five shillings' value from a shop could . . . lead to death. Exile in servitude, usually to America, was a common alternative" (*Moll Flanders,* ed.

J. Paul Hunter, New York, 1970, p. 9n). 26. Mr. Novak (p. 413) regards Defoe's putting into the mouth of his High Churchman his own attack on Occasional Conformity as an example of Defoe's "addiction to paradox" and of his utilizing a common "skeptical" method in debate. Mr. Moore (*Daniel Defoe: Citizen of the Modern World*, p. 107) remarks: "Defoe saw both sides of the problem, and in his unsparing honesty he offended leaders of both parties in the dispute." 27. Apropos of the war in Bohemia the cavalier remarks that its one-time king had been "too much neglected" by his father-in-law, James I of England. One is reminded that in *The Shortest Way* there are complaints from the High Church author about James's policies. 28. *Coleridge's Miscellaneous Criticism*, ed. Thomas M. Raysor (London, 1936), p. 194.

THOSE GAUDY TULIPS
Swift's "Unprintables"

John M. Aden

IT is, happily, no longer necessary to argue the moral case for Swift's "unprintable" poems.[1] We may now, and should, begin assessing them more attentively for their poetical properties. I should like to venture some suggestions toward such a re-assessment in respect to "The Progress of Beauty" (1719), "The Lady's Dressing Room" (1732), "A Beautiful Young Nymph Going to Bed," "Strephon and Chloe," and "Cassinus and Peter" (1734).

All these have in common, in one form or another, the theme of appearance and reality, usually as that relates to the female, though the male is always implicated and is even, in some cases, the principal subject. All undertake to strip down, in one way or another, some delusion to the reality it masquerades for, and all begin that design with some cherished or respected myth or analogy which they proceed to discredit with studious in-difference to shock.[2] For this purpose they usually invoke, among other things, disgusting and scatological imagery and carry on a strategic hide-and-seek with the comic and grotesque. But their debunking serves a serious purpose, and each poem seeks to say something corrective of human psychology, conduct, and morality. They doubtless have other things in common as well, but these are the principal—enough at any rate to begin with if we are not to risk losing the particular poems in a preamble of generalization. We see the truth of this quickly enough, not only in the comic variation of "Cassinus and Peter," but in the first poem, which begins in the manner described—with the myth of Diana or the moon—and which proceeds to do with that what we have said of them all, but in a way quite peculiar to itself.

"The Progress of Beauty" is, of course, not ultimately concerned with Diana or the moon at all, but with Celia. But since that lady (along with her sisters, whoresome or not) is so incorrigibly associated with the moon in that virginal aspect which is, in turn, so incorrigibly predicated of the moon, Swift finds it expedient to discredit the heavenly body along with the earthly, and he does so by a strategy characteristically deceptive: resorting, ostensibly, to the customary comparison, but reversing its customary direction and implicitly collapsing the whole into an *alias* oneness. Instead of likening the human being to the heavenly, he likens the heavenly to the human, and both come tumbling down. And this is accomplished, not by simple straight-on reduction, but by an appropriately alternating, and ever so ambiguous, formula of attrition: now the myth, now the mortal (sometimes both together), now a romantic, now a realistic idiom—knocking the two together, so to speak, until they both shatter. It would not do for either to survive the colliding; that would be to leave a something to breed the hoax all over again. It is possible of course to think of Swift's stratagem in the usual way, as a comparison with a vengeance: you want to compare Dianas, mundane and celestial; very well, we shall compare them, and you will be surprised at the outcome. But it is also possible to think of the strategy as not really leading to comparison at all, however unflattering, but to identification. Two "ladies," yes, but one folly. A hoax by any other name is still a hoax, and the two terms by which it is here romantically entertained must be abrogated if the imposture is to be wholly dispelled. The moon is no more divine than the maid; as "deities" there is no difference between them; they are both the same, a mere fancy.

It is for this reason no doubt that Swift opens the poem in the curiously ambiguous manner that he does:

> When first Diana leaves her Bed
> Vapors and Steams her Looks disgrace,
> A frouzy dirty colour'd red
> Sits on her cloudy wrinckled Face.
>
> But by degrees when mounted high
> Her artificiall Face appears
> Down from her Window in the Sky,
> Her Spots are gone, her Visage clears.[3]

It is doubtful that anyone, on a first reading, could be sure of the subject of these lines, whether Swift is talking about a mortal Diana or about the mythic, lunar one. The uncertainty is almost surely intentional on Swift's part. He confounds response, not only in parody of his reader's failure to discriminate, but also to suggest that discrimination in this instance is misleading anyway. It is not, at any rate, until line 9, with its "'Twixt earthly Femals and the Moon," or line 11, with its "Celia," that one can identify with confidence the lunar subject of the first two stanzas.[4] Until then he is trapped in a Swiftian blindman's bluff.[5]

How Swift plays the game is worth remark. In normal poetic discourse, *Diana* is moon or myth, but it is also the name of mortal maids, and Swift leads the reader a chase in search of which. In the first stanza the beck is mortal, in the second lunar, but in neither is the token decisive. *Diana*, as we say, can point either way, but "Bed" immediately beckons earthward. "Vapors and Steams" only tantalize, since they can apply as easily to the atmospheric as to the cosmetic, though "frouzy," "red," and "wrinckled," along with "Face" draw us maidenly again. Only "cloudy" remains to rekindle the doubt. In the second stanza, "mounted high" suggests moonish identity, and "Down from her Window in the Sky" seems a dead giveaway but for the fact that *all* windows, celestial or oppidan, are in the "sky" to those below. Add to that the fact that "Face," "Spots," and "Visage" pull again, though admittedly with no great assurance, toward the mortal, and we are back where we started from.

Not until stanza three are we resolved of the uncertainty,[6] and by that time, given any sensitivity at all, we probably begin to suspect that the distinction is unimportant anyway, if not downright misleading, for Diana of Drury Lane and Diana of myth are both products of the fancy and neither of them real. Swift's implied simile turns out to be an implied metaphor, and we are not only shocked, but chagrined.

Having collapsed the comparison before he quite begins it, Swift picks up the pieces and, in stanzas 4–14, concentrates on the mortal residue—Celia—and the difference between *her* appearance and reality. But he keeps operative the interplay between the "poetic" or fanciful and the real which complicated his introduction of the subject. This is a technique, not just a point of view, and is rather like the irony with which he elsewhere, in his prose, entraps the unwary or forestalls retreat from embarrassment. Swift teases the reader with the possibility that perhaps things aren't so bad as they seem after all; that if he hangs on a bit longer all will yet be well. "Crakt Lips, foul Teeth, and gummy Eyes" risk the premature loss of audience, and hence the blandishment of "Tresses" (line 19). Similarly with "A mingled Mass of Dirt and Sweat," which is retrieved with the most endearingly pastoral of sounds and scenes: "when the Lilly slipps / Into the Precincts of the Rose, / And takes Possession of the Lips," until that too washes out in the "Purple" of the "Nose," where it remains, on a dead level of ugliness, through the next four stanzas (8–11), until the delusive rhetoric is reinvoked in stanzas 12–14 and hope is rekindled in "Cheeks again to blush" (line 48). If the hope is not requited (as that kind of hope never is by Swift), something more relevant is proffered, though moon-struck Strephons will doubtless continue to overlook it in the shambles of ladies' dressing rooms: "Order from Confusion sprung," "gaudy Tulips rais'd from Dung." Here it is expressed as follows:

> Thus after four important Hours
> Celia's the Wonder of her Sex;
> Say, which among the Heav'nly Pow'rs
> Could cause such wonderfull Effects.
> . . . .
> Love with White lead cements his Wings,
> White lead was sent us to repair
> Two brightest, brittlest earthly Things
> A Lady's Face, and China ware. (Stanzas 14, 16)

This of course is no happy ending, no micro-paradox of fortunate fall. It is but a paradigm of the husbandry of unhallowed soil. Celia isn't redeemed; she is still a slut, but she has put a good face on a bad, and at a distance can, like her "Sister Star," "Delude at once and Bless our sight" (line 70).

Stanza 15 had resumed the mythic formula which we perceive operating in the second of the two stanzas quoted above, the sisterhood of moon and mortal, now taking the form of the whole female conspiracy (Venus and her son; Diana; Celia and her sisters of the flesh) to deceive mankind, which is willing enough to be deceived: "G——d d——m me Jack, she's wondrous fair." For a brief interval (stanzas 15–19), freed of some of the burden of illusion, it effects an escape from the ugly of stanzas 8–11 and wings a fitful flight back toward the atmosphere of make-believe. But the medium is too paltry to sustain it, and the image wanes again, now into eclipse (*swa heo no wære!*), as the matter of beauty empties out of its frail form, which collapses with it, leaving but a wizened moon of "Forehead" and "Chin," driven to the desperation of midnight advent, as it must be with Celia, forced to stroll the street "When sober Folks are all a-bed."

To be like the moon, like Diana, thus proves something else than what is popularly supposed:

> For sure if this be Luna's Fate,
> Poor Celia, but of mortall Race
> In vain expects a longer Date
> To the Materialls of Her Face.

And paint can scarce "restore a Nose," or teeth, or glass eyes and lead a cheek or lip. And so, instead of courtly compliment, we are left with the wryness of mock supplication:

> Ye Pow'rs who over Love preside,
> Since mortal Beautyes drop so soon,
> If You would have us well supply'd,
> Send us new Nymphs with each new Moon.

The progress of beauty has proved a losing battle, not only for Celia (and Diana), but for those who trust its durability and for those, the Strephons of the world, who confound its form and substance and so fall down and worship graven images. This is the poem's meaning, in part, at least. But "The Progress of Beauty," as poetics, is a victory: the scaling down, by ambiguities, redirections, antitheses (alternating tones and images), reversals, ironic pitfalls, and land mines, until we can call a slut a slut without loss of composure and realize that a second-hand rose by any other name will smell as rank.

"The Lady's Dressing Room" is less complex, but not therefore less poignant, in its method. It works by a familiar Swiftian device, the anecdote or episode, beginning with the goddess analogy. The "action" is simple enough: Strephon, a naif, slips into Celia's dressing room, beholds its filth and litter, and finally steals out, despairing in the discovery that "*Celia, Celia, Celia* shits!" Like Gulliver he is overwhelmed by his vision, and concludes that all women are filthy (stinking). To all of which the poet adds a valedictory in which he expresses pity for this over-response:

> I pity wretched *Strephon* blind
> To all the Charms of Female Kind;

> Should I the Queen of Love refuse,
> Because she rose from stinking Ooze?
> To him that looks behind the Scene,
> *Satira's* but some pocky Quean.
> When *Celia* in her Glory shows,
> If *Strephon* would but stop his Nose;
> (Who now so impiously blasphemes
> Her Ointments, Daubs, and Paints and Creams,
> Her Washes, Slopes, and every Clout,
> With which he makes so foul a Rout;)
> He soon would learn to think like me,
> And bless his ravisht Sight to see
> Such Order from Confusion sprung,
> Such gaudy Tulips rais'd from Dung. [7]

Criticism has, not surprisingly, boggled over these lines, for at a glance they seem uncertain enough. Maurice Johnson thinks Swift has lost control. Swift, he says, "pretends ... to be patronizingly amused by the boy's queasy stomach." [8] Swift is amused, I think, but not by Strephon, whom I think he really does pity for his naiveté. But of that more later. Let us return to Johnson, who continues:

> In these lines the tone is somehow wrong. Is it after all one thing for a Restoration wit like the Earl of Dorset to sing "In grey hair'd Celia's wither'd arms / As nightly Lewis lay," and quite another thing for Dean Swift to attempt a similar subject in verse? He appears to have made his own stomach, like Strephon's, somewhat queasy by examination of washes and slops, so that even his Swiftian irony, when he pretends insensitive affection for the gaudy tulips of love, loses its usual force and seems to mock itself. It is as though the reformer has been convinced by his own argument and the preacher has frightened himself with his own description of Man's flaws and failings. [9]

Apart from the judgment about tone, the ability of a dean to write on such a subject, and the falter of Swiftian irony, one must question these conclusions of such a reading: (1) that Swift was himself made "queasy" by his inventory of Celia's dirty linen, (2) that he was pretending "insensitive affection" for the Celias of the world, and (3) that he somehow scared himself into backing off from the reality of human ugliness. Such conclusions simply will not square with the evidence, which points not only to didactic composure and emotional control but to urbanity of reprimand as well. How otherwise account for the affirmation of the "Queen of Love," the bravura of "*Celia* in her Glory," the charge of impiousness in Strephon, or for the last four lines, with their acknowledgment of blessing, ravishment, and order? There is not the slightest evidence that Swift is out of control, himself the victim of trauma; but every evidence of the command which he pities the want of in Strephon.

It is less easy to disagree with D. J. Greene, but here too I must confess to certain misgivings. Greene is right in challenging Norman Brown's conclusion that Swift is advising Strephon to "reconcile himself" to imperfection, but his counter-argument is, it seems to me, rather too weighty for these lines. Greene contends that they express a reminder that all beauty, like Creation itself, is born out of chaos; that, in other words, Strephon is guilty of a theological oversight.[10] True as this proposition is per se (including Strephon's theological ignorance, unsurprising as that is), it does not ring true to the lines as I read them. Such a conclusion would have the effect, it seems to me, of ratifying what is manifestly a meretricious beauty and so, in effect, of getting Celia off the hook, neither of which I can associate with the poem without discounting everything that has gone before. If Swift is here arguing as a divine, which I rather doubt, he could scarcely afford, in the name of Creative Grace, to confer dignity upon the false face of beauty. Some such idea as Greene suggests may well be implicit in the lines, but that it is explicit, i.e., motivational and definitive, I find it difficult to believe.

What the lines really say, I think, is that if Strephon would but discount the argument from his senses (his willingness to be effected by appearances), he could, like the poet, find the spectacle of beauty out of such noisome origins a source of wonder and not, as he has, of despair. Now this is not reconciliation, but neither is it theology; it is simply clear-sightedness, good sense, and wisdom. This, I think, is all that Swift is here asking of Strephon, or of any of us: not that we remember our Creator in the days of our youth, but that we see things for what they are, whereupon much else is apt to follow, including something so mundane, and yet so practically important, as rescue from the snakepit of romantic delusion.

But we have gotten ahead of the poem, or the poetics, which is our chief concern. It opens with a sketch of Celia in her

"Goddess" aspect of "Lace, Brocades and Tissues," who, after five hours dressing, issues from her boudoir, leaving it prey to the snooping eyes of Strephon. What he sees there Swift images by means of another favorite vehicle, the catalogue. In Swift's hand this is always a shock technique, piling up in rapid and merciless succession a display of repulsive images: a smock "besmeared" in armpits; combs clotted with "Sweat, Dandriff, Powder, Lead and Hair"; oily forehead cloth; "Gallypots and Vials" filled with "Slops, / And Ointments good for scabby Chops"; a "filthy Bason" for "The Scrapings of her Teeth and Gums"; and so on, through smelly towels, snotty handkerchiefs, smelly stockings, nose-worm glass, and—the last straw—Celia's close-stool.

But this inventory, like those elsewhere in Swift, is not merely an enumeration of filth, but a witty and dramatically defined event. Here it is largely evoked from and aimed at Strephon, who is hoist on the petard of his own voyeurism. It is as much an indictment of him as of Celia, and, what is more important, as much a picture of his mind as it is of her room. Strephon indicts and mocks himself as he holds aloft the "dirty Smock," turning it about "on every Side"; as he smells the towels, stares into the magnifying glass, raises the lid of the close-stool, and even (it would appear) gropes within it in search of a "*Hope*" he could scarcely have recognized as pathological. There is other texturing, too, relative to Celia and her sex, often allusive, as in the quotation from Milton [11] and the apparently grotesque recall of Belinda's "Puffs, Powders, Patches, Bibles, Billet-doux" in Celia's "Sweet, Dandriff, Powder, Lead and Hair." [12] The close-stool wrought (however futilely) to resemble a cabinet and, compared to Pandora's box, is a little comedy in itself; and the domesticating of the epic simile—"As Mutton Cutlets, Prime of Meat . . . So Things, which must not be exprest"—here, as elsewhere, lends a piquancy to the crude description.

But Strephon, unable to perceive the poetry he makes, and trapped in hopeless naiveté, cannot take it, cannot see it as Swift does, and so slinks out of the race, groaning, "Oh! *Celia, Celia, Celia* shits!" Whereupon Swift invokes, appropriately enough in behalf of one who has till now believed it, the supernatural of the poets, and tells how Goddess Vengeance punished poor Strephon for the offense of peeping, leaving him in that state of pathologic disgust and suspicion of womankind for which Swift suggests the cure we have already remarked.

It is a poor comedy that Strephon enacts, and has no comic ending for him; but it is a comedy, however astringent its middle, and has a comic ending for us, if we will but take it.

I have elsewhere discussed "A Beautiful Young Nymph Going to Bed," pointing out the interplay in it of the comic and the pathetic and suggesting the need for a more nearly *poetic* apprehension of what is going on in the poem. [13] I shall not retrace that ground—I have not changed my mind about it—but only emphasize the importance of the poem as an image rather than as a moral, an image affectively intended, though not as usually perceived (a gross insult to human dignity), but "rueful as well as risible" [14] and ever steady in that honest commixture of responsible satire. Here too Swift begins with the sacrificial analogy—the pastoral—and invokes the catalogue, or inventory, though the latter works in a denser texture of predicament than Strephon's, Corinna not being self-deceived in the fashion of that young man, and her plight being more real than his. It is one of Swift's most tightly woven poems, richly laden, though not, like "Strephon and Chloe," overladen, and impeccable in tone, image, and viewpoint.

I have said that "Strephon and Chloe" is overladen. It is, I believe, the least perfect (successful) of the unprintable poems, not because of any moral fault, but because it fails of poetical economy and thematic consistency. It is, of course, the longest poem in the group, well over twice as long as three of them and better than four times as long as "A Beautiful Young Nymph." On such a theme, in his more corrective mood, Swift does not usually write at such length. Why he did so in this instance is perhaps impossible to guess, but whatever the reason it proved costly. Perhaps too the length of the authorial comments and the curiously subdued and even lyrical character of the conclusion contribute to the sense of imperfection in the piece.

Token of the falter appears from the outset, in the generally fine and satirically essential first paragraph, where the texture is flawed by more than one puzzling if not pointless repetition. Chloe, we are told,

> Would so discreetly Things dispose,
> None ever saw her pluck a Rose.
> Her dearest Comrades never caught her
> Squat on her Hams, to make Maid's Water. [15]

Later, at the end of the paragraph, something of the same sort recurs:

> Her Milk-white Hands, both Palms and Backs,
> Like Iv'ry dry, and soft as Wax.
> Her Hands the softest ever felt,
> Tho' cold would burn, tho' dry would melt.

Whatever the pastoral and allusive effect Swift may have had in mind in this latter, it scarcely dispels the impression of redundancy.

The paragraph that follows (lines 29–38) seems even more gratuitous. It tells us that Venus would do well to keep Chloe out of sight in view of her monopolistic effect on the lovers' market, a point well enough taken and altogether conducive to Swift's purpose, but which he follows with an amplification that adds nothing to the point, tending towards digressive exercise in beau painting:

> Think what a Case all Men are now in,
> What ogling, sighing, toasting, vowing!
> What powder'd Wigs! What Flames and Darts!
> What Hampers full of bleeding Hearts!
> What Sword-knots! What Poetic Strains!
> What Billet-doux, and clouded Cains!

The only part of this that is truly relevant is "What Poetic Strains!" That points to the adoration malady that the poem is about. The rest is dressing. *Ogling* is even out of place, along perhaps with *toasting*, for these imply a kind of male cynicism that is poles removed from the male naiveté that is the subject of the poem. Nor are *bleeding Hearts* quite to the point, which is rather bleeding psyches. *Sighing* and *vowing* will do, no doubt, as perhaps *Flames* and *Darts*, but what is the pertinence of *Wigs*, *Sword-knots*, and *clouded Cains*? Swift has drifted off course, is flirting with another poem, one better suited to Pope.

The paragraph beginning IMPRIMIS—on the wedding— though not so noticeably wide of the mark also smacks of *decor*. Mr. Greene has remarked its "lush paraphernalia of pagan mythology or, perhaps more precisely, the *clichés* of Grub Street, the Madison Avenue of the time: Apollo, Mercury 'with Silver Tongue' (the patron of advertising men), Hebe, Juno, and the rest." [16] "Perhaps," says Mr. Greene, "Swift is making the point that it is emphatically not a Christian marriage, for all that the setting seems to be eighteenth-century 'Christian' London." Even if this is right, it is hard to see what relevance such an intent would have for the poem which contains it, for I don't believe that the poem is about Christian marriage. It is about decent marriage, which Christian marriage may be, but Swift is surely not writing this poem to bespeak the latter. He is writing, as Mr. Greene himself says, to describe "first an irrational state of illusion, and then the equally irrational state of despair when the illusion collapses." [17]

One is left wondering then about the usefulness of the pantheon Swift runs through in this place, the notice of Chloe's *Flammeum*, of Phoebus's *Epithalamium*, of Juno's priest, and of Luna absenting herself from felicity awhile. Some attention to the delusive trappings (more romantic than pagan) of such an occasion would be appropriate enough, but not as much as Swift lavishes. His real subject is, after all, yet to come. Actually, the only lines strictly on target are these: "And pigeons billing, Sparrows treading, / Fair Emblems of a fruitful Wedding." The trouble with the paragraph is not, as Mr. Greene seems to think, that it is pagan rather than Christian, but that it is excessive of its contribution to the point and movement of the poem.

After this Swift settles to his task pretty well for a time, but boggles again in lines 227–234, where he repeats, to no apparent purpose, a point (the dangers of romantic sublimation of female mortality) which he has abundantly and dramatically made already. But a worse error follows, in line 235–250, a paragraph true enough to Swift but not to this poem. It would come closer to fitting a poem like "The Lady's Dressing Room," where the lesson would be more dramatically consistent:

> O *Strephon*, e'er that fatal Day
> When *Chloe* stole your Heart away,
> Had you but through a Cranny spy'd
> On House of Ease your future Bride,
> In all the Postures of her Face,
> Which Nature gives in such a Case;
> Distortions, Groanings, Strainings, Heavings;
> 'Twere better you had lickt her Leavings,
> Than from Experience find too late
> Your Goddess grown a filthy Mate.
> Your Fancy then had always dwelt

On what you saw, and what you smelt;
Would still the same Ideas give ye,
As when you spy'd her on the Privy.
And, spight of Chloe's Charms divine,
Your Heart had been as whole as mine. [18]

In this poem the lines seem gratuitous, for Strephon has apparently accommodated well enough to all such manifestations of his bridal goddess:

Now *Strephon* daily entertains
His *Chloe* in the homeli'st Strains;
And, *Chloe* more experienc'd grown,
With Int'rest pays him back his own. (lines 211–214)

They have learned "to call a Spade, a Spade" (line 204), which makes one wonder about the need for such lecturing.

In still another instance (lines 271–282) does Swift appear to waver. He had just remarked the "various Ways our Females take, / To pass for Wits before a Rake! / And in the fruitless Search pursue / All other Methods but the true," i.e., the method of decency and good sense. The point is entirely apropos, and some illustration of it would not be amiss, but when Swift comes to illustrate it he permits himself to be attracted to satiric magnets outside the strict scope of this poem: women who read freethinking or deistical (even atheistical) literature; who are given to jesting over the natural defects of their fellow human beings; who pride themselves on bawdy; who tell tales out of school—all of which reads more like a digression into the random house of female vice and folly than a canvas of the misdirections of a woman intent on finding a mate. It can of course be rationalized, but that betrays the problem; it has (like so much else in the poem) to be rationalized. The propriety is not self-evident, even if we view the poem, as Herbert Davis does (and rightly), as a "burlesque epithalamium." [19] The passages to which I have objected as blemishes are, in part no doubt, passages that collaborate in this kind of mockery, but my point is that they over-collaborate, that they upstage, so to speak, by over-extension and thematic drift, the ultimate satiric tenor of the poem. But let us look at it briefly under the more positive rubric.

The poem is, as Davis says, a burlesque epithalamium, as "A Beautiful Young Nymph" is a burlesque (city) pastoral and "Cassinus and Peter" a burlesque elegy. Its purpose is to explode the same myth—that women are nymphs or goddesses, without human (biological) properties. Swift pictures this nymph, Chloe, in all the panoply of such repute among her votaries, one of whom, Strephon, out-sighing and out-bidding his competitors, wins her hand in marriage. The wedding scene is described and the couple brought home, Strephon most uncomfortably since he deems himself too merely mortal to lay hands on such a goddess. After agonizing over his predicament, and bethinking him of such precedent as he can of the mating of deities and mortals, he creeps into the wedding bed and observes a fearful distance from his bride. At this point the poet steps in with a word of advice. He would have parents school their daughters in the abstinence or timing of food and drink like tea, beer, and beans, so that they might not be driven to relief abed, since that, as we discover, is what leads to the distresses of this particular nuptial eve. Chloe has swilled twelve cups of tea (and ate her fill of peas as well, it seems) and now abed with her bridegroom, she is forced to seek relief. Her stealth in smuggling a urinal abed is all in vain, however, for Strephon overhears "the fuming Rill," and gives voice to his worst fears: "ye Gods, what Sound is this? / Can Chloe, heav'nly Chloe—?" Thus finding her "*mortal* as himself at least," he follows suit, seeking the "Pot" on his side of the bed: "And as he fill'd the reeking Vase, / Let fly a Rouzer in her Face." Whereupon the hovering cupids vanish, and with them "ravishing Delights, / High Raptures, and romantick Flights." Strephon and Chloe "learn to call a Spade, a Spade," and discharge their functions heedlessly before, and talk coarsely to, one another. Here endeth the drama. The rest is the author's envoi, his advice on marital surety to man and maid. This part is rather long, ninety-five lines, very nearly one-third of the poem, but Swift manages to meliorate its proportion by alternating the advice between man and maid. First the maid (lines 219–234), to secure her beauty's appeal by "Decency." Then the man (lines 235–250), to the effect that it were better to know woman starkly from the outset than to learn at such cost to marital grace that she is, after all, human, like himself. Then the maid again, repeating the lesson of "Decency," with the somewhat excrescent inventory of the false approaches of the sex to male approval. Then the man again, counselling a better foundation for marriage than transient "Beauty." Finally the both of them, in the touching but hardly consonant closing lines:

On Sense and Wit your Passion found,
By Decency cemented round;
Let Prudence with Good Nature strive,
To keep Esteem and Love alive.
Then come old Age whene'er it will,
Your Friendship shall continue still:
And thus a mutual gentle Fire,
Shall never but with Life expire.

I have declared these lines inconsonant, and they are in at least two ways. They do not, like much of the envoi, consort with the tone of the dramatic part of the poem, nor with the dramatic outcome of the poem. No part of the final commentary, in fact, fits the dramatic part of this poem, which is a pity, for these last lines especially deserve a better setting than they have, one which does not compromise their grace and beauty with nagging questions about consistency.

Swift fails to pull this poem together. He wants to image and dramatize the folly of romantic love, to elaborate for its own sake the intrinsically useful burlesque of the wedding hymn, and to enunciate a redemptive doctrine for the victims of the folly he has derided. There is no reason why all this could not be made coherent, but little of it is, and as a result we get the impression of alien elements rebuffing one another in search of a proper setting. There is much in the poem that is pleasing and effective, but it has to be found, and taken, piecemeal.

"Cassinus and Peter, A Tragical Elegy" is the sprightliest, and one of the most successful, of the unprintable poems, and aside from the four-letter word of its closing, it is difficult to perceive why it has remained so long interdicted. Perhaps the new morality of four-letter words will lower that barrier now, if that has been the problem. The poem is unquestionably the most delicious parody of the group, and it illustrates how easily Swift could perform in the romantic style he so greatly resents in others.

"Cassinus and Peter" is an anecdote, or episode (tragical and elegiac)—a conversation (dialogue) in a dormitory between two college sophs, brilliant perennials: literary, amorous, and appallingly unclean. Peter, come to Cassy's for gab and warmth, finds his friend in the profoundest dumps, weeping midst the litter of his room and the filth of his own person. Inquiring the cause, Peter, and we, are made to dangle in maddening yet fascinating suspense until Cassy can at last bring himself to reveal, after much unwitting comedy of romantic posturing, what Celia has done to bring him to such sad pass. She has, it turns out, committed the unbelievable, unpardonable, un-bearable sin of relieving herself of a perfectly natural burden: "Nor wonder how I lost my Wits; / Oh! Cælia, Cælia, Cælia sh—." Those, Victorian and Freudian, who have waxed so horrified over this and comparable passages in Swift have, in their solemnity, missed his wit both great and small; have failed no doubt, in this instance, to perceive the witty seasoning of this comic disclosure in Cassy's Latinate pronunciation, and hence spelling, of the fair Celia's name, something that Strephon, not being a college man, could not bring to his outcry against a like-named lass in "The Lady's Dressing Room."

Swift moves through this poem with the steadiness and certainty that marks his performance in "A Beautiful Young Nymph"; only here he is consistently comic where there he was comic and pathetic by turns. But the comic cloth of "Cassinus and Peter" is woven of several strands, principally with yarn not unlike that of "Baucis and Philemon" (a domestic, amiable stuff), a bit of carpe diem thread, and a great deal spun from the sensitive plants of elegy and pastoral. The poem opens on what I have called the Baucis yarn:

> Two College Sophs of *Cambridge* Growth
> Both special Wits, and Lovers both,
> Conferring as they us'd to meet,
> On Love and Books in Rapture sweet;
> (Muse, find me Names to fix my Metre,
> *Cassinus* this, and t'other *Peter*)
> Friend *Peter* to *Cassinus* goes,
> To chat a while, and warm his Nose.[20]

With the exception of a few strands of scatological yarn (cf. lines 18, 22), Swift weaves with this homespun until, in line 31, he works in a quartet of sprightly threads of carpe diem à la Herrick: "What makes thee," cries Peter to the dolorous slugabed, "lie a-bed so late?"

> The Finch, the Linnet and the Thrush,
> Their Mattins chant in ev'ry Bush:
> And, I have heard thee oft salute
> *Aurora* with thy early Flute.

Peter's going a-maying, and would have Cassy go along. The pastoral and elegiac form the warp to this woof of homespun and carpe diem, and are perhaps familiar enough to need no illustrative reminder, though it is difficult to forbear Cassy's finest elegiac reach:

> Then, leave me to despair and dye.
> Yet, kind *Arcadians*, on my Urn
> These Elegies and Sonnets burn,
> And on the Marble grave these Rhimes,
> A Monument to after-Times:
> "Here Cassy lies, by Cælia slain,
> "And dying, never told his Pain.

Cassy then bids this cruel world adieu and fancies himself on his journey underworld, a vision wherein, it may be, we sense still other threads smuggled into the comic weave, Virgilian, Marlovian, Shakespearean, and Popeian of the apocalyptic *Dunciad*.[21]

But the ultimate comic stimulus of the poem arises from the melodramatics themselves of Cassy, embellished by the various stylistics we have remarked, but also by Swift's inventiveness in the substance of the swan-song and in the use of Peter to elicit that. "Is Cælia dead?" asks Peter, fearing the worst. Would she were, cries Cassy. Has "she play'd the Whore?" then, asks Peter, obviously framing his questions from the worst possibilities downwards, unaware that his order of importance is exactly the opposite of Cassy's. Would she had done no more, responds despondent Cassy. Does she have the Pox? Ah, "Beauty's but a Varnish," says Cassy; you could never guess what she has done. Aha, cries Peter, it's "the Barber's Boy." This "I could excuse," says Cassy. No, it is a crime beyond belief, and quite singular in the annals of female history. It is here that Cassy goes into his mock farewell, after which Peter, desperate, recommends purging and bleeding and entreats Cassy to tell him what dread thing it is that Celia has done. Alas, says Cassy, you will tear it from me, but I abjure you (by a curse he shortly utters) never to tell it, neither to Celia ("How would her Virgin Soul bemoan / A Crime to all her Sex unknown!"), the reeds, the rocks, the college, nor the "chatt' ring feather'd Race." Whereupon he tears it from his tortured breast: "Oh! Cælia, Cælia, Cælia sh—."

Once more Swift has refused to compromise. He holds the romantic, as he has the realistic, to the full penalty of satiric assessment, and the result is neither preachment nor psycho-therapy, but poetry—the product of an imagination as dazzling and a pen as steady as any in English literature.

Notes

1. One of the most recent, and one of the best, arguments for the thematic dignity of the poems is that by D. J. Greene, "On Swift's 'Scatological' Poems," *Sewanee Review*, LXXV (1967), 672–689. Greene discusses "The Lady's Dressing Room," "Strephon and Chloe," and "Cassinus and Peter."   2. Others have remarked Swift's habit of working from analogy. See, e.g., Irvin Ehrenpreis, *Swift: The Man, His Works, and the Age* (Cambridge, Mass., 1967), II, 246.   3. Swift's poetry is cited here and hereafter from *The Poems of Jonathan Swift*, 3 vols., ed. Harold Williams (Oxford, 1958). "The Progress of Beauty" appears in I, 266–229.   4. I have spoken of a *lunar* Diana. I suspect Swift intends us to assimilate, along with everything else, the *lunatic* association, and that this is one reason why, later in the poem (line 105), he uses the name itself, *Luna*.   5. The technique is very similar, on a smaller scale, to that of delayed disclosure in the *Modest Proposal*.   6. Actually, of course, Swift does not even then make the distinction explicit. Swift's satiric tact in such matters is impeccable.   7. *Poems*, ed. Williams, II, 530.   8. Maurice Johnson, *The Sin of Wit* (1950; rpt. New York, 1966), p. 118.   9. Ibid., p. 119.

10. Greene, p. 680.   11. "Those Secrets of the hoary deep!" (line 98), from *Paradise Lost*, II, 890–891. See *Poems*, ed. Williams, II, 528n.   12. If this is an allusion, one is tempted to suppose that Celia's *Tripsy* is likewise a meiotic counterpart of Belinda's *Shock*. The whole scene in fact reads like a burlesque of Belinda's toilet.   13. "Corinna and the Sterner Muse of Swift," *ELN*, IV (1966), 23–31.   14. Ibid., p. 30.   15. For "Strephon and Chloe," see *Poems*, ed. Williams, II, 584–593. See also "pluck a Rose," in Eric Partridge, *A Dictionary of Slang and Unconventional English*, 2nd ed. (London, 1938).   16. Greene, p. 681.   17. Ibid., p. 680. Cf. (pp. 683–684) "but surely Swift's *real* advice to us in the poem is not to let our minds work at all in the way Strephon's works!" But Mr. Greene is tenacious of the Christian reading (cf. p. 685).   18. I say the lines are more appropriate to a poem *like* the "Dressing Room," not to that poem itself, where, though more proximate, they would not fit either by virtue of the fact that that is not a marriage poem or the fact that Strephon does not learn the lesson these lines claim he would from the experience he had.   19. *Jonathan Swift: Essays on his Satire and Other Studies* (Oxford, 1964), p. 195.

20. "Cassinus and Peter" appears in *Poems*, ed. Williams, II, 593–597.   21. "Avaunt—ye cannot say 'twas I" has been traced by Williams (*Poems*, II, 596n) to the two familiar utterances of Macbeth. The passage also calls up Faustus's foreclosing devils and anguished outcry, especially in "*Medusa*, see, / Her Serpents hiss direct at me." Cassy's "I come, I come" (as well as

his grim depiction of Hades) reminds one not only of Virgil (and other classical sources) but of the "all composing Hour" of Pope's *Dunciad*, with one particularly analogous formula: "She comes! she comes!..."

GULLIVER'S FOURTH VOYAGE
"Hard" and "Soft" Schools of Interpretation

James L. Clifford

SOME literary masterpieces apparently defy exposition. The changing taste of the times, rise and fall of new methods of analysis, individual commitments of each explicator, and the refusal of the author himself to be explicit all combine to render the job virtually impossible. Yet we keep trying. Each eager enthusiast comes up with his own brilliant interpretation, hoping to settle the matter forever, but he never quite convinces his colleagues, not to mention posterity.

The fourth book of *Gulliver's Travels* is one of these difficult cases. What exactly did Swift intend his basic message to be? Can we ever know? Certainly through the years there has never been any complete agreement, but at least in our day the argument seems to fall into two main camps. I realize the dangers of any such simple division. It can only represent an attempt of one person to isolate what appears to him to be the central issues involved. Still, it does appear to me that the present split can be described as a struggle between a "hard" and a "soft" approach. By "hard" I mean an interpretation which stresses the shock and difficulty of the work, with almost tragic overtones, while by "soft" I mean the tendency to find comic passages and compromise solutions.

But before attempting to analyze the principal points of disagreement, let me say something about the nineteenth-century background, which naturally led to the present argument. The story of the early reactions to the fourth voyage of Gulliver was well summarized by Merrel D. Clubb some thirty years ago.[1] There should be no need for me to repeat all the evidence here. As Clubb clearly shows, the gradual assumption that Swift was a bitter, disappointed misanthrope developed from a too literal interpretation of the allegory. Many readers assumed without question that Gulliver was Swift himself, that the

Yahoos were meant to represent the human race, and that the Houyhnhnms were real horses. The result of such a reading inevitably turned Swift into the gibbering monster, "filthy in word, filthy in thought, furious, raging, obscene," so vividly described by Thackeray. By the late nineteenth century Gerald Moriarty could assume an identification of horses as the imaginary rulers and men as beasts, all of which proved Swift's belief that human beings were "abominable to the very core." The description of the Yahoos, with its terrible defamation of the human race, so Edmund Gosse put it, banished "from decent households a fourth part of one of the most brilliant and delightful of English books."

By the early twentieth century the standard textbook descriptions echo such remarks as "In the fourth part he represents humanity as infinitely contemptible from the standpoint of a commonwealth of horses," or "Human nature indignantly rejects her portrait in the Yahoo as a gross libel," or "Swift thus heaps scorn and contempt on the race to which he belongs."

The customary explanation of the cause of Swift's horrible misanthropy was a supposed early appearance of his mental breakdown. So Sir Walter Scott could allude to the "soured and disgusted state of Swift's mind"—and to his incipient mental disorder. Of course, there were some isolated defenses of the fourth voyage in the eighteenth century—by Monck Berkeley and William Godwin, and later by such men as William Hazlitt, Henry Morley, and Cecil Headlam. But these failed to stem the general tide.

When the reaction came in the twentieth century, the first step was to rescue Swift from the libelous assertion that he was a half-crazy misanthrope. It was easy for such careful scholars as Louis Landa to show that his mental breakdown—actually his senility—did not begin until at least fifteen years after writing *Gulliver's Travels*.[2] Swift was as sane in the early 1720s as he ever was. Other critics emphasized the fact that Gulliver must not be equated with his creator. He did not always represent Swift, or parrot his opinions. He was a fictional character, sometimes a satiric *persona*, and sometimes merely a character in a narrative. Moreover, the Houyhnhnms and the Yahoos should not be interpreted literally. Nor should the latter be thought of simply as a libel on the human race. The allegory in Book IV is much more complicated than that.

As has often been pointed out, one of the first significant forerunners of the new approach was T. O. Wedel. In 1926, in *Studies in Philology*,[3] he stressed the fact that Gulliver, being himself part beast and part reason, was meant to be between the Yahoos and the Houyhnhnms. Swift was really attacking the philosophic optimists of his time, with their unrealistic faith in reason and progress, and their denial of the old doctrine of original sin. Ricardo Quintana and Arthur Case, adopting this approach, made perfectly clear that Swift's purpose was not complete identification of any sort.[4] Rather there were two themes—the bestiality of man under the control of the irrational and the utopian possibilities of a life of reason. As Case put it, the Houyhnhnms and the Yahoos represent the "extremes between which human behavior may range." Swift did not think man could ever reach either such heights or depths, but he felt that, since at the moment man's tendency was downward, strenuous efforts were needed if he were to be saved. The first step must be to show the inherent dangers of human pride.

Once it was recognized that man stands between the two extremes, it seemed natural to assume that Swift was pointing to some kind of golden mean, and that the fourth voyage was meant to force readers to such a conclusion. Thus irresistibly scholars came to explore this middle-ground interpretation, thus forming what I like to call the "soft" school. It was to dominate Swift criticism of the 1940s and early 1950s.

One of the most influential of these approaches, though it took some time to be fully recognized, was John F. Ross's "The Final Comedy of Lemuel Gulliver," which appeared in 1941.[5] Everyone, Ross insisted, has misunderstood the fourth voyage of Gulliver. Swift's target throughout is not mankind, but the insufficiency and foolishness of misanthropy itself. It is Gulliver who is being satirized, his stupid attacks on human weakness, his credulity in believing the Houyhnhnms to be ideal. In the end the joke is turned by Swift against himself. To prove this point, Ross stressed the ridiculous qualities of the Houyhnhnms and the places where Gulliver is himself shown to be inadequate and absurd. The final comedy of the book is that "Swift should make an elaborate and subtle joke at the expense of a very important part of himself."

Ross's theory was so "far out" that it took some time for it to be assimilated. Indeed, eight years later, Edward Stone in

Modern Language Quarterly could make something like the same discovery without ever having heard of Ross.[6] He, too, comes to the same basic conclusion that the work is comic. It is a parody of the beast fable and of the idea that beasts are better than men. Gulliver's denunciations of human behavior are much too ludicrous to be taken seriously. Swift must have had his tongue in his cheek throughout. He is laughing at us. When he purposely in the end turns Gulliver into a mad railer, he is satirizing people who take the whole business too seriously.

The *locus classicus* of the new "soft" approach may be found in the work of Kathleen Williams—her articles beginning in 1951 and her book, *Jonathan Swift and the Age of Compromise* in 1958.[7] Admittedly the word "compromise" in her title was a mistake. She herself is quick to agree that another word might have been more descriptive of what she means. Today "compromise" has a pejorative implication, suggesting something a bit shoddy, somehow lacking in firmness. This is not at all what she intended. She means a middle position—something more approximating the golden mean of classical ideals. Because Swift was a representative of what we call a neoclassical age, so Miss Williams suggests, he must have advocated a central position—a sensible, attainable norm. Even though he may give the impression of being violent and harsh in attack, he always implies a reasonable alternative which man ought to strive for. It is the duty of the modern critic to cut through Swift's apparent misanthropy and find the rational core at the center. One can do this in the fourth book of *Gulliver's Travels* by showing the unattractive qualities of the extremes. This is easy with the Yahoos. Everyone recognizes their nastiness and grossness. But what of the Houyhnhnms? Gulliver says that they are the perfection of nature. But Swift must have meant this to be taken ironically. When carefully examined, they are as full of faults—though of a different sort—as the Yahoos. They lack many of the qualities which everyone admires. Basically, then, they represent a point of view which Swift, an Anglican clergyman, surely would have detested—the new stoical and deistic self-sufficiency, which was becoming more and more popular. Consequently they must have been intended to show the inadequacy of the life of reason. Swift is balancing extremes, and in the end pointing to an attainable norm. What is it? Obviously there is only one truly admirable creature in the fourth book, the Portuguese captain who brings Gulliver back home. He must function as the norm. Captain Mendez must be the key to the meaning of the satire.

Such an interpretation has many advantages. It rescues Swift from the traditional claims that he was a mad misanthrope. It also shows that he himself saw the futility of such an approach and had the wit to laugh at all those who rail about the depravity of man. As a person of taste and common sense, he clearly saw the value of striving for a sensible position. Although it was often well hidden, he had a sane, reasonable program for mankind. From this point of view, then, Swift is displayed in a good light, and our own comprehension is flattered in being able to discern the truth underneath the sensational surface violence.

For a time the "soft" approach seemed to have won. Scholar after scholar joined the ranks. The list is impressive: Ernest Tuveson, Samuel Monk, Maynard Mack, Harold Kelling, Clarence Tracy, Martin Kallich, Calhoun Winton, and many others.[8] Tuveson, for example, insists that in *Gulliver's Travels* Swift's basic attack is not upon man but upon the various false ideals which have misled him—rationalism, inevitable progress, and the essential goodness of human nature.[9] Since in his own day traditional Christian doctrines were being discarded indiscriminately, Swift thought it time to protest. The moral at the end of the tale is the treachery of man's pride,[10] the bankruptcy of human desires, and the necessity of finding guidance "beyond our own resources." Certainly the Houyhnhnms are not the answer. Thus a relatively "soft" Christian interpretation comes on the scene.[11]

All of these scholars assume the insufficiency of the Houyhnhnms as a model and try to show that they really represent positions and ideas which Swift personally abhorred. In an earlier essay, which he has since disclaimed, Irvin Ehrenpreis even suggested that the Houyhnhnms typified a kind of deism associated with Bolingbroke.[12] Amusingly enough, Swift once had a horse named "Bolingbroke." But to assume that the Houyhnhnms were meant to stand for any specific belief is, as Louis Landa succinctly put it, to identify "the *language* of rationalism with the *substance* of deism."[13]

It was this kind of interpretation which finally brought a vigorous rebuttal. In 1958 George Sherburn blasted the attempt to make deism a central issue. In a trenchant short piece in *Modern Philology* entitled "Errors Concerning the Houyhnhnms" he initiated the "hard" school interpretation. Sherburn insisted that, despite surface weaknesses, the Houyhnhnms were obviously meant to be ideals.[14] They cannot be regarded as objects of satire, for Gulliver's final reaction is not comic but deeply serious. He has seen a vision of perfection and cannot speedily recover. Swift means us to be deeply moved, not amused.

Sherburn's position was amplified by his former colleague at the University of Chicago, Ronald Crane, in what might be called the *locus classicus* of the "hard" approach. To be sure, his tough-minded analysis of the problem came together slowly. It was first given in a talk at the Modern Language Association meeting in Chicago in 1955. Then in the spring of 1959 he read another version at Oxford, and the next year he delivered a still further revision to the English Graduate Union at Columbia. Each time it had been radically changed. Happily a portion of one of the early versions is preserved in Robert A. Greenberg's annotated text of the travels (1961), and the final text was printed in 1962 in the festschrift for Marjorie Nicolson.[15] There is no need here to sum up all of Crane's arguments—his skeptical and detailed analysis of what he considered the false assumptions made by earlier historians of ideas, his discovery of one specific source of Swift's allegory of the horses in popular rhetoric texts used by Swift in college, and his insistence on the harsh purpose of the entire work. I will have more to say about all this later when discussing individual points.

Crane's remains the dominant work in the "hard" school approach, the one which must be controverted by those on the other side. To be sure, he has had the support of another Chicago scholar, Edward Rosenheim, of Charles Peake of London, of Louis Landa, Conrad Suits, and Donald Greene, to name only a few.[16] If the "hard" school is still not accepted by a majority of eminent eighteenth-century scholars, it has enlisted a number of vigorous advocates.

Of course, the "hard" and "soft" antithesis is much too pat and narrow to cover all the recent approaches to the fourth book of *Gulliver's Travels*. Every kind of new critical technique has been used. Martin Price approaches the problem through the examination of prevailing metaphors.[17] Dick Taylor, Jr., uses an archetypal approach.[18] Roland Frye and others use biblical themes and symbols.[19] Inescapably there continues to be a variety of interpretations. Some of them, while not strictly "soft," could be called "spongy" or "mushy," or even "soggy," although others could more fairly be termed "firm" or "hard of center." One of the most intriguing comes from John Traugott, who suggests that it is possible to be "hard" and "soft" at the same time.[20] Swift, Traugott proposes, is saying that man can hold to an impossible ideal and at the same time make all the compromises and adjustments which modern society demands; that he can believe in perfection, and yet also play the knave when necessary. When one follows Traugott's own rather tortuous rhetoric to his final conclusion, his is a challenging piece with obvious further ramifications. Boswell and Sterne, we know, could occasionally delight in foolish actions and at the same time evaluate their own stupidity. They could be sentimental and satirical at the same moment, without any sense of incongruity. Could Swift, too, have been thoroughly committed to an impossible ideal, accepting at the same time an attainable human norm? Possibly. Yet how can we ever be sure?

In passing, let me also note briefly a few more recent approaches which appear to me to be neither completely "soft" nor "hard." Ricardo Quintana, for example, is difficult to place.[21] Throughout, he seems to be taking a fairly central position, with a concentration on the importance of Swift's comic approach coupled with a refusal to consider the Houyhnhnms as objects of satire. Or does the Houyhnhnms' cool, passionless existence embody, as Denis Donoghue suggests, "Swift's desire for ease and rest. To be relieved of passion he was prepared to pay a high price"?[22] Irvin Ehrenpreis now appears to be moving steadily from "soft" to "hard." His assessment of the problem in *Review of English Literature* for July 1962 might best be called "firm" or at least "hard of center."[23] He now accepts the Houyhnhnms as meant to represent an ideal of sorts, as set up against man's irrationality, and he does not stress the comic elements of the ending.

In this short résumé I have been able to give only a cursory account of the recent differences of opinion. Let me now mention what seem to me to be the basic problems involved, and then stress four crucial points. In trying to evaluate the position of each of the combatants, or even of one's own fundamental stance, we must somehow answer these basic questions.

In the first place, should *Gulliver's Travels* be considered as a single, isolated work of art, or as an integral part of Swift's total output as a writer? Second, what are Swift's overall goals, if it is possible to discover them? And does he ever in his other works present an easily attainable norm?

Without openly taking sides on these important decisions, let me suggest that viewing *Gulliver's Travels* independently, cut off from what we know about his career and his other works, has sometimes resulted in strange, distorted interpretations. On the other hand, I am forced to admit that there is no generally accepted view of what Swift's overall intentions were. Thus there can be no guarantee that placing the fourth book of *Gulliver* in the context of Swift's other satires will make our task any easier. For example, Kathleen Williams surveys Swift's whole career and comes to the conclusion that he was always searching for some acceptable middle ground, some workable compromise.[24] Edward Rosenheim, on the contrary, sees Swift's principal purpose as shock treatment, setting impossible goals and leaving to others the task of teaching mankind reasonable solutions.[25] Others on his side come to similar conclusions. Swift, they say, did not think it his duty to provide rules of conduct, or any sensible answers. His job was to strip bare the conscience of man, to shock each reader into making an honest appraisal of his own condition. In the end each reader has to work out for himself the kind of compromise he is willing to accept.

Such an emphasis on shock technique does not necessarily imply a lack of serious moral purpose in Swift. If he seems to be largely negative in his approach, this does not mean that he has no positive assumptions. The point that the "hard" school makes is that Swift's norms are rigorous and ascetic. They are usually impossible of ordinary achievement. No golden mean will satisfy him as an objective. Swift accepted the orthodox Christian position. Man is fallen and corrupt; he is, for the most part, ruled by selfishness and bestiality. But God has also placed in man a small core of reason—too little to do much to improve his condition—but enough to show him the falsity of too much pride. Since he does not have the power to determine his own destiny, his reason should keep him from making foolish claims.

The "soft" school generally would support the notion that the fourth voyage of Gulliver must be judged by what we can guess of Swift's intention at the time. So judged, it turns out to be a comic satire on man's foolish pride and his gullibility in taking too seriously all impossible and unattractive ideals. The "hard" school replies that it is difficult to find anywhere else in Swift's work such compromise thinking. Except in pieces designed for some special political emergency—as in the *Contests and Dissentions*—Swift rarely comes out with any middle-ground solution. Although Martin in *A Tale of a Tub* may have been intended to represent Swift's own Church of England position, Swift consistently undercuts him. Certainly no contemporary reader thought of the work as conciliatory or preaching a golden mean. The *Drapier's Letters* suggest no compromise. The only answer must be complete surrender by Wood and the English. *A Modest Proposal*, at least for most of us, is shocking and painful. And it might be argued that Swift's general suggestion concerning the relationship of man and woman, as exemplified by his own ties to Stella, involves an almost impossible ideal of a complete negation of sex. His norm is never easy of attainment.

Maynard Mack pointed out some time ago that in the *Argument Against Abolishing Christianity* Swift's basic position is one which is devastating to the reader's own complacency.[26] Irvin Ehrenpreis, indeed, now suggests that a similar interpretation might be used in getting at the overall meaning of the fourth voyage of Gulliver.[27] In the earlier work Swift implies that if men really did practice true Christianity it would destroy everything they cherish in their civilization. So at the close of *Gulliver's Travels* he is addressing all the people of his day who had easy solutions, and who kept repeating their allegiance to reason. If you really lived by your avowed principles, he says, you would uproot society as Gulliver wrecks his family. Yet ardent "soft" school adherents would insist that this is a false analogy—that the situations are different, and conclusions valid for one work cannot be grafted to another. And so the argument continues.

In addition to these general problems concerned with the possibility of discovering Swift's overall purpose—some might call it the biographical or the intentional fallacy—there are particular questions which seem to me just as crucial. Of course, the areas of disagreement cover a wide range of topics, but I should like to suggest that they may largely be classified in four specific categories—(1) the meaning of the Yahoos, (2) the meaning of the Houyhnhnms, (3) the significance of Captain Mendez, and (4) the interpretation of the ending.

I might have eliminated the question of the Yahoos, since there has been less argument lately about them than about the other points. No one today accepts the older identification of the Yahoos with mankind, or assumes that they represent a crazy slander on human beings. For the most part, current theories accept them as descriptions of the limits to which man may degenerate if his passions are unrestrained, or, using biblical and theological symbols of sin, as the orthodox representation of the natural depravity of man.

The interpretation of the Houyhnhnms, on the other hand, is central to our understanding of the book. Yet Swift's intent is never completely clear. The result is that there are almost as many divergent explications as there are of the character of Hamlet, and they vary almost as widely. Merely to list a few will indicate the nature of the problem. Do they represent (1) a vision of prelapsarian perfection, unattainable by man, or (2) an unattainable ideal which man should nevertheless strive to reach, (3) an ideal limited by Swift's view of the nature of man, (4) not an ideal objective, but an insulting impossibility, (5) mere absence of vice, (6) one of the two opposing sides of man's nature, (7) pure reason, but not ideal, (8) cold, inhuman beings, lacking Christian benevolence, (9) deistic rationalism, which Swift hated, (10) Bolingbroke and the rationalistic thinkers of his type, (11) merely rhetorical devices through which to attack man's pride in thinking himself better than animals, (12) Trojan horses designed to betray credulous mankind, (13) a narrative device in the classical Menippean tradition?[28] And there are many other interpretations which people take seriously.

How are we to explain this wide spectrum? As I intimated earlier, much depends on the standards by which the Houyhnhnms are judged. Are they to be evaluated by human standards? Or in some superhuman frame of reference? If the latter, how is it possible to assess the results? As human beings ourselves, how can we judge correctly the nature of Swift's fictional horses? While there is no easy answer, one thing is certain: we must try to avoid anachronistic approaches based on twentieth-century beliefs. Let me cite in passing what seems to me to be one example of this kind of mistake—Hugo Reichard's essay in the *Satire Newsletter*, in which he claims that the attitude of the Houyhnhnms turns Gulliver into a snob, a condition obviously deplorable.[29] But this is to assume in Swift a modern liberal dislike of snobbery. How can we be certain that he would have disapproved of qualities and actions we now term snobbish? I suspect that he firmly believed in social gradations, in hierarchy and subordination. We cannot blandly assume today his agreement with social evaluations which we take for granted.

Another kind of mistake—so it appears to me—made by scholars attempting to find specific sources for Swift's satire is epitomized in an article by James R. Wilson in *Tennessee Studies in Literature* in 1958.[30] Assuming that Swift's Houyhnhnms are not intended as ideal utopian creatures, Wilson triumphantly shows that in the Old Testament there are at least six places where one can find passages stressing the danger of putting one's trust in a horse rather than in God. Here are a few samples:

> Some trust in chariots, and some in horses;
> but we will remember the name of the Lord our God.
> Psalms 20:7

> Be ye not as the horse, or as the mule, which have no understanding. . . .
> Psalms 32:9

> A horse is a vain thing for safety:
> neither shall he deliver any by his great strength.
> Psalms 33:17

Moreover, there have been many other attempts to show that the horses are merely narrative devices, needed to carry the story along.

More important than such peripheral quibbles is the basic decision as to whether the Houyhnhnms represent some kind of ideal, flawed or not, or should be viewed as butts for Swift's satire. Or if not meant to be perfect, are they satirized as proof of the impossibility of any utopian standards whatsoever, or as proof of Gulliver's gullibility in taking them seriously, or even of his faulty reporting about them? Is Gulliver being made fun of through his view of the Houyhnhnms? Or the reader? Or both?

Central to the "hard" school approach is the conviction that the Houyhnhnms do indeed represent some kind of an ideal. They are not being satirized or attacked in the same manner as the Yahoos. They do not represent an excessive position to be judged from a middle-ground norm. But if not, how to explain their many unattractive qualities, their lack of warm benevolence, the rigidity of their social outlook? If they are to be admired, why do they lack so many of the attributes we would like to see in an ideal? But this, answer those of the "hard" school, is to judge them by human standards. We do not like them, but we are human beings. Swift meant them to represent a kind of perfect reason which obviously would not appeal to normal human beings. For example, imagine trying to have a conversation with a prelapsarian being. How could one communicate with him? How could one argue? There would be only one side to every question, the true one. There would be no need to think of such matters as kindness, benevolence, sympathy, since with no sin and no weakness there would be no gradations or inequalities. Suppose you tried to talk to him about some philosophic problem. He would settle it at once and that would be the end of it. He would have no need whatsoever for any of the qualities we prize most in mankind.

Now it is quite obvious that Swift's Houyhnhnms do not represent such a standard of perfection. Judged by absolute, prelapsarian standards some of them are definitely flawed. They do not know everything, and are willing to listen for days on end to Gulliver's interminable accounts of European life (of course, for narrative and satiric reasons all this is vitally necessary). Indeed, it could be argued that Gulliver's Houyhnhnm master was significantly corrupted by his association with Gulliver, a sign that even perfect beings are susceptible to corruption. Gulliver's master is willing to break the accepted laws of Houyhnhnmland, on occasions showing almost human kindness, and exhibiting various degrees of benevolence. Does this mean that Swift is satirizing the Houyhnhnms by showing that even they have some human qualities? Or is it a simple flaw in Swift's artistry? Or a decision on his part not to make the Houyhnhnms completely unacceptable? Or merely his desire to make the story more entertaining on the purely narrative level?

There can be no doubt that in places Swift is poking fun at the Houyhnhnms. Yet does this necessarily mean, as the "soft" school insists, that he intends the horses to be ludicrous, and not to be taken seriously? It is a crucial point. Irvin Ehrenpreis, in his 1962 article, suggests that the laughable qualities of the Houyhnhnms may be easily explained by Swift's habitual inability to resist having a joke. "Like Shaw, he often could not resist a comic opening even when the indulgence would obscure a satirical design."[31] And so he cannot resist

ridiculing the anthropocentricity in the Houyhnhnms. Yet
Ehrenpreis sees that, despite surface weaknesses and peripheral
joking, Swift did clearly intend the Houyhnhnms to represent
some kind of an ideal—cold and unemotional, to be sure, and
not particularly attractive to a warm-hearted human reader—
but an ideal just the same. For Swift's purpose this must be so.

Another recent analysis which supports the view that Gulliver
was "right to propose the horses as a model for imitation" is
that held by M. M. Kelsall.[32] As he points out, Gulliver, when
on the island of the sorcerers on his third voyage, called up the
spirits of the mighty dead, and conversed with Brutus, Junius,
Socrates, Epaminondas, Cato the Younger, and Sir Thomas
More. Why, Kelsall asks, did Swift select these six men as special
heroes? Was it because their virtues were similar to those of the
Houyhnhnms? A careful analysis of their qualities and careers
would seem to suggest that this is so. To be sure, the whole thing
is "utterly ridiculous." But "the more ridiculous it becomes, the
blacker the pessimism."

Advocates of the "hard" school tend to shrug off the
significance of Captain Mendez, the kindly Portuguese sea
captain, but for the "soft" school he is vital. If, as they insist,
the Houyhnhnms and the Yahoos represent unattractive
extremes to be avoided in a search for a stable, central
norm, then there must be somewhere else in the fourth voyage
a character who represents this ideal of human excellence. Swift,
they argue, was too sensible a man not to present us somewhere
with a viable solution. He must have meant the reader to see
through the flawed allegory of the horses and the beastly ape-
like creatures, to a proper goal. Even though occupying a minor
position in the plot, Captain Mendez is obviously the only
wholly attractive person in the book. He must represent Swift's
carefully considered model for human behavior. When Gulliver
loses all sanity after his exposure to the false vision, Houyhnhnmland, and thus becomes the butt of the final comic satire, the
admirable sea captain remains with us as the epitome of human
excellence and benevolence. He is what we should try to emulate.

This kind of argument naturally leads me to the last bloody
battleground of twentieth-century scholars—the question of
the meaning of the ending. If the "soft" school is right about
Captain Mendez, then the ending must be comic or satiric,
with Gulliver and the reader raked over the coals for their
credulity in having been taken in, even for a moment, by the

so-called "perfections of nature," the Houyhnhnms. But for the "hard" school adherents, who see Don Pedro as merely a minor character in the narrative, being Swift's ironic admission that even such an admirable person is basically a Yahoo, the description of Gulliver's return home is meant to shock and not to amuse the reader. There is no such viable solution. Thus Swift savagely twists the knife. To see it any other way, they say, is to misinterpret his basic satirical approach. We must always be careful not to be diverted by surface comic effects or attractive rationalizations.

Of course, there is a wide variety of exegesis coming from both "soft" and "hard" school camps. Some critics like W. B. C. Watkins think that in the fourth voyage Swift leaves the realm of satire altogether and enters that of pure tragedy.[33] Even though Gulliver does survive in the end, he is caught just as inextricably as are the protagonists of classical drama. But most "hard" core adherents stress shock as basic in Gulliver's return home. As Robert B. Heilman puts it, Gulliver had undergone "an almost annihilating experience, and at the end is recovering as best he may."[34]

Sherburn suggests that the analogy to be always kept in mind is the case of St. Paul on the way to Damascus, struck blind by the light of heaven, and remaining so for days.[35] Crane similarly uses Plato's myth concerning the prisoner of the cave, who was completely blinded by his vision of the sun, and could not easily adjust to his old surroundings.[36] Like this prisoner, Gulliver has undergone a deeply disturbing, even terrifying revelation about mankind, and he cannot be expected to act sanely thereafter. All his subsequent actions, foolish though they may appear from one angle, are the result of this searing experience. The reader is supposed to be torn out of his own complacency by a realization of the terrible predicament of the human race, unable to attain perfection and yet with no other intermediate choice for imitation.

Those who find the ending satiric rarely agree as to the identity of the targets, or how seriously they are being attacked. Swift could be lashing out merely at man's foolish pride in thinking he could ever be like the ideal Houyhnhnms, or he could be poking fun at Gulliver's credulity, or the reader's gullibility, or the impossibility of all utopian schemes. Is there one single target? Or are there many? The answers keep multiplying.

I have listed four basic approaches to the ending—interpreting it as tragic, shocking, comic, and satiric. To these might be added another—didactic. Suppose one were to concentrate on the final paragraphs of the fourth voyage where Gulliver refers to his gradual attempts at reconciliation with the human species by instructing the members of his own family and by attempting to eradicate the stupid vice of pride everywhere. In this way, he intimates, it might be possible to render the society of an English Yahoo supportable. The implication is that the slow process of education is a possibility, though certainly Gulliver has no illusions as to any speedy progress toward Houyhnhnm ideals.[37]

One trouble with such an interpretation is that it depends upon the isolation of a few passages, rather than on overall motivation. Many may find it difficult to believe that Swift intended his reader, as he comes to the end of the book, to rush off with zeal for pedagogical schemes.

To conclude—perhaps what Swift is saying is basically this. Absolute standards are unattainable by fallen man, and even if they could be reached would prove unattractive and unsatisfactory. Moreover, all attempts at middle-ground solutions involve a certain amount of selfish rationalization and hypocrisy. This is man's predicament. He knows he can never attain perfection, yet his attempts to set up alternative solutions involve choices which he cannot wholly justify. And so he is caught in a great dilemma.

Gulliver's reaction to this discovery, fictionally represented in melodramatic terms, clearly sets up the problem. How we interpret it depends largely on our own beliefs. For some his reaction appears comic, representing an unrealistic attempt to take the confusions of life more seriously than necessary. For others it is ironic—an amused, almost disdainful guffaw over the whole idea. For myself, and for most others of the "hard school," it is poignantly moving, a truly tragic realization of man's flawed condition, trapped in a situation which he cannot control. Swift's genius has confronted us with a work which, like other masterpieces of literature, can never be explicated with absolute certainty.[38]

Notes

1. "The Criticism of Gulliver's 'Voyage to the Houyhnhnms,' 1726–1914," *Stanford Studies in Language and Literature*, ed. Hardin Craig (1941), pp. 203–232. Quotations in the following three paragraphs come from this source.   2. See Louis A. Landa, "The Critical Significance of Biographical Evidence: Jonathan Swift," *English Institute Essays, 1946* (1947), pp. 20–40.   3. Theodore O. Wedel, "On the Philosophical Background of *Gulliver's Travels*," *SP*, XXIII (1926), 434–450.   4. Ricardo Quintana, *The Mind and Art of Jonathan Swift* (New York, 1936), and Arthur E. Case, *Four Essays on "Gulliver's Travels"* (Princeton, 1945).   5. *Studies in the Comic*, University of California Publications in English, VIII, no. 2 (1941), 175–196.   6. "Swift and the Horses: Misanthropy or Comedy?" *MLQ*, X (1949), 367–376.   7. "Gulliver's Voyage to the Houyhnhnms," *ELH*, XVIII (1951), 275–286; "'Animal Rationis Capax': A Study of Certain Aspects of Swift's Imagery," *ELH*, XXI (1954), 193–207; *Jonathan Swift and the Age of Compromise* (Lawrence, Kans., 1958).   8. Milton Voigt, *Swift and the Twentieth Century* (Detroit, 1964), discusses most of them. Ernest Tuveson's collection of critical essays on Swift, in the Prentice-Hall Twentieth-Century Views series (Englewood Cliffs, N.J., 1964), stresses this side of the argument.   9. "Swift: The Dean as Satirist," *UTQ*, XXII (1953), 368–375.

10. Samuel Monk, "The Pride of Lemuel Gulliver," *Sewanee Review*, LXIII (1955), 48–71.   11. J. J. McMammon, "The Problem of a Religious Interpretation of Gulliver's Fourth Voyage," *JHI*, XXVII (1966), 59–72. A recent proponent of the religious interpretation is Martin Kallich, *The Other End of the Egg: Religious Satire in "Gulliver's Travels"* (Bridgeport, Conn., 1970).   12. *The Personality of Jonathan Swift* (Cambridge, Mass., 1958), pp. 103–109.   13. Review of Irvin Ehrenpreis, *The Personality of Jonathan Swift*.   14. LVI (1958), 92–97.   15. "The Houyhnhnms, the Yahoos, and the History of Ideas," *Reason and the Imagination*, ed. Joseph Mazzeo (New York, 1962), pp. 231–253.   16. For example, see Edward Rosenheim, Jr., "The Fifth Voyage of Lemuel Gulliver," *MP*, LX (1962), 103–119, and his *Swift and the Satirist's Art* (Chicago, 1963); Charles Peake, "Swift and the Passions," *MLR*, LV (1960), 169–180; Louis A. Landa, Review of Ehrenpreis, *PQ*, XXXVIII (1959), 351–353; Donald J. Greene, "The Sin of Pride: A Sketch for a Literary Exploration," *New Mexico Quarterly*, XXXIV (1964), 8–30; Conrad Suits, "The Rôle of the Horses in 'A Voyage to the Houyhnhnms,'" *UTQ*, XXXIV (1965), 118–132; and Ronald S. Crane, Review of Martin Kallich, "Three Ways of Looking at a Horse . . . ," *PQ*, XL (1961), 427–430.   17. *Swift's Rhetorical Art* (rpt. Hamden, Conn., 1963).   18. Dick Taylor, Jr., "Gulliver's Pleasing Visions: Self-Deception as a Major

Theme in *Gulliver's Travels*," *Tulane Studies in English*, XII (1962), 7–61.   19. Roland M. Frye, "Swift's Yahoo and the Christian Symbols for Sin," *JHI*, XV (1954), 201–217. See also W. A. Murray, "Mr. Roland M. Frye's Article on Swift's Yahoo," *JHI*, XV (1954), 599–601.

20. "A Voyage to Nowhere with Thomas More and Jonathan Swift: *Utopia* and *The Voyage to the Houyhnhnms*," *Sewanee Review*, LXIX (1961), 533–565.   21. *PQ*, XXXVII (1958), 354–355; and his *Swift: An Introduction* (Oxford, 1955).   22. Denis Donoghue, *Jonathan Swift: A Critical Introduction* (London, 1969), p. 14.   23. "The Meaning of Gulliver's Last Voyage," *REL*, III (1962), 18–38.   24. *Jonathan Swift and the Age of Compromise*.   25. See n. 16.   26. In his anthology, *The Augustans* (Englewood Cliffs, N.J., 1950), pp. 10–12.   27. See n. 23.   28. W. E. Yeomans, "The Houyhnhnm as Menippean Horse," *College English*, XXVII (1966), 449–454. For a few other recent attempts at explication see Martin Kallich, "Three Ways of Looking at a Horse," *Criticism*, II (1960), 107–124; Calhoun Winton, "Conversion on the Road to Houyhnhnmland," *Sewanee Review*, LXVIII (1960), 20–33; Clarence Tracy, "The Unity of Gulliver's Travels," *Queen's Quarterly*, LXVIII (1962), 597–609; W. B. Carnochan, "The Complexity of Swift: Gulliver's Fourth Voyage," *SP*, LX (1963), 23–44; Conrad Suits (see n. 16); William H. Halewood and Martin Levich, "Houyhnhnm est Animal Rationale," *JHI*, XXVI (1965), 273–281; John H. White, "Swift's Trojan Horses: 'Reasoning But to Err,'" *ELN*, III (1966), 185–194; Anselm Schlösser, "Gulliver in Houyhnhnmland," *Zeitschrift für Anglistik und Amerikanistik*, XV (1967), 375–382; Steward LaCasce, "The Fall of Gulliver's Master," *Essays in Criticism*, XX (1970), 327–333, and "Gulliver's Fourth Voyage: A New Look at the Critical Debate," *Satire Newsletter*, VIII (1970), 5–7.   29. Hugo M. Reichard, "Satiric Snobbery: The Houyhnhnms' Man," *Satire Newsletter*, V (1967), 51–57.

30. "Swift, the Psalmist, and the Horse," *TSL*, III (1958), 17–23.   31. See n. 23.   32. "*Iterum Houyhnhnm*: Swift's Sextumvirate and the Horses," *Essays in Criticism*, XIX (1969), 35–45.   33. *Perilous Balance* (Princeton, 1939), p. 23.   34. Introduction to Modern Library edition of *Gulliver's Travels* (1950), p. xv.   35. "Errors Concerning the Houyhnhnms," *MP*, LVI (1958), 97.   36. "The Houyhnhnms, the Yahoos, and the History of Ideas," p. 233.   37. Donald J. Greene points this out as a possibility in "The Sin of Pride," pp. 26–27.   38. Since the completion of this essay some years ago a number of works bearing on the subject have appeared. Three might be mentioned: James E. Gill, "Beast over Man: Theriophilic Paradox in Gulliver's 'Voyage to the Country of the Houyhnhnms,'" *SP*, LXVII (1970), 532–549; Raymond Bentman, "Satiric Structure and Tone in the Conclusion of *Gulliver's Travels*," *SEL*, XI (1971), 535–548; and Larry S. Champion, "*Gulliver's Travels*: The Framing Events as a Guide to Interpretation," *Texas Studies in Language and Literature*, X (1969), 529–536.

THE RIVALRY OF THE *FEMALE TATLERS*
Periodical Piracy in the Early Eighteenth Century

Robert B. White, Jr.

THE *Female Tatler*, which first appeared on Friday, 8 July 1709,[1] is one of the more important and interesting of the various periodicals issued in imitation of the *Tatler* in an effort to capitalize on Steele's obvious financial success. In an era when many periodicals were born and died in the same issue and when a run of a month or two constituted a substantial life span, the *Female Tatler*, omnisciently edited "By Mrs. Crackenthorpe, *a Lady that knows every thing*," survived for one hundred fifteen thrice-weekly numbers and a life of almost nine months. This journal, unlike some of its contemporaries, was not totally without literary merit, and Walter Graham thought it quite the most important of Steele's rivals.[2] Mrs. Crackenthorpe survived a scolding match with the *British Apollo*, was presented as a public nuisance to a Grand Jury in the company of Defoe's *Review*, and, in the middle of the *Female Tatler's* career, resigned her editorial duties to "*a Society of Modest Ladies*," who conducted the journal from number 52 until its termination several months later. The identity of the authors behind the eidola has been fiercely debated in critical journals, the weight of evidence seemingly favoring Thomas Baker for the first fifty-one numbers and the unlikely combination of Susanna Centlivre and Bernard Mandeville for the subsequent numbers.[3] Furthermore, as one of the earliest periodicals to make a direct and consistent appeal to feminine readers, the *Female Tatler* has importance in a nonliterary area as well.

Probably the most interesting aspect of the career of the *Female Tatler*, however, occurred following number 18 when with number 19 there were two *Female Tatlers*, issued by different publishers, each claiming authenticity and each branding the other as spurious.

The first issue of the *Female Tatler*, 8 July 1709, was, according to its colophon, "Sold by *B. Bragge*, in *Pater-Noster-Row*; where

Advertisements are taken in." For the next six weeks, until Wednesday, 17 August, the first eighteen numbers of the periodical duly made their appearance over the colophon of Bragge. On Friday, 19 August, however, two *Female Tatlers* appeared. As might be expected, one was number 19, "Sold by *B. Bragge* in *Pater-Noster-Row*"; the other, however, was a *Female Tatler*, number 19, "Sold by *A. Baldwin* at the *Oxford-Arms* in *Warwick Lane*," according to its imprint. Except for minor typographical variations these two papers were identical in format; in content they were entirely different.

This condition, the simultaneous issue of two *Female Tatlers*, one presumably "genuine" and the other "spurious," continued through the appearance of number 44, Monday, 17 October. On this date the final issue of the Bragge series was published; Mrs. Baldwin's serial continued to appear three times a week until one hundred and fifteen numbers had been issued.

Which of these two papers with their conflicting claims to authenticity was the real *Female Tatler?* Because of the scarcity of the copies of these papers,[4] the earlier historians of the periodic press apparently were unaware that the rivalry had existed and made no mention of it.[5] On the other hand, J. H. Burn was aware of the rivalry, but he showed a lack of certainty concerning the problem of authenticity.[6] George A. Aitken also knew of the rival papers—"This paper was issued by Thomas Baker, but with number 19 another periodical with the same title appeared, 'printed for A. Baldwin'"—but he does not discuss the problem of authenticity.[7]

In spite of the comments by earlier critics, Walter Graham in his *English Literary Periodicals* (New York, 1930) gave no indication of the fact that for a time there were two *Female Tatlers*, although his discussion makes it apparent that he was familiar with issues from both the initial Bragge numbers and the Baldwin continuation.[8]

Paul Bunyan Anderson, in the course of writing a dissertation on the literary career of Mary de la Rivière Manley,[9] became aware of the rival *Female Tatlers*. Without citing any real evidence to support his conclusion, Anderson showed no doubt concerning the authenticity of the Baldwin continuation, of its explanation of the rivalry, and of the spuriousness of the Bragge numbers subsequent to number 18, accepting as evidence of authenticity the claims made by the author of the more successful of the two.

After the publication of Anderson's study,[10] Graham re-entered the debate and was inclined to accept the same sort of evidence that seems to have convinced Anderson, that is, the claims to authenticity made by one of the periodicals. He used it, however, to substantiate his assumption that the Bragge series was the genuine one and the Baldwin continuation spurious: "In this debate between the rival *Female Tatlers*, the advantage at this point seems to be with the paper published throughout by Bragge, which could furnish 'complete setts from the beginning.' The other 'Mrs. Crackenthorpe' met this argument by declaring that she had been disingenuously treated by her first printer, and desired to leave him, then had been chagrined to find that 'authors cannot even command their names and titles.'"[11] Finally, John Harrington Smith, in a study primarily concerned with the controversy surrounding the authorship of the *Female Tatler*, attempted to reestablish the claim to authenticity of the Bragge-Baldwin series of papers, listing several "respects in which continuity can be traced from the first eighteen numbers printed by Bragge into the continuation by Baldwin."[12]

None of these critics, however, exhausted the testimony of the papers themselves, and an examination of them, their content, and their conflicting claims throws considerably more light on the problem than has yet been perceived. Furthermore, most of the people concerned with this complicated web of literary piracies, authors, and publishers, turn out to have been involved in similar kinds of piracy later in connection with other periodicals. Mrs. Baldwin, particularly, seems to have learned much from her experiences with the rival *Female Tatlers*.

In the first of the papers printed by Mrs. Baldwin (number 19), the reader is presented with the announcement that "*Mrs. Crackenthorpe desires her Friends hence forward, when they have anything to insert, that they'd direct their Letters to her, at Mrs. Baldwin's at the Oxford Arms in* Warwick-lane."[13] Little can be determined on the basis of this announcement alone: it will fit the story that this Mrs. Crackenthorpe will present in the next issue of her disagreement with her first printer and her removal of her paper to another publisher, in which case it is simply an announcement of her new address as would be expected under such conditions; or it will fit equally well into a situation in which a publisher deliberately set up a rival publication, pirating title, eidolon, and format, and made such an announcement for the deception of his readers.

Bragge's first paper of the rivalry, on the other hand, closes with an announcement in which the author clearly seems to be anticipating the rivalry and establishing an explanation for it:

> Mrs. *Crackenthorpe* acquaints the Publick, that her Man *Francis* has of late deserted her Service, and carried away with him several Letters and Papers of Moment, which he is requir'd to return; and if any Person can give Notice of him to her, they shall be gratefully rewarded: He is a pretty Fellow, as times go; middle fix'd, a pleasant Aspect, fitted for Ladies Company, which made way for this Temptation, for he is suppos'd to be seduc'd by a scandalous, lewd Wench, a Cast-off Miss to a Quondam Quack Doctor in the City, who had been seen in his Company very lately. If any Person light on him, they are desir'd to give Notice to Mrs. *Crackenthorpe*, or have him press'd aboard the *Scoundrel Galley.*

The charge that Francis has defected and has taken with him "Letters and Papers of Moment," which presumably were intended for future papers, is followed up four issues later in a notice in Bragge number 23:

> Mrs. *Crackenthorpe* takes this Opportunity of returning Thanks to the Gentlemen and Ladies who have all along encouraged her Paper; and doubts not of the Continuance of their Favour. But being now inform'd, of a certain, that the Spurious Paper foisted into the World under her Name, is contriv'd and carry'd on by the Villany of her Man *Francis;* she thinks her self oblig'd to let the Publick know she disowns being any ways concerned in the Publishing thereof, and to give a caution to all Gentlemen and Ladies that they be not imposed on by that Scandalous and Trifling Pamphlet.

The rivalry had begun with number 19, and Bragge's author was prepared in that number with an explanation for it; it was not until number 20 that Mrs. Baldwin's publication was ready with its own explanation of the two *Female Tatlers* and a rebuttal to the claims of the Bragge journal:

> Mrs. Crackenthorpe finding herself disingenuously treated by the first Printer of this Paper, thought she might take the same Liberty of removing it, as a Gentleman that is trickt does his Taylor or Perriwig maker; but such is the Probity of Pyracing Printers, that Authors can't command even their Names and Titles, and this fellow has set up

some pitiful Scoundrel, whose Principles are as wretched as his Circumstances, to impose upon the Town a sham Paper, upon another Person's Foundation, and talks of Ladies Drawing-Rooms, who was never yet admitted into tolerable Company: But as the Ladies gave the first reputation to this Paper, 'tis hoped they'll so warmly espouse it, as to have a just Abhorrence for such base Proceedings, who are the only Court of Judicature, to be applyed to, in this matter. As they have hitherto found nothing rude, to affront 'em in Publick, or immodest to shock them in Private, their Protection may be the more reasonably expected in opposition to the other which at its abortive appearance in the World, has entertained 'em with an odious filthy Story of Mr. [sic] *Crackenthorpe's Man, Francis* —Francis is so angry, he intends to indict 'em for Scandal, to make a Thief, a Renegado, and a Beastly Fellow of him, when his Mistress has intrusted him with untold Gold; never lay out a Night without leave, and his Modesty is so Universally known, that he never had the assurance to Salute a Woman in his Life. As for pressing him Aboard the *Scoundrel Galley*—Contemptible Wretches! 'tis well known he is a Freeholder, has Ten Pounds a Year in *Cumberland*, and gives his Vote for Sir *Tunbelly Clumsy*.

The charges and countercharges continued unabated, and these are the points of evidence accepted by Graham in defense of one publisher and by Anderson in defense of the other. In the following issues of the papers the Bragge journal was by far the more vehement, protesting its genuineness and its opponent's spuriousness with great frequency and pungency. Mrs. Baldwin's periodical changed its format with number 21, and included a portrait of Mrs. Crackenthorpe as a portion of its title. In number 22, Bragge's Mrs. Crackenthorpe protested the portrait, declaring "she never had a *Hair-Lip*, *Wry-Neck*, *Cataract on her Eye* or *Cancer'd Breast*, as People will generally believe, seeing her exhibited like a *Patient* on a *Mountebank's* Bill." Mrs. Baldwin's author later devoted the whole of number 35 to a scathingly satiric caricature of her opponent which was presented as a character sketch submitted by a reader who had actually met the author of the spurious papers.

The primary significance of these various claims and accusations would seem to lie in the very first of the Bragge notices, which announced the defection of Francis with "several Letters and Papers of Moment," in number 19. The inference to be drawn from this notice is that the author of this paper knew that there was to be a rivalry as he prepared his copy for the very first issue of that rivalry. Only the enterprising author of the spurious journal would have such information at that time. The author of the genuine paper, having no idea what the future held as he prepared his copy of number 19 for the printer, would have been unable to take note of a rival until that rival had appeared, that is, in number 20 at the earliest. Thus the evidence seems to suggest that the story of "disingenuous" treatment is accurate and that the genuine Mrs. Crackenthorpe probably did transfer her editorial venture from B. Bragge to Mrs. Baldwin between number 18 and number 19. Bragge apparently refused to admit defeat in this enterprise and continued to publish a *Female Tatler*. Doubtless he also continued to market it through the outlets he had developed for the genuine paper.[14]

The story of "disingenuous" treatment may be further supported by examining a portion of the subject matter in the various papers concerned. The first eighteen papers, published by Bragge, contain allusions to plays, productions of plays, players, and playwrights. These allusions continue unabated during the period of the rivalry in the papers published by Mrs. Baldwin. In sharp contrast the numbers published by Bragge during the rivalry, numbers 19 through 44, contain no allusions to theatrical subjects. Thus a theory which assumed continuous authorship for the Bragge series of papers would face at once the almost insuperable task of accounting for both the abrupt disappearance of theatrical allusions in that series after number 18 and the remarkable coincidence of the appearance in Mrs. Baldwin's periodical of a series of very similar allusions. It is far more reasonable, then, to assume that Bragge numbers 1 through 18 and Baldwin numbers 19 through at least number 51 are the product of a single author who changed publishers following number 18 and that Bragge numbers 19 through 44 are indeed "spurious."

Ann Baldwin, however, seems to have learned her lessons in publishing practice well; she was now ready to do unto others as she had been done unto. When Steele terminated the *Tatler* on 2 January 1711 there were four different attempts made to continue it.[15] One of these, which seems to have lasted but two issues, is, curiously enough, attributed to Thomas Baker, who had had his *Female Tatler* pirated earlier by B. Bragge. A second continuation was published by John Morphew, the publisher of the original sheets, and a third, written by William Harrison, a protégé of Swift, was published by Ann Baldwin. Following the publication of number 284 with Mrs. Baldwin, Harrison went over to Morphew, and on 3 February, when her number 285 should have appeared, Mrs. Baldwin had no *Tatler*. She did have one on 6 February, however, and again there is an attempt by a publisher to continue a periodical after the author has taken his work to another publisher. This last issue from Mrs. Baldwin's shop probably should be considered doubly spurious, for it was a spurious issue of Harrison's spurious *Tatler* continuation.

Once again, in 1712, Mrs. Baldwin engaged in piracy. She had published the original series of the *Medley* in 1711 and was engaged as publisher again when that journal was revived in a second series in 1712. After twenty numbers had appeared, some difference arose between author and publisher. Two *Medley*s appeared on 12 May: one was number 21 written by Oldmixon, the author of the original series, but bearing the imprint of J. Baker; the other, also number 21 and by an author never identified, bore Mrs. Baldwin's colophon. These two papers, one published by Baker and genuine, the other published by Mrs. Baldwin and spurious, continued to appear simultaneously twice a week through number 43, 28 July 1712.[16]

Mrs. Baldwin was the fortunate publisher to whom Thomas Baker took his *Female Tatler* when that author had a disagreement with his original publisher, Benjamin Bragge. For eight weeks thereafter both Baker and his new publisher were the victims of piracy as Bragge continued to publish a *Female Tatler* in spite of his loss of an author. As much as they protested through Mrs. Crackenthorpe this lack of ethics on Bragge's part, both Mrs. Baldwin and Baker were quite willing to attempt a very similar form of piracy upon the demise of Steele's *Tatler*. Mrs. Baldwin went on to reenact the attempted theft of the *Female Tatler* when the author of the *Medley* attempted to shift publishers, but this time she became the pirate rather than the victim. Her spurious *Medley*, however, was more successful than Bragge's piracy had been, for it survived until the Stamp Tax put an end to both *Medley*s.

Notes

1. There is an undated handbill in the British Museum, Harl. 5995 (172), which notes: "Whereas a *New Paper*, entitled the FEMALE TATLER, was expected to be Published to day, this is to inform the Town, that the said *Paper* will certainly be Publish'd on Friday next, by *B. Bragge* at the *Black Raven* in *Paternoster Row;* and will be deliver'd *gratis* the first time, in hopes of Future Encouragement." For this detail, and others in this essay, as well as for general guidance, it is a pleasure to record my indebtedness to Richmond P. Bond.   2. Walter Graham, *English Literary Periodicals* (New York, 1930), pp. 69, 88.   3. Paul Bunyan Anderson put forward Mary de la Rivière Manley as a candidate for authorship of the *Female Tatler* in "Mary de la Rivière Manley, A Cavalier's Daughter in Grub Street" (Ph.D. diss., Harvard University, 1931); "The History and Authorship of Mrs. Crackenthorpe's *Female Tatler*," *MP*, XXVIII (1931), 354–360; and "Mistress Delariviere Manley's Biography," *MP*, XXXIII (1935), 261–278. The traditional ascription to Thomas Baker was defended successfully by Walter Graham, "Thomas Baker, Mrs. Manley, and the *Female Tatler*," *MP*, XXXIV (1937), 267–272, and John Harrington Smith, "Thomas Baker and *The Female Tatler*," *MP*, XLIX (1952), 182–188. The Centlivre ascription was made by Anderson in "Innocence and Artifice: or, Mrs. Centlivre and *The Female Tatler*," *PQ*, XVI (1937), 358–375; his claim for Mandeville appeared in "Splendor out of Scandal: the Lucinda-Artesia Papers in *The Female Tatler*," *PQ*, XV (1936), 286–300. The Mandeville attribution is supported by Gordon S. Vichert, "Some Recent Mandeville Attributions," *PQ*, XLV (1966), 459–463.   4. The *Union List of Serials* indicates that there are complete files of the *Female Tatler* at both Harvard University and the University of Illinois. In fact, the Harvard University Library has only numbers 1–19 bearing Bragge's imprint and numbers 20–111 (115) bearing the A. Baldwin colophon (Letter from Luise B. Mallinger, Library of Harvard University, 24 February 1964). The Library of the University of Illinois has a photo-facsimile of the Harvard Library holdings and a photographic reproduction of Baldwin number 19 and the balance of the Bragge papers from the Bodleian Library (Letter from Isabella F. Grant, Rare Book Room Librarian, University of Illinois Library, 30 January 1964). The only complete file of both *Female Tatlers* listed in the *Bristish Union Catalogue of Periodicals* is the file in the Bodleian Library.   5. The rivalry went unnoticed by Nathan Drake, *Essays, Biographical, Critical, and Historical, Illustrative of the Rambler, Adventurer, and Idler . . .* (London, 1809); by H. R. Fox Bourne, *English Newspapers* (1887); and by George S. Marr, *Periodical Essayists of the Eighteenth Century* (New York, 1924).   6. Jacob Henry Burn, comp., *Catalogue of a Collection of Early Newspapers and Essayists, Formed by the Late John Thomas Hope* (1865), p. 18.   7. *The Life*

of Richard Steele (1889), I, 298.   8. Pages 69, 77, 87–89, 112.   9. Paul Bunyan Anderson, "Mary de la Rivière Manley, A Cavalier's Daughter in Grub Street."

10. Paul Bunyan Anderson, *MP*, XXVIII (1931), 355.   11. Graham, *MP*, XXXIV (1937), 268. It is curious to find Graham here espousing the cause of the Bragge *Female Tatler*, for in his book, *English Literary Periodicals*, he had quoted liberally from the Baldwin paper to demonstrate the literary ability of this rival to Steele's *Tatler*.   12. John Harrington Smith, *MP*, XLIX (1951–1952), 183–184.   13. This notice was repeated in Baldwin numbers 20, 22–27, 32–34, 36, 37.   14. Two further pieces of evidence which tend to support the theory that the Bragge-Baldwin series is the genuine *Female Tatler* need to be considered. The following announcement appeared in the *Daily Courant*, number 2446, 26 August 1709, and was repeated in number 2448, 29 August: "The original Author of The FEMALE TATLER thinks fit to give Notice to the Publick, that they may no longer be impos'd on, that the true FEMALE TATLER is now publish'd by Mrs. Baldwin in Warwick-Lane, and not by Mr. Bragge since No. 18. And that all others that shall be publish'd by the said Mr. Bragge will be false and spurious, as being contrary to his Knowledge. All Gentlemen and Ladies are desir'd to send what they would have inserted to Mrs. Baldwin aforesaid. Note, The right has Mr. [sic] Crackenthorpe's Picture at the beginning." Even more effective evidence for the assumption that Mrs. Baldwin's paper represents a continuation of the original *Female Tatler* may be found in a broadside lampoon published by "Benj. Bragg" and titled "THE CHARACTER OF THE TATLER." This sheet bears no date, but in the course of presenting a satiric character sketch of Isaac Bickerstaff, its author says, "Mrs. *Crackenthorpe*, hearing that Esq; *B*. was acquainted with Mr. *Flamsted*, writ an Ingenious Letter to him by the Peny-Post, to meet her at the said Philosopher's House in *Greenwich-Park* at the Hour One, by Moon-light, (knowing that the Esq's; Bashfulness, how loth he was to be seen Publickly Barefac'd,) that they Three might be Merry together, and Dance the Hay. She comes to the Place appointed, when behold who should she meet there but the Devil upon Two Sticks; the poor Lady fell in Fits, and from that Fright has never been able to write Sense, of which sad Mischance her Printer gives the World an Account Three Times a Week." Such an attack on Mrs. Crackenthorpe would probably not have been published by Bragge until the end of his *Female Tatler*, 17 October. Thus this sheet must have reference to Mrs. Baldwin's *Female Tatler* while Mrs. Crackenthorpe was still the putative author, i.e., before the Society of Ladies took over on 4 November. If this is the case, the paragraph just quoted seems to imply an admission on Bragge's part of the genuineness of Mrs. Baldwin's Mrs. Crackenthorpe. See Robert B. White, Jr., "*The Character of the Tatler*," *PQ*, XLV (1966), 450–454.   15. The continuations of the *Tatler* have been studied by Robert Joyce Hooper, "A Study of the Continuations of the *Tatler* (1711)" (M.A. thesis, University of North Carolina at Chapel Hill, 1955); by Robert C. Elliot, "Swift's 'Little' Harrison, Poet and Continuator of the *Tatler*," *SP*, LXVI (1949), 544–559; and by Robert B. White, Jr., "A 'New' Continuation of the *Tatler*," *N&Q*, III (1956), 104–105.   16. M. L. Poston, "*The Medleys* of 1712," *Library*, 5th ser., XIII (1958), 205–207.

CAMBRIDGE AND THE COPYRIGHT
ACT OF QUEEN ANNE (1710–1814)

J. C. T. Oates

THE last of the Licensing Acts expired on 3 May 1695; the first of the Copyright Acts became law on 10 April 1710. It had been introduced into Parliament in response to several petitions presented by publishers during the years 1703–1709 asking for legal protection against the piratical exploitation of their property by their less scrupulous colleagues.[1] Entitled *An Act for the Encouragement of Learning, by Vesting the Copies of Printed Books in the Authors or Purchasers of such Copies, during the Times therein mentioned*, it gave not the perpetual copyright which owners had virtually enjoyed under the Licensing Acts but twenty-one years' copyright from the date of the act in works already published, and fourteen years' copyright in works published after the act came into force, with a reversion of the copyright to the author, if he was still living at the end of that period, for a further fourteen years. Moreover, whereas the Licensing Acts required copies to be sent only to the Royal Library and to the universities of Oxford and Cambridge, the Copyright Act added to the list of privileged libraries Sion College in London, the Advocates' Library at Edinburgh, and the universities of Edinburgh, Glasgow, St. Andrew's, and Aberdeen. Thus in return for a protection which they themselves deemed inadequate the publishers were required to give away not, as under the Licensing Acts, three copies of every new book or reprint with additions, but nine; and they were understandably disappointed and annoyed at being fobbed off half the old loaf at three times the old price.

The provisions of the act were explicit enough as regards the deposit of copies, save in one essential particular. First, copyright protection was made dependent upon entry of the title before publication in the Stationers' Register (or upon advertisement in the *Gazette* if entry was omitted by the refusal or neglect of the Stationers' Clerk); secondly, the printer was required to deliver to the Stationers' warehouse-keeper before publication "Nine copies of each Book, or Books, upon the best Paper"; and thirdly, the warehouse-keeper was required to deliver the copies to the privileged libraries within ten days of receiving a demand for them from the librarians concerned or their authorized agents. Specific penalties were incurred by a printer who failed to deliver the copies to the warehouse-keeper, and by the warehouse-keeper if he failed to deliver them to the libraries on proper demand: but any action at law for the recovery of these penalties by the libraries had to be "Brought, Sued, and Commenced within Three Months next after such Offence Committed."

But the act specified no penalty for failure to enter a title in the register at all. The publishers therefore argued that registration was not obligatory, and that they need enter and so deposit at Stationers' Hall only those books for which they wished to obtain copyright protection. Thus the librarian of Sion College, writing when the act had been in operation some fifteen years, complained that the booksellers "enter such English Sermons, Histories, Poems and Pamphlets, as they are apprehensive will quickly be reprinted by others in cheaper Paper and Character: but commonly neglect to enter large and learned Works, which are not easily reprinted, or not vendible in lesser Forms."[2] Similarly Edmund Law, writing anonymously in 1770 (the year after he had ceased to be principal librarian at Cambridge), observes that "very few books of value have been obtained, the Booksellers being determined not to lose so many Copies of the largest Paper, as this Act requires to be delivered, and chusing rather to forfeit all the benefit of it, and trust one another, by never entering their Books in the Register." When it might be dangerous not to enter a book, he continues, they would enter one volume of a set only and would refuse to send the remaining volumes to the libraries or even to sell them to them unless they paid for the whole set; and against obstruction such as this the libraries were defenseless, for it proved in practice impossible to establish the fact of a bookseller's refusal and to begin a prosecution within the statutory limit of three months.[3] Indeed it does not appear that any legal action of this kind was ever undertaken before 1812, when the case of *Cambridge University* v. *Bryer* established that a publisher could not evade his liability to deposit copies of a book simply by refraining from registering it.

A fairly clear picture of the mechanics of deposit at Cambridge can be pieced together from the university's audit-books and from the vouchers, preserved in the university archives, from which the audits were compiled. The stationers' parcels usually arrived twice a year, at or soon after Lady Day and Michaelmas. In return for his labors the warehouse-keeper (who was also usually the treasurer) or sometimes the clerk received a quarterly fee of five shillings, raised to a guinea a year in 1758.[4] These payments were made with fair regularity from 1722 onward, but the university sometimes fell into arrears, and when it did so the sum eventually paid was sometimes below the standard rate. Thus in 1751 Thomas Simpson received eight guineas only for arrears of fees since 1737, and in 1755 three years' arrears were discharged at 10s. 6d. a year. Soon afterward, the university withdrew altogether from these grave administrative problems by delegating them to a succession of Cambridge booksellers, to whose premises the stationers' parcels were accordingly delivered, though it does not appear that they were the university's official "authorized agents" in the meaning of the act.[5] This system continued until the second decade of the nineteenth century, when, following the Copyright Act of 1814, the great increase in the number of copies deposited and delivered compelled the university to make different and more responsible arrangements.

What books the university library received under the first act is a question which cannot be exactly answered. Its eighteenth-century accessions-book does not begin until 1758, and it has no file of correspondence from Stationers' Hall before 1814; and the enthusiasm which some university librarians—sometimes justifiably—have applied to undoing the work of their predecessors has rearranged and rearranged its eighteenth-century collections so frequently that all chronological order of accession on the shelves has been lost. These defects are to some extent made good by surviving eighteenth-century shelf-lists, the copy of the *Catalogus impressorum librorum Bibliothecae Bodleianae* (1738) which the library bought in 1752 to serve, interleaved and annotated, as its own catalogue, and the extensive series of binders' bills which are preserved in the university archives. Some sections of the shelf-lists were however destroyed during a rearrangement of the library at the end of the eighteenth century, and the university audit book shows that a few of the binders' bills have been lost. Moreover, in 1751 the university authorized its librarian to sell such copyright accessions as he did not think worth keeping, so that from 1755 to 1815 the bills furnished by the library's Cambridge booksellers show regular credits in such terms as "Received by books," "for some odd Articles laid aside of the Stationers' Company," and "By refuse pamphlets &c. from the Stationers' Company." These factors, combined with the accumulated losses which an open-access library could not escape and the ejection from time to time of duplicates or editions thought to be superseded, make it very difficult to compile even approximate statistics.

A comparison of the Accessions Book with the Stationers' Register for the years 1758–1767 and 1771–1773 suggests that about one-third of the books registered was received into the library, and for the period 1766–1814, during which some seventeen thousand items were registered, about one-sixth.[6] In seeking the reasons which caused so meager a harvest several factors (at some of which I have already hinted) must be borne in mind. On the one hand, each entry in the register was technically a receipt for "nine copies," and entrance was not complete until the copies were deposited. There should therefore have been available at Stationers' Hall nine copies of every book that was registered, and the supposition must be that the warehouse-keeper in the normal run of events forwarded each and every copy to its respective library; and when St. Andrews University, suspecting that it had not received many of the books to which it was entitled, made personal enquiry at Stationers' Hall through one of its professors in 1771, the stationers' treasurer George Hawkins asserted in reply that he could furnish proof that he had forwarded to the libraries all the books which had been delivered to him.[7] On the other hand, the law required only that the books be forwarded within ten days after demand by the librarians or their authorized agents, so that the warehouse-keepers were under no compulsion, legal or moral, to deliver books which had not been demanded. As we have seen, Cambridge did not employ, so far as we can tell, an authorized agent in this sense, and if regular demands were made by successive Cambridge librarians themselves (as was done twice a year at the Bodleian Library) all trace of their activity has disappeared save for a solitary letter of 17 February 1725/6 written to the librarian from Stationers' Hall by the clerk Thomas Simpson sending him "according to Your desire" thirteen titles, "being all which are Entred & come to my hands, Since my Letter to you."

It would seem therefore that the university made but weak and occasional efforts to use to its advantage an act which was itself incompetent to enforce its own purpose, and we need not be surprised that the results of such a situation were casual and confused. A parcel of stationers' books delivered to Cambridge in 1770, for example, included nine publications of 1753–1758 and one of 1763, and other examples can be cited of books arriving long years after their title-page dates.[8] A natural corollary of late delivery was that stationers' parcels were sometimes found to contain books which the library had already bought (and on such occasions forthwith returned to the suppliers), with the result that all manner of complications attended the getting of multivolume sets or a long series like the *Annual Register*, there being no possibility of predicting which volumes would be delivered and which would not.

The disastrous effect of this inefficiency—both of the law and of the library—may be readily imagined, and can be briefly illustrated. In the realm of fiction and near-fiction the library received during the first thirty years of the act Mrs. Manley's *Memoirs of Europe* (1710) and *The Power of Love in Seven Novels* (1720); the English translation published by J. Tonson in 1710 of the first two volumes of *Gil Blas;* both parts of *Robinson Crusoe* (1719) and perhaps a copy, since lost, of *Moll Flanders;* an incomplete set, wanting the third and fifth volumes, of Samuel Croxall's *Select Collection of Novels in Six Volumes* (1720–1722); Ozell's translation of the *Persian Letters* (2 vols., 1722); *Gulliver's Travels* (1726); John Lockman's *Travels of Mr. John Gulliver* (1731), translated from the French; Andrew Ramsay's *Travels of Cyrus* (1727); *Memoirs of an English Officer. By Capt. George Carleton* (1728), by Defoe; and *The Travels and Adventures of James Massey* (1733), from the French of S. Tyssot de Patot. The list is meager enough, yet it represents a far greater proportion than might be supposed of the new works of fiction registered during the first quarter-century of the act.[9] By 1740, however—the year of the publication of *Pamela*—the library's authorities seem to have decided that there was no future for the English novel. They did not keep, or did not claim, as far as I can discover, any registered novel published during the next forty years except *Sir Charles Grandison*, in six octavo volumes, 1754;[10] and while not all the fiction titles of those years were registered, the items which the library failed to procure or did not think fit to keep included *Joseph Andrews* (1742), *Tom Jones* (1749) and *Amelia* (1751), *Roderick Random* (1748), *Peregrine Pickle* (1751) and *Humphry Clinker* (1771), *The Prince of Abissinia* (1759), and *A Sentimental Journey* (1768), as well as Robert Paltock's *Peter Wilkins* (1751), Francis Coventry's *History of Pompey the Little* (1751), Mrs. Haywood's *Betsy Thoughtless* (1751) and *Jemmy and Jenny Jessamy* (1753), and Dr. John Hill's *History of a Woman of Quality, or the Adventures of Lady Frail* (1751). On 8 January 1781, however, we find admitted to the library among the books "from Lady to Michaelmas 1780" Sir Herbert Croft's *Love and Madness* (new edition, 1780), a curious production in which the alleged love letters of James Hackman to Martha Reay (whom he murdered on 7 April 1779 because she preferred to be the mistress of the Earl of Sandwich) are augmented by a critical and biographical essay on Chatterton containing material which Croft had obtained from the dead poet's sister. Perhaps the librarian decided that this work was not fiction at all, or that Hackman's meditations in the condemned cell would provide useful moral lessons for an academic society; at any rate, fiction began soon afterwards to trickle in once more, and by the middle of the nineteenth century the library's "Novel Room" was one of the most frequented places in it and a memorably impressive sight to lady visitors.[11]

If we turn to the poets and dramatists of the century the picture is no brighter. The only publications of Pope received under the act, apart from his translations of Homer, were the folio *Works* of 1717, the quarto *Dunciad, Variorum* of 1729, printed for A. Dod, with the leaf of addenda, and the octavo *Dunciad. With Notes Variorum*, "the second edition, with some additional notes," also 1729, published by Lawton Gilliver a few days after he had established his claim to the copyright by recording in the Stationers' Register on 21 November 1729 its reassignment to him by Burlington, Oxford, and Bathurst.[12] Thomson is represented only by the *Works* of 1750 and Gay only by the *Fables* of 1727 (the latter being reported missing from the library in 1784); the nine parts of Young's *The Complaint: Night Thoughts* were received, but not the five parts of his *Universal Passion*. Addison's *Works* in four volumes (1721) was received, but *Cato* and *The Campaign* were not. Goldsmith's *Survey of Experimental Philosophy* (1776) appears in the library's eighteenth-century catalogue but not *The Deserted Village* and *She Stoops to Conquer*. Original editions of Akenside and Churchill are entirely absent. Johnson is represented by his *Dictionary* but not by *Irene*, and Nicholas Rowe by his translation of Lucan but not by his *Tragedy of Jane Shore* and *Tragedy of Lady Jane Gray;* and a search for copyright copies of registered plays by Carey, Cibber, Robert Dodsley, Foote, Garrick, and Hill has proved barren. Drama, however, like fiction, began to make an appearance in the 1780s, the earliest examples which I can trace being three works of 1785—Arthur Murphy's comedy *The Way to Keep him*, Thomas Holcroft's comic opera *The Choleric Fathers*, and *The Patriot, a Tragedy: From a Manuscript of the Late Samuel Johnson. Corrected by Himself.*[13]

As I have already hinted, peculiar difficulties attended the delivery of periodical publications. The registration of literary periodicals was frequently irregular, and in many instances only an odd issue was entered. Thus of the nine numbers which made up the run of Steele's *Town-Talk*, only the fifth (of 13 January 1715/16) was registered, this being the issue in which Steele printed and answered the Pretender's Declaration of 25 October 1715 (with the result that, though sold at twice the usual price, it went into five editions). Other examples of occasional registration are provided by *The Entertainer* (no. 18), *The Grumbler* (nos. 29, 30), and *Kapelion, or The Poetical Ordinary* (no. 1). Some registrations, however, lack the usual note of the receipt of nine copies. Thus Steele's *Guardian* is entered in four batches (nos. 1–72, 72–104, 104–150, 150–173), but only the last is receipted. There is no receipt for *The Freeholder*, entered "compleat" in fifty-five numbers on 29 June 1716, or for the original *Spectator*, numbers 1–40 (18 April 1711), 40–66 (16 May), 66–163 (5 September), 163–216 (7 November), [216]–232 (26 November), 232–338 (28 March 1712), and 232–523 (30 November), though nine sets of numbers 232–555 were deposited on 2 February 1712/13. Numbers 105–112 of *The Monitor* were registered and deposited at various dates between 23 July and 10 September 1757; number 113 was registered on 17 September but there is no note of deposit; and numbers 1–104 were registered in the two-volume reprint on 20 September, when nine copies were duly supplied. The intention to reprint a periodical in volume form probably accounts for failure to deposit original issues, but such irregularities must have proved an additional difficulty to the copyright libraries. A bill of work done by the bookbinder Henry Crow in 1716 shows that the library had received seven volumes of *The Spectator*, two of *The Guardian* and one of *The Englishman*, all in the duodecimo reprints; and Charles Povey's anonymous *Visions of Sir Heister Ryley*, numbers 1–80 (21 August 1710–21 February 1710/11), apparently the original issues with the addition of a title-page, preface, and table, appears on Francis Hopkins's binding-bill of March 1713/14. Otherwise a trial of some thirty of the periodicals registered in whole or in part before 1775 has revealed only the reprints of *The Intelligencer* (1729) and *The Monitor* (nos. 1–104, 2 vols., 1756–1757); and in the period immediately following I find only the reprints of *The Lounger*, "the second edition, corrected" (3 vols., Edinburgh, 1787), and *The Looker-on*, "third edition" (4 vols., 1795), and both the original folio issues of *Olla Podrida* (44 numbers, Oxford, 17 March 1787–12 January 1788) and their octavo reprint ("the second edition," London, 1788). Books issued in fascicules are also poorly represented. Of the fourteen which were registered before 1750[14] the Library appears to have received only Edward Ward's *Adventures of Don Quixote*, "merrily translated into Hudibrastick verse" (parts I–IV of vol. I only, 1711), Fleury's *Ecclesiastical History* (the first four of the five volumes only, 1727–1730), and Cantemir's *History of the Othman Empire* (1734), though it is perhaps allowable to add to these John Russell's anonymous *Letters from a young Painter abroad*, in two volumes, received when he re-registered the whole work three years after its first appearance. *The Modern Story-Teller, or General Entertainer* (2 vols., 1748–1749) and Mrs. Teresia Constantia Phillips's *Apology* may well have been discarded, if they were ever received, and the library may perhaps have supposed the fourth edition of Chambers's *Cyclopaedia* (1741) superfluous since it already owned the second (1738); but it is difficult to find excuses for the absence of such books as Dennis De Coetlogon's *Universal History of Arts and Sciences* (2 vols., 1745), John Marchant's *Expositions* of the New and Old Testaments (1743, 1745), and William Duff's anonymous *New History of Scotland* (1749), all of which were delivered to the Bodleian.

Two less substantial kinds of publication may lastly be considered—popular ephemera and sheet music. The former were commonly registered only during the first year or two of the act, and a number of such pieces from this period survive in the library. They include *The Amazing Wonder* (being "a Full and True Relation of the Dismal Condition of one John Sexton, a Blew-Coat-Boy in Christ Hospital"), *The Lives and Characters of the Dutchess of Marlborough's Four Daughters* (with woodcut portraits highly prejudicial to those ladies), *Have at you blind Harpers* ("Three Ballads concerning the Times. Sold by J. Baker and by all her Majesty's Running-Stationers"), *The World's Wonder. Being Great News from divers Places in Yorkshire* (describing "a Strange and Fiery Serpent that was seen in the Air on Holy-Thursday last"), and two pieces about the "Four Kings of Canada" who came to England in 1710 to ask for a more vigorous prosecution of the war against the French. I suspect, however, that the survival of the two volumes containing these and other items is no more than a fortunate accident, for the first item in one of them has the initials of Jonathan Pindar, under library-keeper at the time, written on its title-page. His initials also occur in a volume of political pamphlets of 1710–1711 (*Faults on both sides* and seven others) and in a volume of theology (Bishop Trimnell's *Sermon preach'd on Monday in Easter-Week,* 1710 and five others), and it seems at least possible that he made off with these trifles for his own private edification and that they found their way back to the library subsequently.

Music, according to the *Report from the Select Committee on the Copyright Acts* of June 1818, [15] was rarely entered till 1776–1777, and single songs not till April 1783, though thereafter they formed a large proportion of the items registered. Thus the Accessions Book records only one book of copyright music before 1776 (John Burton's *Ten Sonatas for Harpsichord, Organ, or Piano Forte,* 1766), followed by twelve folio volumes of music in 1790 and in 1796 by "six Concertos by Dr Arne. Bound up in 8 p^{ts}. Lond. 1795," "4 Musick Books," and a volume of "Opera Dances & Marches." Another volume, "Haydn's &c.," came with the parcel "to Lady 1796," and from 1798 onward music arrived intermittently, though the contents of the parcels are rarely described in any detail.

Such references in the Accessions Book to "volumes" of music mean no more than that the pieces received made up the stated number of volumes after the library had got them bound, their entry in the Accessions Book being delayed until the binder had done his work. All copyright accessions, in fact, down to the second decade of the nineteenth century were received unbound, the earliest deposited books in boards with printed labels that I have found being publications of 1815. [16] Some books certainly arrived in unfolded sheets; Charles Wright's bill of January 1718/19 includes a charge of 1s. "for folding & stiching of pamphlets" and Francis Hopkins's boy spent "One Day & a Quarter folding up Books in Quires, unbound" in October 1722. In general, however, books were delivered in quires, and when James Bruce's *Travels into Abyssinia* (5 vols., 1790) arrived from the hall "in sheets" the fact was thought curious enough to be noted in the Accessions Book.

The delivery of copies to the hall unbound clearly gave stationers the opportunity, if they wished to take it, of fobbing off on the libraries deposit copies which were in one way or another defective or imperfect, and there would also be a natural temptation to collate sheets or quires which had to be given away less carefully than those which were intended for commerce. I have, indeed, found copyright books which are defective or imperfect, but they are very few, and so far as my search has gone the stationers must be acquitted of any general attempt to defraud in this way, at any rate before the controversial Copyright Act of 1814. Freind's *History of Physic*, part 1 (8°, 1725), has the inner form of the last gathering blank, and the librarian Samuel Hadderton has duly noted the fact on a flyleaf: "Mem. ye Reiteration of ye Half Sheet X in this Vol. is unprinted. Quaere, How it may be supplied, & whether or not it were so in the whole Impression"; William Sewel's *History of the Quakers* (1722) wants gathering 4L^4 and the inner sheet of 4Y^4; and William Smellie's *A Collection of Cases and Observations in Midwifery* (1754) is somewhat better than perfect since it has sheet F in duplicate—which is but poor consolation to the Bodleian Library, whose copyright copy wants sheet K.[17] In other instances time and a binder's oversight have overlaid what might once have seemed a defect with the patina of bibliographical desirability. Thus Gilliver's "second edition" variorum *Dunciad* of 1729 has D3 and E2 slit for cancellation but not replaced, Walter Harte's *Poems on several occasions* has both the cancellandum *A3 in the dedication and the cancellans, and Lyttelton's four-volume edition of Thomson's *Works* of 1750–1752 has both printings of the preliminaries (as has the British Museum's copyright copy), in the later of which Lyttelton suppressed his earlier mention of "many redundancies being pruned away, and many faults of diction corrected"—a statement which to Thomson's devotees must have seemed superfluous indeed since Lyttelton had "pruned away" no fewer than fourteen hundred lines from *Liberty*.

It will be remembered (to conclude this survey) that the act called upon printers to deliver copies "upon the best paper," and if "best paper" can be equated with "large paper" it would seem that in this particular the act worked well. I know of no easy way of discovering exactly what books, or what proportion of registered books, were issued on large paper, but I find no fewer than twenty-five such (including *Gulliver's Travels*, Pope's folio Homer, and Prior's *Poems on several occasions*) among some two hundred titles listed in the binders' bills from 1717 to 1729, when the fashion for large-paper copies was perhaps at its height; I have not however pursued this somewhat rarefied topic through the century's later years.

It is, I hope, unnecessary to add that the Cambridge University Library has since been at some pains to obtain for money books which it might once have got for nothing, or that its eighteenth-century English collections, though inferior to some, are yet rather better than most. Nevertheless, something must be said in explanation, if not extenuation, of its failure to rise to an occasion which was potentially so advantageous to itself and of a performance so sadly inferior to what it should have been.

We must, then, first remember that the library had always been essentially a private preserve for senior members of the university and occasional visiting scholars; it expressly excluded undergraduates and had nothing to do with higher education as any form of organized activity. It did not foresee that the act of Queen Anne began a process which (whether it liked it or not) would turn it into a repository of national literature in which two hundred years later scholars would seek out and earnestly study not only the works of other scholars but also the reading-matter of former generations at all levels of society. Why, then, should it stoop to competition with booksellers like "Maps" Nicholson, in whose shop in Trumpington Street the weaker spirits might find "the most choice collection of Lounging Books that the genius of Indolence could desire . . . Rabelais in English, several copies of the Reverend Mr. Sterne's Tristram Shandy, Wycherly and Congreve's Plays, Joe Miller's Jests, Mrs. Behn's Novels, and Lord Rochester's Poems"?[18]

Secondly, we must remember also that, though some of the colleges were rich, the university as a whole was not; until the closing years of the eighteenth century all the practical work of its library, together with the general superintendence of the whole group of buildings of which it formed a part, fell on the shoulders of a solitary under-library-keeper, assisted only in times of special crisis by temporary help. Above him were two grandees of the university, the librarian and (from 1721) the principal librarian, the latter being charged with the special (though largely nominal) superintendence of the library of thirty thousand printed books and manuscripts, formerly the property of the recently deceased Bishop of Ely, John Moore, which King George I presented to the university in 1715. This was a scholar's library, beside which the products of the contemporary press must have seemed for the most part wholly insignificant, and the problems of its accommodation and arrangement (all Cambridge dons being then, as now, enthusiastic amateur architects) diverted such energies as the university could corporately muster into a controversy which lasted for nearly forty years while rival schemes were successively promoted and discussed. The Cambridge of which I have written was, without doubt, shortsighted and administratively incompetent, and perhaps idle as well. Yet Bentley walked its courts and avenues, and did it not see Gray and Wordsworth plain? Let not hindsight pass too harsh a judgment.

Notes

1. For the historical background of the act and its full text, see Harry Ransom, *The First Copyright Statute* (Austin, 1956). R. C. B. Partridge, *The History of the Legal Deposit of Books* (London, 1938), p. 300, prints the clauses relating to deposit.   2. W. Reading, "The History of the Ancient and Present State of Sion-College" (p. 38), at the end of his *Bibliothecae cleri Londinensis in collegio Sionensi catalogus* (1724); he adds, however, that even learned works were sometimes entered and that the books received by Sion "have been worth about five Pounds *per Annum*, one Year with another."   3. [Edmund Law], *Observations occasioned by the contest about Literary Property* (1770), pp. 3–5. The [University] Copyright Act of 1775 attempted to stop this kind of evasion by requiring the delivery to the hall of "the whole book, and every volume thereof" (see Partridge, pp. 42–43, 306–307).   4. St. Andrews paid 5s. a year only, beginning in 1723 (Philip Ardagh, "St. Andrews University Library and the Copyright Acts," *Edinburgh Bibliographical Society Transactions*, III, 1948–1955, 186); Oxford at this time paid the same fee as Cambridge (I. G. Philip reviewing Ardagh in *The Library*, 5th ser., XII, 1957, 69); Sion first paid a guinea in 1772, having previously paid 10s. 6d. (Partridge, p. 42).   5. As were, for example, W. & J. Innys for Oxford, Gavin Hamilton for Edinburgh, and William Strahan for Glasgow (Partridge, pp.

301–302; Ardagh, pp. 187–188; and Audrey Nairn, "A 1731 Copyright List from Glasgow," *The Bibliotheck*, II, 1959–1960, 30–32).   6. For the annual totals of registrations down to 31 December 1826 see *Parliamentary Papers*, 1826–1827, XX, 509 (reprinted by Partridge, pp. 315–316). A different set of figures, giving the totals by decades from 1710 to 1810 and by four-year periods from 1811 to 1818, is printed in *Parliamentary Papers*, 1818, IX, 254. The figures given can be misleading: many of the earliest registrations were "old copies," which were not depositable; periodicals, including "number-books," were entered an issue or a few issues at a time, and from 1783 the totals are greatly inflated by registrations of sheet music (see below).   7. Ardagh, p. 188.   8. Joseph Downing, *Treatise on the disorders incident to Cattle*, published 1797, received 1801; Edward Pearson, *Art of Catechising*, published 1810, received 1813; A. F. C. Kollman, *Essay on musical harmony*, published 1796, received 1802; Thomas Winterbottom, *Account of the Native Africans in Sierra Leone*, published 1803, received 1817. Similar delays were experienced at Glasgow (see Audrey Nairn).   9. Or so I conclude, having compared the titles in part II of A. Esdaile's *List of English Tales and Prose Romances printed before 1740* (London, 1912) with the *Index of Titles and Proprietors of Books entered in the Book of Registry of the Stationers' Company from 28th April 1710 to 30th Dec. 1773* (n.d., n.p.).

10. *Grandison* was published simultaneously in six volumes octavo and in seven volumes duodecimo. The edition registered was the octavo.   11. I have traced the following titles (excluding translations) received under the act before 1800: [Andrew M'Donald], *The Independent* (1784); Elizabeth Todd, *The History of Lady Caroline Rivers* (1788); Charlotte Smith, *Emmeline, the Orphan of the Castle* (1788), no longer in the library; [Cassandra Hawke], *Julia de Grammont* (1788); [John Moore], *Zeluco* (1789); [W. Combe], *The Devil upon two Sticks in England* (1790); Ann Radcliffe, *The Mysteries of Udolpho* (1794); [Richard Cumberland], *Henry* (1795); and Fanny Burney, *Camilia* (1796).   12. See *The Dunciad*, ed. James Sutherland, 3rd ed. (London, 1963), pp. 462–463.   13. The title-page is fraudulent. The play was written some twenty years earlier (with the title *Leonidas*) by Joseph Simpson, whose unpublished manuscript came into Johnson's hands.   14. See R. M. Wiles, *Serial Publication in England before 1750* (Cambridge, 1957), Appendix B.   15. *Parliamentary Papers*, 1818, IX, 254.   16. *Theresa; or, The Wizard's Fate*, 4 vols., by "a Member of the Inner Temple"; Selina Davenport, *Donald Monteith, the Handsomest Man of the Age*, 5 vols.; Mrs. Ross, *The Family Estate; or, Lost and Won*, 3 vols.; *Lady Jane's Pocket*, 4 vols., by "the author of *Silvanella*"; A. F. Holstein, *The Discontented Man; or, Love and Reason*, 3 vols.; and Catharine Smith, *Barozzi; or, The Venetian Sorceress*, 2 vols. All were published by A. K. Newman & Co.   17. Information from Mr. I. G. Philip, who also tells me that one volume of the Bodleian's set of Pope's *Odyssey* was received imperfect, but the missing sheets were procured by the Bodleian's agent.   18. *Gradus ad Cantabrigiam* (1803), p. 85.

ORDERING CHAOS *The Dunciad*

B. L. Reid

EVEN reluctant readers of Pope confess the greatness of the end of *The Dunciad*. Most students of poetry would call those fifty lines, in which the enormous yawn of the Goddess Dulness speaks her final uncreating word and completes the incursion of universal darkness, the grandest thing in Pope and one of the triumphs of English genius. "Crowded thoughts and stately numbers"[1] Samuel Johnson found there, and the lines surely express power, intelligence, taste, grandeur of conception, mastery of medium, ease and energy of movement:

> More she had spoke, but yawn'd—All Nature nods:
> What Mortal can resist the Yawn of Gods?
> Churches and Chapels instantly it reach'd:
> (St. James's first, for leaden Gilbert preach'd)
> Then catch'd the Schools; the Hall scarce kept awake;
> The Convocation gap'd, but could not speak:
> Lost was the Nation's Sense, nor could be found,
> While the long solemn Unison went round:
> Wide, and more wide, it spread o'er all the realm;
> Ev'n Palinurus nodded at the Helm:
> The Vapour mild o'er each Committee crept;
> Unfinish'd Treaties in each Office slept;
> And Chiefless Armies doz'd out the Campaign;
> And Navies yawn'd for Orders on the Main.
> O Muse! relate (for you can tell alone,
> Wits have short Memories, and Dunces none),
> Relate, who first, who last resign'd to rest;
> Whose Heads she partly, whose completely blest;
> What Charms could Faction, what Ambition lull,
> The Venal quiet, and entrance the Dull;
> 'Till drown'd was Sense, and Shame, and Right, and Wrong—
> O sing, and hush the Nations with thy Song!
> . . . .

In vain, in vain—the all-composing Hour
Resistless falls: The Muse obeys the Pow'r.
She comes! she comes! the sable Throne behold
Of *Night* Primæval, and of *Chaos* old!
Before her, *Fancy's* gilded clouds decay,
And all its varying Rain-bows die away.
Wit shoots in vain its momentary fires,
The meteor drops, and in a flash expires.
As one by one, at dread Medea's strain,
The sick'ning stars fade off th' ethereal plain;
As Argus' eyes by Hermes' wand opprest,
Clos'd one by one to everlasting rest;
Thus at her felt approach, and secret might,
Art after *Art* goes out, and all is Night.
See skulking *Truth* to her old Cavern fled,
Mountains of Casuistry heap'd o'er her head!
Philosophy, that lean'd on Heav'n before,
Shrinks to her second cause, and is no more.
Physic of *Metaphysic* begs defence,
And Metaphysic calls for aid on *Sense!*
See *Mystery* to *Mathematics* fly!
In vain! they gaze, turn giddy, rave, and die.
Religion blushing veils her sacred fires,
And unawares *Morality* expires.
Nor *public* Flame, nor *private*, dares to shine;
Nor *human* Spark is left, nor Glimpse *divine!*
Lo! thy dread Empire, CHAOS! is restor'd;
Light dies before thy uncreating word:
Thy hand, great Anarch! lets the curtain fall;
And Universal Darkness buries All.[2]

The effect is massive and horrific, literally stunning, as it is meant to be. The lines make most of their point even in isolation, freestanding. But that solitary impressiveness is itself obscurely disturbing. Has Pope done more than make a "moment" of Longinian sublimity? Do the ending and the main body of the poem deserve each other? Is the conclusion a true one, an honest rounding of a unified design? For the questions of the unity of this big poem of four books and 1,754 lines, of the part structure plays in its achievement, of the size of the achievement itself are still vexed and complicated.

The dubieties as to structure are obvious and significant: Pope's dithering with the names of the individual dunces; the spurious anonymity of the first versions; alterations in the text and additions to the apparatus culminating in the "Variorum" three-book *Dunciad* of 1729; the addition to the "completed" poem, thirteen years later, of a fourth book nearly twice as long as any of the others; the mechanical dethronement there of Lewis Theobald in favor of Colley Cibber as Prince of Dulness; the continued absence of any true hero as a figure of focus controlling the action within the mock-epic form. None of this suggests any great clarity in the original conception or any firm purpose in the long piecemeal history of the execution of the "design." Is the poem a shape or an agglomeration, a more or less efficient set of accidents? And if the structure is casual and fortuitous, are Pope's command of satirical penetration, of scenic and dramatic movement, and of figurative precision and logic powerful enough to order that looseness into fluency and coherence? Nobody who has compared the original and the revised versions of *The Rape of the Lock* will ever again doubt Pope's artistic nerve or the altering and synthesizing powers of his imagination, the lordly command of purpose and medium that can rebuild a "finished" work and raise it to a higher order of excellence. And whereas *The Dunciad* never achieves the seamless fabric of *The Rape of the Lock*, it does grow to a massive comeliness of form thoroughly suited to its very different nature.

From Johnson on down, Pope's critics have naturally compared his two mock-epics. It is enchanting to watch the lobster-claw delicacy with which Johnson handles the jewel-work of *The Rape*: "the most airy, the most ingenious, and the most delightful of all his compositions," he called it; "the most exquisite example of ludicrous poetry."[3] Johnson treats *The Dunciad*, in the main, respectfully but coolly: it is "one of his greatest and most elaborate performances"; it "affords perhaps the best specimen that has yet appeared of personal satire ludicrously pompous."[4] Among recent critics Geoffrey Tillotson's formulation I take to be decisive: "*The Dunciad*, like *MacFlecknoe*, is the ludicrous, grotesque, lifesize shadow cast by a piece of an epic poem, *The Rape of the Lock*, an exquisitely diminished shadow cast by an entire epic, by the august epic form itself."[5] That carries one a long way: *The Rape* (794 lines) is a brilliant miniature of a complete grand original; *The Dunciad* mocks a fragment of the grand original in terms of equivalent size. The distinction means a fundamental difference in scale, in the general manner of attack. The satirical arithmetic of the two epical mockeries is very different, and so is the angle of observation.

In *The Rape of the Lock* the subject is the absurdity of human vanity and pettiness, and Pope observes his creatures and his scene from a position a bit raised and oblique. His figures are slightly distanced by this slight removal, but they are not really shrunk in size as in Swift's kind of geometry—though there occurs an insistent trivializing of the figures due to the not-quite-present omnipresence of the tiny sylphs, just barely not caught every so often in a flicker at the corner of one eye. But the real reduction of the persons and the action is less a matter of size than of limitation, less vertical than horizontal: an abstracting that is achieved by narrowing the thing seen, by applying a kind of fanatical tunnel vision. An unspoken metaphor of concentration controls the whole poem. We see only the world of the poem's society because that *is* the world as limited and redefined by the madly inflated social issue, taking over life: a hermetic world, tiny passions making a great noise under a bell jar. Pope's persons have no thought, no action, no character that is not related to the ridiculous affair of the rape of the lock. That is the point. We see nothing but this world because it is what is left, the trivial absolute created by absolute vanity.

In *The Dunciad* we are in the same city but a different world. Rather than control by a metaphor of concentration and exclusion, we are in the hands of grandiosity, a burly, slovenly inclusiveness. The vision is extensive rather than intensive. Instead of the fanatically intensified, fastidiously neat mannikin world of *The Rape*, a world folded inward, we see London folded outward to become a race, a time, a landscape of the national mind, a culture preempted. The master metaphor is that of seizure, of occupation, of dispossession and repossession: a whole society hollowed out and replaced by its antiself. As Tillotson says, it is all both grotesque and lifesized. We move on the London bricks and mud here, and we meet the swarming citizens of Dulness's kingdom eye to eye. Except for the great Queen herself, that "ample presence," they are not really larger than ourselves though they are, thank God, grosser, for the moment. The mirror of vision in *The Dunciad* is convex rather than concave. What we see is ourselves unhealthily plumped out, a bit swollen and softened, with a certain pompous ductility of outline and an air of inconsequential busyness.

The basic difference in the shape and feeling of the two poems rests then less upon the scale of the persons observed than upon the arena of their movement and the manner of their moving.

The theater of *The Rape of the Lock* is an elegant drawing room approached by a narrow corridor of river and city. There the lovely sillies dance out a clear narrative-dramatic line, sharply defined and brightly lit. They do it beautifully, for they have nothing else to do. Every movement is stylized and stylish, graceful, to the point of the action, with no waste at all. The theater of *The Dunciad* is the sprawl of the city, folding out to seize, to "involve" the whole Augustan world. The scene is crowded, filthy, flaring, frenetic: a favorite word of the text is "swarm." Here the dance is a disorderly cockney Kermess, observed by Hogarth or Gilray. Movements are violent and awkward because they share no coherent impulse: the only conscious purpose here is the gross chthonic malevolence of Dulness herself, the force "inertly strong" of her implacable "deep Intent." *The Dunciad* does not move in linear and progressive ways, along a line of "plot" as in *The Rape of the Lock*. Movement is lateral, side-to-side, echoic, repetitive, an agitation in place at once clumsy and efficient; it winnows and harrows the complex city scene as it moves to accomplish not so much a plot as an action.

Shapeliness is a word one does not easily associate with *The Dunciad*. Its knobby symmetry is a very queer aesthetic phenomenon, and it takes one a long time to find it and give it a name. Certainly the sense of a developing shape fulfilling a commanding purpose does not dominate one's first readings of the poem. What one feels first is a general hectic busyness of no clear point or tendency; numerous single foci of satirical brilliance, varied and scattered tableaux and processions; semi-dramatic burlesque episodes. Fairly soon we begin to see that something big is going on but we cannot quite say what it is: we still feel a discrepancy between part and whole.

The peppering of the page with the initials or names or pseudonyms of the individual dunces is a famous difficulty, a litter of persons we no longer know and can hardly be brought to care about. This particularity of the names is the first formidable barrier to a perception of the big design of the action. With rereadings the names come clearer and clearer and mean less and less. Ultimately they lose identity and become so many counted neutral syllables. One sees the point then of Austin Warren's assurance that the names of the dunces are "annually replaceable"[6] : what matters is not who a dunce was but what he stood for, his intellectual character in Pope's view. When

the dunces have become types or symbols, an effect will have
been achieved that Pope did not quite intend, I suspect, and he
will have built even better than he knew. *The Dunciad* is first
of all a profoundly occasional poem, and we should be wrong
to forget the fact. Pope was attacking real persons for real or
supposed injuries or errors, out of an animosity that was private
before it was public or general, particular before it was typo-
logical. Though it was easier to say then than now, Johnson's
description continues accurate: "personal satire ludicrously
pompous."

But the poem is more than that, and the more that it is
is timeless. I think Pope knew that too, for he made it so at great
cost of labor and genius. It is the structure, the design, the
ordering of the action, not the dunces nor yet their annual
replaceability, that turns the poem toward the universal, and
we need to try to understand the means, chiefly those of the
grand figures, that accomplish this aggrandizement.

If we turn back to the closing lines of *The Dunciad* with which
we began, we find in those crowded thoughts and stately
numbers the great creeping, sweeping, annihilating gesture
that perfects the action of the poem. The action of *The Dunciad*
is just what Pope said it was in his note of "Martinus Scriblerus
of the Poem" attached to the *Variorum* of 1729: "the restoration
of the reign of Chaos and Night, by the ministry of Dulness
their daughter." Chaos and Night is to say shapeless and dark,
the void, the abyss. Pope's superb invention casts the final movement of the poem in the trope of a "Yawn *of extraordinary virtue*"
(Argument to Book IV) which spreads to paralyze and engulf
the instruments and institutions of church, state, and art, the
whole visible civility of the world.

It is noteworthy that the yawn of Dulness hushes even her
own speech. In the grand last *scena* that culminates her "progress"
Dulness is distributing prizes and making a state address to her
collected children, presenting her program to "MAKE ONE MIGHTY
DUNCIAD OF THE LAND":

> Then blessing all, "Go Children of my care!
> To Practice now from Theory repair.
> All my commands are easy, short, and full:
> My Sons! be proud, be selfish, and be dull." (IV, 579–582)

But her oration is interrupted by her own yawn: "More she
had spoke, but yawn'd . . . ." What she speaks, then, is the

yawn, the last "word," the "uncreating word" before which "light dies": the yawn is the word, or the word is the yawn—in any case, the death of the mind. The iconography of the scene seems medieval, a kind of abstract graphic absolute: the maw of Dulness into which the yawn opens becomes among other things a Hell Mouth. That gaping awfulness emits a narcotic vapor and between them they work the annihilation, the paralysis, and engulfment. The line of movement is epidemic and inclusive: "Wide, and more wide, it spread o'er all the realm" (IV, 613); it misses nothing living and significant. Churchmen, statesmen, military men, artists, and learned men succumb in turn. The Muse is called to read the catalog of victims, to "sing, and hush the Nations with thy Song" (IV, 626). But she too "obeys the Pow'r" and lies mute. The triumph of Dulness is proclaimed: "She comes! she comes! the sable Throne behold / Of *Night* primæval, and of *Chaos* old!" (IV, 629–630). Her "Hour" is come and it is "all-composing": an order and a paralysis, at once a new construct and a negative absolute, a life that is a death. Her composition is littered with the stunned forms of her victims: "In vain! they gaze, turn giddy, rave, and die" (IV, 648). The way is cleared for the terrible last couplets.

All of this is obvious enough, perhaps, and all the more imposing for its union of clarity and massiveness. What is less obvious, and what I hope to document, is the fact that the main lines of movement at the end of the poem are true ends of ligaments of action and thought that have girded and shaped the poem from the outset. The stunning power of the Goddess, her ability to drop curtains between sense and effective energy, and the "sick'ning" capitulation of her subjects, are cases copiously proven by the end of the awful comedy: the great yawn both includes and concludes.

First and last, *The Dunciad* is a poem of the mind in trouble, intelligence and good will beset by implacable mindlessness. The mock-epic form, by mocking, becomes itself the most inclusive metaphor of the work, and we must take that as given. In his first lines, by brisk and brilliant mockery of the myths of Eden and the Golden Age, Pope establishes a context of size and significance that is never lost. The uncreating word speaks at the beginning as well as at the end. Milton's Holy Spirit "dove-like satst brooding on the vast Abyss / And madst it pregnant"[7]: the divine will to life. Pope presents a gross malign fowl: "Here pleas'd behold her mighty wings out-spread / To hatch a new Saturnian age of Lead" (1, 27–28). In the anticreation of his epic proposition, the Goddess has "pour'd her Spirit o'er the land and deep" (1, 8) and "bade Britannia sleep" (1, 7). The miasma of her stupefying spirit, in vapors, veils, mists, fogs, excrements, pervades the poem, saturating the air we breathe.

Dulness is "Daughter of Chaos and eternal Night" (1, 12) and from them naturally takes her genetic equipment: she is "gross as her sire, and as her mother grave" (1, 14). Before the awakening of intelligence, "in eldest time, e'er mortals writ or read" (1, 9), Dulness had ruled over all, in "native Anarchy" (1, 16). Now, her sway having been interrupted by the march of mind, she moves to reinstate her power: "Still her old Empire to restore she tries " (1, 17). There is the subject of our epic action. Its ways of moving derive from the qualities of the Goddess's personal presence: "Laborious, heavy, busy, bold, and blind" (1, 15).

As the mock-epic form makes a comprehensive metaphor, so does the city. The city is London, and London is Britannia, and Britannia is the civilized world. The city is the theater of the arts of life: statecraft, religion, art, learning. It is the head and heart of the race, and it shows itself sick and vulnerable. The work of Dulness is to make a conquering "progress" through these kingdoms and establish her dominion, to "occupy" the city. She discovers or creates vacuums and fills them with her own vague and awful plenitude. Her ramshackle, rabble-engulfing progress is the axial movement of the poem, varied by pauses for complex posturings, disorderly agitations *in situ*, grotesque and vulgar *scenae*, audiences of the Goddess instated amid her thralls or holding levee over their drowsing forms in anticipation of the great sleep that closes all. The general rhythm and the pictorial logic, again, feel vaguely and massively medieval: crude processions lapsing into crude tableaux, a big, ugly, profane Book of Hours.

In fact most of Book 1 is composed of tableaux of one kind or another, clusters of persons, gestures, themes that establish an arena and a climate for the action to come. The secret throne room of Dulness, where she "shines" in "clouded Majesty" (1, 45), is appropriately situated near the gates of the madhouse, Bedlam Hospital. It is a cavernous, hollow place, full of the howling winds that are "emblem of Music caus'd by Emptiness" (1, 36), the retreat of the nameless bards of Grub-street, wont

to "escape in Monsters, and amaze the town" (I, 38), taking
protean shapes to startle and confound the city audience. What
the "cloud-compelling Queen" (I, 79) contemplates "with
self-applause" (I, 82) is the "wild creation" (I, 82), the chaos of
unreason that her influence induces in the world of art:

> How hints, like spawn, scarce quick in embryo lie,
> How new-born nonsense first is taught to cry,
> Maggots half-form'd in rhyme exactly meet,
> And learn to crawl upon poetic feet.
> Here one poor word an hundred clenches makes,
> And ductile dulness new meanders takes;
> There motley Images her fancy strike,
> Figures ill-pair'd, and Similies unlike.
> She sees a Mob of Metaphors advance,
> Pleas'd with the madness of the mazy dance:
> How Tragedy and Comedy embrace;
> How Farce and Epic get a jumbled race;
> How Time himself stands still at her command;
> Realms shift their place, and Ocean turns to land.
> Here gay Description Ægypt glads with show'rs
> Or gives to Zembla fruits, to Barca flow'rs;
> Glitt'ring with ice here hoary hills are seen,
> There painted vallies of eternal green,
> In cold December fragrant chaplets blow,
> And heavy harvests nod beneath the snow. (I, 59–78)

Ironically, what holds it all together is formlessness, the nonsense
that vainglorious stupidity makes of form, discipline, tradition,
logic. The passage is a storehouse of images—of incongruous
conjunctions, swarming embryos, busy indeterminate shapes,
crowds of creatures in frantic and indecisive movement—that
go on to control the poem. Fundamental is the idea of endless
ugly generation, the remorseless will of mindlessness to spawn
and survive.

It is this line of her generation that the Goddess inspects with
peculiar satisfaction: "She saw, with joy, the line immortal
run, / Each sire imprest and glaring in his son" (I, 99–100). Her
gaze sweeps to the worthy new Prince, Cibber, as he sits "swearing and supperless" in an ectasy of frustration:

> Then gnaw'd his pen, then dashed it on the ground,
> Sinking from thought to thought, a vast profound!
> Plung'd for his sense, but found no bottom there,

> Yet wrote and flounder'd on, in mere despair.
> Round him much Embryo, much Abortion lay,
> Much future Ode, and abdicated Play;
> Nonsense precipitate, like running Lead,
> That slip'd thro' Cracks and Zig-zags of the Head;
> All that on Folly Frenzy could beget,
> Fruits of dull Heat, and Sooterkins of Wit. (i, 117–126)

He is moved finally to build a votive pyre of his own writings and those he had plundered, and to address a prayer to Dulness, whom he salutes as "Great Tamer of all human art" (i, 163), and begs to keep him "obliquely wadling to the mark in view" (i, 172), to "spread a healing mist before the mind" (i, 174), to hang on the weights to keep his clockwork moving. He ignites the heap and "the rowling smokes involve the sacrifice" (i, 248). It is the first use of this inconspicuous but important verb which in its literal sense conveys the manner of Dulness's movement through the city and through the mind. Dulness "whelms" the fire—another of the verbs specified to her nature—then manifests herself to her chosen Prince. It is our first full, if not clear, view of the Goddess and it establishes once and for all her basic nature and her way of working: her dreadful ductile amplitude, her overbearing sufficiency, her power to occupy a space and to substitute her gross vague self for any former content or emptiness:

> Her ample presence fills up all the place;
> A veil of fogs dilates her awful face:
> Great in her charms! as when on Shrieves and May'rs
> She looks, and breathes herself into their airs. (i, 261–264)

The grateful Prince is led to her throne room and shown her state treasure of heaped nonsense:

> Prose swell'd to verse, verse loit'ring into prose:
> How random thoughts now meaning chance to find,
> Now leave all memory of sense behind:
> How Prologues into Prefaces decay,
> And these to Notes are fritter'd quite away:
> How Index-learning turns no student pale,
> Yet holds the eel of science by the tail:
> How, with less reading than makes felons scape,
> Less human genius than God gives an ape,
> Small thanks to France, and none to Rome or Greece,

A vast, vamp'd, future, old, reviv'd, new piece,
'Twixt Plautus, Fletcher, Shakespear, and Corneille,
Can make a Cibber, Tibbald, or Ozell. (I, 274–286)

The book closes parodically as it began, with the anointment and proclamation of the Beloved Son, the burlesque Messiah: Cibber to be Poet Laureate. The Queen then summons the first of the poem's mad processions, the Holiday of Misrule of the Mind:

> Lift up your gates, ye Princes, see him come!
> Sound, sound, ye Viols, be the Cat-call dumb!
> Bring, bring the madding Bay, the drunken Vine;
> The creeping, dirty, courtly Ivy join.
> And thou! his Aid de camp, lead on my sons,
> Light-arm'd with Points, Antitheses, and Puns.
> Let Bawdry, Billingsgate, my daughters dear,
> Support his front, and Oaths bring up the rear. (I, 301–308)

She looks ahead in rapture to the final perfection of her power when "all be sleep" (I, 318), and the shouts of the acquiescent mob, "God save king Cibber!" ricochet from point to point and enroll the city in the cause of Dulness: from the Chapel Royal, to White's gaming house, to Drury Lane, to Mother Needham's brothel, to the Devil Tavern in Fleet Street, to the bear-gardens in Hockley Hole.

The mock-epic simile that closes Book I,

> So when Jove's block descended from on high
> (As sings thy great forefather Ogilby)
> Loud thunder to its bottom shook the bog,
> And the hoarse nation croak'd, "God save King Log!"
> (I, 327–330)

rounds the opening movement by presenting the national voice choked and vulgarized by the thick wash of stupidity. At the same time it names the master element of Book II and a controlling figure of the entire poem, filth, assorted forms and densities of the miasma of the mind that emanates from Dulness and is a sign of her "ductile," "ample" presence: fogs, veils, mists, clouds, opium, mud, drains, excrement, polluted lakes and streams. Certainly these essences imbue the "high heroic Games" (II, 18) that comprise the action, again mainly a movement-in-place, of the second book.

The book opens on Cibber enthroned (again flanking both Milton's and Pope's deities) and we see that he has learned overnight how royalty behaves in the Kingdom of the Dull: "The proud Parnassian sneer, / The conscious simper, and the jealous leer, / Mix on his look" (II, 5–7). He has swiftly acquired, too, some of the Gorgon powers of the Queen: "All eyes direct their rays / On him, and crowds turn Coxcombs as they gaze" (II, 7–8). But the full deadliness of this Incarnation and its malign outreach into morality is better suggested by Pope's comparison of Cibber to the burlesque Roman laureate Camillo Querno, "the Antichrist of wit" (II, 16). The heralds' summons to the games in Drury Lane draws forth the jumbled swarm of Dulness's citizenry:

> An endless band
> Pours forth, and leaves unpeopled half the land.
> A motley mixture! in long wigs, in bags,
> In silks, in crapes, in Garters, and in rags,
> From drawing rooms, from colleges, from garrets,
> On horse, on foot, in hacks, and gilded chariots. (II, 19–24)

The various contests, for their various tawdry prizes, need not be recalled in detail, but they do need to be recognized as common in kind, and as archetypes of behavior in a mental kingdom so enthralled, so dispossessed and repossessed as this. Booksellers, hacks, and critics expose their greed, their vanity, and their awkwardness without shame, indeed with besotted eagerness, in movements appropriately laborious, heavy, busy, bold, and blind. Filth is everywhere and in it the contestants joyfully slide, sink, plunge, grope. Curll's headlong surge, for example, "swift as a bard the bailiff leaves behind" (II, 61), comes a cropper in the lake his Corinna "chanc'd that morn to make" (II, 70). As he "lies bewray'd" he directs his prayer to Jove whose throne is a kind of celestial close-stool where "amus'd he reads, and then returns the bills / Sign'd with that Ichor which from Gods distils" (II, 91–92). His petition preferred, Curll rallies and sweeps on through his native element:

> Renew'd by ordure's sympathetic force,
> As oil'd with magic juices for the course,
> Vig'rous he rises; from th' effluvia strong
> Imbibes new life, and scours and stinks along. (II, 103–106)

But of course the absolute of filth is the diving contest held at the sewer mouth.

The plan of this book devoted to the serial games is frankly and naturally episodic. Yet the book possesses a curious and instructive coherence. It is held together by the concord of its discords: the dirt, the noise, the ugliness, the blatancy and ineptitude that are everywhere. The brilliant mockery of the epic similes, here generally heavy or grotesque, is a major factor in this unity. Here is Lintot's gross gallop:

> As when a dab-chick waddles thro' the copse
> On feet and wings, and flies, and wades, and hops;
> So lab'ring on, with shoulders, hands, and head,
> Wide as a wind-mill all his figures spread,
> With arms expanded Bernard rows his state. (II, 63–67)

Here is Pope's analog of the din raised by the "Monkey-mimics" as they try the "wond'rous pow'r of Noise" (II, 222):

> As when the long-ear'd milky mothers wait
> At some sick miser's triple-bolted gate,
> For their defrauded, absent foals they make
> A moan so loud, that all the guild awake;
> Sore sighs Sir Gilbert, starting at the bray,
> From dreams of millions, and three groats to pay.
> So swells each wind-pipe; Ass intones to Ass,
> Harmonic twang! of leather, horn, and brass. (II, 247–254)

But it is in the episodic movement of Book II that the "involvement" of the city is particularly dramatized, and that action works strongly for unity. The topography of Pope's similes of the braying asses and the defecating Dutchman suggests the strategy of his design here:

> Walls, steeples, skies, bray back to him again.
> In Tot'nam fields, the brethren, with amaze,
> Prick all their ears up, and forget to graze;
> Long Chanc'ry-lane retentive rolls the sound,
> And courts to courts return it round and round;
> Thames wafts it thence to Rufus' roaring hall,
> And Hungerford re-echoes bawl for bawl. (II, 260–266)
> . . . .
> As what a Dutchman plumps into the lakes,
> One circle first, and then a second makes;
> What Dulness dropt among her sons imprest
> Like motion from one circle to the rest;

> So from the mid-most the nutation spreads
> Round and more round, o'er all the sea of heads. (II, 405–410)

What occurs in each case is a powerful "communication" from a center of malign energy, radiating outward to occupy the city spaces and to take physical and spiritual possession of the populace. The din raised by "sonorous Blackmore's strain" (above) is stupefying, stunning the whole city's sense. The epidemic movement of Dulness takes several shapes and rhythms; the raucous bouncing echo; the spreading circles of the Dutchman's deposit; the wavelike progression of sympathetic influence, as in the simile of the nodding pines:

> Then mount the Clerks, and in one lazy tone
> Thro' the long, heavy, painful page drawl on;
> Soft creeping, words on words, the sense compose,
> At ev'ry line they stretch, they yawn, they doze.
> As to soft gales top-heavy pines bow low
> And lift them as they cease to blow;
> Thus oft they rear, and oft the head decline,
> As breathe, or pause, by fits, the airs divine.
> And now to this side, now to that they nod
> As verse, or prose, infuse the drowzy God (II, 387–396);

the cynosure effect of the enchanted crowds, "turning coxcombs as they gaze" at Dulness's shows; and a rolling, tumbling linear movement that seems to lick up the city's streets and the river's banks. Cibber's ecstatic vision prefigures a condition perfected:

> "And oh! (he cry'd) what street, what lane but knows,
> Our purgings, pumpings, blankettings, and blows?
> In ev'ry loom our labours shall be seen,
> And the fresh vomit run for ever green!" (II, 153–156)

The "involving" force of this movement can be shown by the single couplet that brings the crowd back into the old City at the end of its eastward return: "Thro' Lud's famed gates, along the well-known Fleet, / Rolls the black troop, and overshades the street" (II, 359–360).

The movement of the fable itself, admittedly hazy and desultory in the first two books, is of course that of a mock Lord Mayor's Procession, east to west and back again, along Fleet Street, the Strand, the Thames, from the City to Westminster and return, bringing "the Smithfield Muses to the ear of Kings" (I, 2), bringing vulgarity to polite and learned life. The progress of Dulness throws a long slovenly noose about the heart of London, a garrotte about the city's throat.[8] At the end of Book II even the dunces are choked into silence; the reading clerks subside into mutters; Centlivre "felt her voice to fail" (II, 411). No head can resist the opiate of Dulness, and prefiguring, now gently, the end of the poem, "the soft gifts of Sleep conclude the day" (II, 419). Dulness has begun her work of "hushing the Nations."

Partly because it is the most static, the action of Book III is the most orderly and homogeneous of the four books. Though the mental eye moves with great range and agility here, the angle of the artist's observation is single and fixed, and the fictive theater is entirely intracranial. But of course Cibber's is presented as a fairly hectic cranium. The action is that of a vision, busy and complicated, of the past and present history of Dulness and "a glimpse, or Pisgah-sight of the future Fulness of her Glory" (Argument to Book III). Cibber is discovered in a posture that continues the last movement of the preceding book, asleep like a huge baby in the lap of Dulness in the sanctum of her temple: a posture "of marvellous virtue," the Argument assures us. The shrouding, brooding attitude of mother and son, a profane Madonna and Child, forms a womb at the center of the concentric circles of her kingdom, at the radial point of her labyrinths. Attitude and atmosphere both shield and inspire the snoring Prince:

> Him close she curtains round with Vapours blue,
> And soft besprinkles with Cimmerian dew.
> Then raptures high the seat of Sense o'erflow,
> Which only heads refin'd from Reason know. (III, 3–6)

Being refined from reason, Cibber's head is free to wander "on Fancy's easy wing" to the Dunciadic underworld, where "a slip-shod Sibyl led his steps along, / In lofty madness meditating song" (III, 15–16).

There is neither space nor need to canvass these visions in detail. I am more concerned with showing how the main fibers of the action as a whole also shape the principal images of the dreams, for in content they too are effectual actions. What dominates Cibber's first view of the soporific realm of Bavius, for example, is another of Pope's swarming undifferentiated multitudes:

> Millions and millions on these banks he views,
> Thick as the stars of night, or morning dews,
> As thick as bees o'er vernal blossoms fly,
> As thick as eggs at Ward in Pillory. (III, 31–34)

So Cibber's own history is treated as a type of the endless genetic chain of the lineage of stupidity: "Who knows how long thy transmigrating soul / Might from Bœotian to Bœotian roll?" (III, 49–50). So too the rhythmical outreach and ingestion of Dulness's malign plenitude is caught in a single swift and homely simile:

> Or whirligigs, twirl'd round by skilful swain,
> Suck the thread in, then yield it out again:
> All nonsense thus, of old or modern date,
> Shall in thee centre, and from thee circulate. (III, 57–60)

So Cibber is invited to view the range of Dulness's power to encompass and smother: Earth's wide extremes "her sable flag display'd, / And all the nations cover'd in her shade!" (III, 71–72). All of this within the first seventy-two lines of the book.

It is this sense of inexorable progression that unifies the series of visions unveiled by Settle for the enraptured Prince. The march of Dulness through space and time calls forth some of Pope's grandest synoptic couplets:

> How little, mark, that portion of the ball,
> Where, faint at best, the beams of Science fall:
> Soon as they dawn, from Hyperborean skies
> Embody'd dark, what clouds of Vandals rise!
> Lo! where Mæotis sleeps, and hardly flows
> The freezing Tanais thro' a waste of snows,
> The North by myriads pours her mighty sons,
> Great nurse of Goths, of Alans, and of Huns!
> See Alaric's stern port! the martial frame
> Of Genseric! and Attila's dread name!
> See the bold Ostrogoths on Latium fall;
> See the fierce Visigoths on Spain and Gaul!
> See, where the morning gilds the palmy shore
> (The soil that infant arts and letters bore)
> His conqu'ring tribes th' Arabian prophet draws,
> And saving Ignorance enthrones by Laws.
> See Christians, Jews, one heavy sabbath keep,
> And all the western world believe and sleep. (III, 83–100)

The phantasmagorias of present and future foretell the restoration of England to Dulness's possession: "This fav'rite Isle, long sever'd from her reign, / Dove-like, she gathers to her wings again" (III, 125–126). The huge vision now concentrates and grows more particular as the scene returns to the occupation of the city as the type of her triumph:

> Not with less glory mighty Dulness crown'd,
> Shall take thro Grub-street her triumphant round;
> And her Parnassus glancing o'er at once,
> Behold an hundred sons, and each a Dunce. (III, 135–138)

Settle's vision of the city arts, based on the wild popular stage fare of the day, shows the products of perfected unreason:

> Thence a new world, to Nature's laws unknown,
> Breaks out refulgent, with a heav'n its own:
> Another Cynthia her journey runs,
> And other planets circle other suns.
> The forests dance, the rivers upward rise,
> Whales sport in woods, and dolphins in the skies;
> And last, to give the whole creation grace,
> Lo! one vast egg produces human race. (III, 241–248)

Cibber's predicted conquest will "involve" the city:

> Happier thy fortunes! Like a rolling stone,
> Thy giddy dulness still shall lumber on,
> Safe in its heaviness, shall never stray,
> But lick up ev'ry blockhead in the way.
> Thee shall the Patriot, thee the Courtier taste,
> And ev'ry year be duller than the last.
> 'Till rais'd from booths, to Theatre, to Court,
> Her seat imperial Dulness shall transport. (III, 293–300)

And finally Cibber is accorded the ensign of the poppy, a new proclamation and acclamation, and the book closes with enthusiastic prophecies of general disaster to ensue.

It is impossible to say whether Pope realized that the revised and expanded *Dunciad* would be his last published work. But the great fourth book, added after an interval of thirteen years and including relics of other proposed but unattempted works, takes on special elevation and poignancy in the context of the close of "this long disease, my Life." One seems to hear swan song airs particularly at the beginning and end of the book. The second sentence, for example, conveys both a continuing anathema and a weary resignation:

> Ye Pow'rs! whose Mysteries restor'd I sing,
> To whom Time bears me on his rapid wing,
> Suspend a while your Force inertly strong,
> Then take at once the Poet and the Song. (IV, 5–8)

The "sickness" of the sun seems to express not only the Dog Star's "unpropitious Ray" (IV, 9) but the poet's own mind and heart as once more he sees the stubborn daughter of Chaos and old Night ever ready "to blot out Order, and extinguish Light" (IV, 14). The voice of the heartbroken priest, always audible within the ventriloquism of the Tory satirists, sounds with special resonance here. It is a bitter joke, the new invocation in Miltonic parody that opens Book IV, begging only a little light, "one dim Ray" (IV, 1), just enough "as half to shew, half veil the deep Intent" (IV, 4). The full view is too awful to bear. And in this book treating the "consummation of all" (Argument to Book IV) even the prayer of the poet is addressed to Chaos and Night as powers confirmed in state.

The fourth book is altogether a court scene, and as such relatively static, mostly lateral in movement. The panoramas and processions move toward a central point, "by sure Attraction led, / And strong impulsive gravity of Head" (IV, 74–75), to the throne where Dulness sits with her head in a cloud and her "Laureat son" still lolling in her lap, and there they caper and freeze into tableaux, convenient to the yawn that will engulf them and their betters at the end. The throne of Dulness is evidently now the throne of the kingdom, and the jumbled *scena* of the opening view shows her situated at the peak of a heaped pyramid of vanquished and spurned disciplines of the mind: "Beneath her foot-stool, *Science* groans in Chains, / And *Wit* dreads Exile, Penalties and Pains. / There foam'd rebellious *Logic*, gagg'd and bound" (IV, 21–23). The catalog fills twenty-three lines.

With the Goddess fixed on her throne, her swarming disciples cluster busily "conglob'd" about their "Centre." The "rolling," "involving" movement of the mobs through the city is more intense than ever in Book IV, though its effect is more centripetal than processional now, converging on the

Queen, moving toward the eye rather than past it. Here is the general picture:

> The gath'ring number, as it moves along,
> Involves a vast involuntary throng,
> Who gently drawn, and struggling less and less,
> Roll in her Vortex, and her pow'r confess. (IV, 81–84)

And even when the rowdy scene is more or less fixed, the disorderly local movement of "crowds on crowds" as one or another party presses for attention continues the rhythm of dispossession and possession. Here is the mass of black-gowned academics, for example: "Prompt at the call, around the Goddess roll / Broad hats, and hoods, and caps, a sable shoal: / Thick and more thick the black blockade extends" (IV, 189–191). And the rout of travelled fops who displace them: "In flow'd at once a gay embroider'd race, / And titt'ring pushed the Pedants off the place (IV, 274–275).

With the mincing "Harlot form" of Opera, the first of the serial petitioners of Book IV, Pope plays an interesting variant on his theme of unbalanced and inefficient movement: not merely awkward this time, but an incoherent and meretricious prettiness with no musculature and no tensile strength, no body and no brain. "*O Cara! Cara!*" she trills, glancing scornfully at the prostrate Muses; "silence all that train: / Joy to great Chaos! let Division reign. . ." (IV, 53–54). The successive petitioners are archetypes of vanity and anti-intellectualism, perverters of faith and reason, purveyors of egotism, triviality, and false doctrine. They achieve a hectic unity by their common tendency to special pleading, partial views, short and straitened programs to which they adhere with obsessed enthusiasm. Opera's punning imperative, "Let Division reign," could stand as a rubric for the whole book.

These spokesmen perform at greater length and in stricter oratorical modes than those of earlier books, with heavier gravity and more extended resonance, and the effect is that of a ponderous and ominous thickening of spiritual and intellectual crisis. The schoolmasters boast of their "narrowing" potency, their enmity to dubiety and speculation, their command of rote learning and formulaic language by which they "hang one jingling padlock on the mind":

> Plac'd at the door of Learning, youth to guide,
> We never suffer it to stand too wide.

To ask, to guess, to know, as they commence,
As Fancy opens the quick springs of Sense,
We ply the Memory, we load the brain,
Bind rebel Wit, and double chain on chain,
Confine the thought to exercise the breath;
And keep them in the pale of Words till death. (IV, 153–160)

The university men, led by "that awful Aristarch" Bentley, handle language and learning in more sophisticated forms of the same false values. "The critic Eye, that microscope of Wit, / Sees hairs and pores, examines bit by bit" (IV, 233–234): woods are lost in trees, wholes are drowned under a shoal of parts. As sworn servants of Dulness, they use the instrument of language in her obfuscatory and stultifying spirit:

... For thee explain a thing till all men doubt it,
And write about it, Goddess, and about it:
So spins the silkworm small its slender store,
And labours till it clouds itself all o'er. (IV, 251–254)

The pedants are "pushed off the place" by the "gay embroider'd race" of continental travelers, led by "Whore, Pupil, and lac'd Governor from France" (IV, 272), a "finished" youth with his harlot and his bear-leader, who assures the Queen that "Europe he saw, and Europe saw him too"[9](IV, 294). If the young man showed any prospect of English yeomanly sturdiness, it has been sloughed in a tide of continental perfumes. As he "saunter'd Europe round, / And gather'd ev'ry Vice on Christian ground" (IV, 311–312), he has

... Dropt the dull lumber of the Latin store,
Spoil'd his own language, and acquir'd no more,
All Classic learning lost on Classic ground;
And last turn'd *Air*, the Echo of a Sound! (IV, 319–322)

It is in this sense that the young man is Dulness's "accomplish'd Son" (IV, 282). The Governor presents the youth and his consort to the Queen with the prophecy that they will fit smoothly into the endless genetic chain of Dulness: "So may the sons of sons of sons of whores. . ." (IV, 332). The Queen receives them gladly, wraps them in her veil, "and frees from sense of Shame" (IV, 336). The extravagances of the Virtuosi—of coins, flowers, insects—who follow move the Goddess to an ecstatic apocalyptic vision:

> O! would the Sons of Men once think their Eyes
> And Reason giv'n them but to study *Flies!*
> See Nature in some partial narrow shape,
> And let the Author of the Whole escape:
> Learn but to trifle; or, who most observe,
> To wonder at their Maker, not to serve. (IV, 453–458)

"Be that my task," promptly offers a "gloomy Clerk, / Sworn foe to Myst'ry, yet divinely dark" (IV, 459–460), speaking for free thinkers and mechanic philosophers who have perverted reason to be an enemy of both revelation and experience:

> Let others creep by timid steps, and slow,
> On Plain Experience lay foundations low,
> By common sense to common knowledge bred,
> And last, to Nature's Cause thro' Nature led.
> All-seeing in thy mists, we want no guide,
> Mother of Arrogance, and Source of Pride!
> We nobly take the high Priori Road,
> And reason downward, till we doubt of God. (IV, 465–472)

So the demonstrations of Book IV, and hence of the poem, come to a point in absolute Ego, the ultimate vulgarity. Enthralled and fixed in Self, the dunces are ready to be swept up in the harvesting yawn of Dulness. In a book that treats largely of the misuse of reason and of language its vehicle, the yawn that speaks the uncreating word, the antilogos, the anticreation, is the powerful and suitable conclusion. And the yawn rightly concludes the poem as a whole.

It is no use to argue for a neat or obvious unity in *The Dunciad*. It is not a well-made work. It is a big harsh poem with a lot of violent work to do, which it does with some waste and awkwardness that are incidents of its energy, defects of its virtues. Its unity is not that of straightforward narrative march toward a dramatic end always in view, as in *The Rape of the Lock*. One can force out of the scenario of the four books a specious linear sequence of a more traditional sort: perhaps Coronation, Celebration, Consecration, Consummation, if we wish to be fancy about it. But the alignment of the four books is less linear and progressive than parallel and iterative: they are laid not end to end but side by side. But I insist that the poem does march forward, a unity, and the yawn of Dulness does reach upward and outward to enclose the ends of all four books. The unifying movement is that of common cause, of energy, of passion, of intellectual outrage that emerges in visions that have the insistent recurrence of nightmare and merge finally into a single vision, sufficiently apocalyptic.

Size is of the essence in *The Dunciad*: the size of the issue, of the scene, of the fictive events. I have tried to suggest the unity that comes from the proper iteration of images specified to function, especially images of movement appropriate to the nature of Dulness, and more especially her movement through the city of the mind. After the great yawn and the awful Nothing-filled silence that follows, perhaps the strongest lingering effect is that of sheer size, size as significance: of a grand ethical and aesthetic displacement, of the robustness of Pope's vision and the prodigality of his gesture in writing this poem. The effect may lead one to think back over his work as a whole —past our bemusement with his frail childlike figure, his addiction to the tiniest of stanza forms, and the filigree delicacy of his most famous poem—to recognize that his satirical grasp, his way of seizing and moving a subject, had always been direct and stout. Even in *The Rape of the Lock*, is not the sensibility, the manner and spirit of attack, fundamentally robust and largeminded? Looking at Pope from our own day one thinks how nice it would be to have him back: our times could use him.

Notes

1. "Life of Pope," *Rasselas, Poems, and Selected Prose*, ed. Bertrand H. Bronson (New York, 1958), p. 400.   2. *The Dunciad*, ed. James Sutherland (London, 1943), pp. 605–607. All future references will be to this edition and will be given in parentheses in the text.   3. "Life of Pope," pp. 317–318, 319. 4. "Life of Pope," pp. 340, 399.   5. *On the Poetry of Pope*, 2nd ed. (Oxford, 1950), p. 55.   6. "Alexander Pope," *Rage for Order: Essays in Criticism* (Ann Arbor, 1959), p. 50.   7. *Paradise Lost*, I, 21–22.   8. The map on pp. 34–35 of *Pope's "Dunciad": A Study of Its Meaning*, by Aubrey L. Williams (Baton Rouge, 1955), is a great help in visualizing these matters.   9. One may recall the American recruiting poster: "Join the Marines and Let the World See You!"

SENTIMENTALISM AND THEATER REFORM IN THE EARLY EIGHTEENTH CENTURY

Calhoun Winton

LITERARY history, being an aspect of human history, is not provided to us in neat packages of equal shape and size—anthologies and handbooks to the contrary notwithstanding—but in untidy bundles of varying dimension always coming unwrapped at the ends and spilling over into the adjoining bundle. When, however, some period or genre or topic can apparently be fitted into a symmetrical package critics and anthologists will rush to do so, and seeing the genre or period or topic in its proper measurements, restoring it to its natural boundaries, so to speak, will thenceforth be very difficult.

A case in point is the relationship between sentimentalism and theater reform in the eighteenth century. It has been taken as something of a received truth that there was such a relationship: sentimentalism in the drama was associated with or produced by the movement for theater reform, so goes the assumption. Both sentimental drama and theater reform were demanded by an expanding middle-class audience and the whole operation was set in motion by the Reverend Jeremy Collier's *Short View* in 1698. Thus the editor of an anthology often used in graduate and undergraduate classes summarizes the change:

> [The eighteenth century] was an era marked by the decay of the old aristocracy and the rise to power of the new middle classes, the nation of shopkeepers who proudly paraded their wealth, deemed poverty a crime, and—however sinfully they behaved in private—insisted on the forms of bourgeois morality. . . . A crusade against the immorality of Restoration drama, led by Jeremy Collier's *Short View of the Immorality and Profaneness of the English Stage* (1698), and supported by societies for the reformation

of manners, had brought about the enforcement of laws against bawdiness and blasphemy on the stage. Decency returned to the theatres, and dullness came along for company. In the new century most of the old stock plays were cleansed and purified.[1]

This model of theatrical history, which is, I believe, quite widely accepted, has the pedagogical virtues of simplicity and clarity, and the additional merit of possessing two convenient villains or scapegoats, Collier and the middle-class audience, at whose door blame for the resulting mess can be laid. The more one looks into the question, however, the less clear the relationship between sentimentalism and theater reform appears, and the greater the need one feels to discriminate not only between these two main currents but indeed among the various movements for theater reform itself. It is the purpose of this essay, after a necessarily brief comment on sentimentalism, to provide some notes for the study of the different calls for theater reform in the eighteenth century and to underline the relationship between some aspects of the reform movement and the exemplary drama. It is intended as an introduction to a large and potentially interesting subject. The discussion will center on the London stage with some attention to Edinburgh but the topic could profitably be extended to France, to Dublin, and to the infant American theater as well.

Thorny questions about sentimentalism in the drama have been raised in recent years and most of them are by no means resolved, such questions as: whether there is such a genre as sentimental drama at all and if there is, when did it begin and what was its literary history? Which plays should be included in the category and which ones left out? Satisfactory answers are not easily arrived at.[2] For example, one might ask at what point drama became sentimental. Collier's *Short View* and the turn of the century do provide a convenient, mnemonic solution. But if by the adjective sentimental one refers to the inclusion of stage action specifically framed to elicit audience sympathy, it is clear that there were sentimental elements in various plays years before the appearance of the *Short View*. One recalls Dryden and Howard's Montezuma in *The Indian Queen* (1663): "Into my eyes sorrow begins to creep; / When hands are ty'd it is no shame to weep." Four characters including the doughty warrior himself are shedding tears on stage simultaneously in this scene. If this is sentimentalism, as it appears to be by any of several definitions, one would nevertheless be hard put to enroll Dryden among those advocating reform. Several decades later, in 1696, Colley Cibber saw produced his *Love's Last Shift*, which B. R. S. Fone has argued "through and through, reflects the language of the sentimental tradition." The play (produced two years before the appearance of the *Short View*) though sentimental is not a document in the history of stage reform, Dr. Fone maintains: "It takes small knowledge of Cibber to be sure that he intended no reform."[3]

The evidence, in fact, does not indicate that most or even many of those calling for reform of the theaters were interested in introducing sentimental elements as such into the drama. Many theorists of stage reform were, however, concerned with the exemplary effect of the stage, the manner in which they supposed drama influenced the audience; indeed, agreement on this point among both critics and defenders of the theaters is one of the interesting aspects of the controversy. There was, that is to say, widespread agreement that the stage was capable of influencing, for good or ill, the conduct of the audience.

It is at this point, perhaps, that the disentangling process should begin, in emphasizing what will be the product of a moment's reflection: that there is no necessary connection between sentimentalism and exemplary drama. A play may be intended as exemplary without being sentimental in any respect. Shaw's *Caesar and Cleopatra* was planned to effect a change in the modes of thought and action of those who saw and read it. A television serial of the present day, on the other hand, may be written so as to draw tears without any intention on the part of the screenwriters of providing guideposts for audience conduct beyond guiding the housewives by means of the commercials to a particular brand of detergent. Important issues in aesthetic theory are involved here, of course, but these garden-variety examples may be enough to demonstrate that discussion of the exemplary effects of the drama does not imply anything one way or the other about the attitude of the discussant towards sentimentalism, whether sentimentalism is defined as exemplifying a benevolent view of the nature of man or as utilizing stage action to elicit audience sympathy.

Although the function of exemplary drama was an important element in the debate over stage reform, it was by no means the only element. Various segments of the population had differing views on the subject. A large measure of difficulty in discussing theater reform derives from the circumstance that eighteenth-century controversialists would sometimes employ identical terms with different, or even opposite, denotations. What the dramatic author had in mind, for example, when he demanded reform of the theaters might not at all be what the Lord Chamberlain wanted when he voiced the same demand. There seems, in truth, to have been agreement on one and only one point, that is, that reform had not taken place. Our popular view that Collier had cleaned up the stage like Hercules in the well-known stables, that decency "returned to the theatres, and dullness came along for company," was emphatically not shared in the early eighteenth century.[4] The Reverend Arthur Bedford, eight years after the *Short View*, issued his *The Evil and Danger of Stage-Plays: Shewing their Natural Tendency to Destroy Religion, and introduce a General Corruption of Manners* which contained 227 pages of detailed analysis somewhat in Collier's manner. Few would term it sentimental.

This was in the reign of Queen Anne. Soon after the accession of King George I, Richard Steele, who had expressed himself many times in his periodicals on the necessity for dramatic reform, received his royal patent as governor of Drury Lane with a specific injunction from the Crown to eject "all Scandalous and Mutinous Persons" from the house and to see that "no New Play, or any Old or Revived Play be Acted . . . containing any Passages or Expressions offensive to Piety and good Manners, until the Same be Corrected and Purged by the said Governor. . . ."[5] During the first year of Steele's tenure, in 1715, however, Defoe complained that "the Youth of the Kingdom receive [at the theaters] a general Tincture of Debauchery and Wickedness. . . ."[6] Arthur Bedford was back on the spoor of the drama four years later with 383 pages of complaints significantly entitled: *A Serious Remonstrance In Behalf of the Christian Religion, against the Horrid Blasphemies and Impieties which are still used in the English Play-Houses. . . . From almost Seven Thousand Instances, taken out of the Plays of the present Century, and especially of the five last Years. . . .* The anonymous author of *Plays and Masquerades* that same year (1719), though differing from Bedford in his point of view, agreed that there had been little or no reform: "The modern Stage is calculated and design'd to fill the Mind with false Notions of Honour, and wrong Sentiments of Things; to corrupt the Imagination, to fire the

Passions of unexperienc'd Youth, to wear out Impressions of Virtue, and to dispose, by Degrees, to every Evil."[7]

The manager of one of the leading playhouses in 1719 and for the previous five years was of course the reformer Sir Richard Steele. In 1721, nonetheless, the youth of England were still being misled right on the doorstep of Drury Lane, as it were. The records of the Middlesex Court of Sessions report a meeting that year between the Lord Chancellor of Great Britain and the Justices of the Peace for Middlesex and Westminster on the question of public vice, at which meeting all present agreed that the "profaneness and debauchery which prevails and increases in this town and country, proceeds chiefly from the mascorades and gameing houses, and from the encrease of play houses."[8] Vice and immorality have, they found, increased "among all degrees of persons."

Two aspects of this statement by the chief officers of law enforcement in the region merit attention. First, their voices are added to that chorus which proclaimed that all sermons read before Parliament, all orders on the Royal Sign Manual, all manifestos by Sir Richard Steele to the contrary notwithstanding the stage had not been reformed getting on to a quarter of a century after Collier's volley. That hypothetical audience of "shopkeepers who . . . insisted on the forms of bourgeois morality" were uncommonly slow in making their wishes known. Did the audience, in fact, exist? The Middlesex Court of Sessions at any rate felt that the debauching effect of the playhouses extended to "all degrees of persons."

The second aspect of the statement by the Middlesex Court which one might pause to consider is their concern, which was like that of Defoe, not merely with dramatic literature but with the general environment of the theater. It was not only the blasphemies and indecencies of the plays to which they objected but also the moral atmosphere in which the plays were produced. This was a line of attack which William Law was to exploit with devastating force in his *The Absolute Unlawfulness of the Stage-Entertainment Fully Demonstrated* (London, 1726). Writing twenty-eight years after Collier, Law would have no part of any nonsense about the stage's having been reformed. "Let it therefore be observ'd, that the Stage is not here condemn'd, as some other Diversions, because they are dangerous, and likely to be the Occasions of Sin; but that it is condemn'd, as Drunkenness and Lewdness, as Lying and Prophaneness are to be condemn'd; not as Things that may only be the Occasions of Sin, but as such as are in their own Nature grossly sinful."[9] Law rejects out of hand all talk about the usefulness of the stage—everyone knows it is a sink of iniquity, pit, box, gallery, and green room. Acting an honorable occupation? "Perhaps you had rather see your Son chained to a *Galley*, or your daughter driving [a] *Plow*, than getting their Bread on the *Stage*, by administering in so scandalous a manner to the vices and corrupt Pleasures of the World."[10] And so it went. The call for reform was raised, and raised again, but never answered. In 1729 an anonymous observer examined the year's offerings and asked the rhetorical question: "Can you look on these Plays, as any better than Nurseries of *Atheism, Lewdness* and *Debauchery?* For there they endeavour to represent *Vice* as profitable and pleasant; and there they treat Religion with Ridicule. . . . There you have Oaths and Cursing, and taking the Name of God in vain. . . . There you have the most obscene and filthy Words and Actions——."[11] Eight years later an anonymous parson addressed a verse epistle to Charles Fleetwood, manager of Drury Lane, in which he enjoined Fleetwood to pursue theater reform "with steady Zeal. . . . / Thy Stage reform'd, may stem the present Tide, / And turn the Stream as strong on Virtue's Side."[12] Mid-century came and conditions were no better, or so at least thought the anonymous author of *An Address to the Ladies on the Indecency of Appearing at Immodest Plays*, who surveyed the scene and concluded that very few decent plays were being written. He was, however, still hopeful: "May the ensuing Winter, of *Seventeen Hundred* and *Fifty-six*, stand distinguished in *British* Annals, as the glorious Aera, when Bawdry and Obscenity were banished the publick Stage. . . ."[13]

How came it about that, almost sixty years after Collier, so little appeared to have been accomplished in the way of theater reform? In the twentieth century we may assume that Collier and the reformers carried all before them but this was an assumption that Steele's and Garrick's contemporaries would not have shared, if we may judge from the evidence which has survived. How could this be?

As indicated earlier, much of the controversy seems to have stemmed from confusion over the meaning of "reform" itself. An analogy might be drawn to the present day, when everyone agrees that "something must be done" about commercial television in the United States but no consensus can be reached among broadcasters, sponsors, writers, viewers, and critics as to what. So, in the first half of the eighteenth century there would seem to have been at least three areas in which reform was called for at various times, by one or another group of critics. These might be termed (1) jurisdictional or administrative, (2) authorial, and (3) theatrical, the latter including the reform of dramatic literature. The interests involved were sometimes mutually exclusive; that is, reform of one area would work against reform of another, as will be seen.

Although Collier's principal target had been dramatic literature, bawdry and obscenity in the plays themselves, one of the century's most notorious reform controversies, that between the managers of Drury Lane and the Lord Chamberlain in 1719–1721, had almost nothing directly to do with dramatic literature but was instead jurisdictional and personal.[14] It was part of a continuing struggle between political leaders and theatrical management for control of the stage. Important issues were involved, perhaps the principal one in the long view being whether the London stage would be under effective government control or not. In the context of this controversy and of those in the 1730s which culminated in the Licensing Act of 1737, the term "reform" connoted control. It was a type of reform the theater managers could gladly have spared.

Not so in every case the authors, the playwrights themselves. Some authors, Charles Gildon for example, supported the cause of increased political control over the theaters because they believed friends in the ministry would see to it that their plays were produced.[15] Authorial reform, securing better plays by better authors, was in all respects a touchy business. Did it imply, for example, that the monopoly theaters would produce the best plays or the best plays of living authors? The "reform management" of Drury Lane after the accession of George I announced their intention of producing the best plays available, and in the season 1715–1716 mounted no fewer than ten of Shakespeare's plays, as well as others by Jonson, Beaumont and Fletcher, Dryden and Otway. The policy met the approval of the scholarly Lewis Theobald in *The Censor* and fulfilled part of the management's pledge but it undermined another portion of Steele's program, to give "due Encouragement to Men of Abilities, as well by a careful Performance of what they should Act, as a just Recompence for the Purchase of their Works. . . ."[16] The two aspects of reform worked against each other and inevitably living playwrights felt that they were edged aside by their great predecessors. Whether or not this was due to a dearth of talent among the living, the practical effect was to produce a group of writers who thought of theater managers as virtual dictators. These managers were thus depriving audiences of the opportunity for seeing truly fit, or reformed, drama, prepared according to the prescriptions of the complaining playwrights. This opinion was put with amusing directness by John Dennis, who after lamenting for years about the state of the drama finally saw his tragedy *Coriolanus* produced at Drury Lane and die after three performances. The reason for the failure, Dennis asserted, was that the managers had put so much money and effort into a preceding revival of *All for Love*, the design for which play, Dennis informed the public in a pamphlet, was "pernicious" and "criminal." "*Coriolanus* . . . [has] a just Moral . . . Whereas *All for Love*" has not.[17] Fielding presents the difficulties confronting a dramatist in *The Author's Farce*, where the author Luckless presents his new play for approval to the theater managers Marplay and Sparkish (who represent the Drury Lane managers Robert Wilks and Colley Cibber). He is told the play will not do. "What faults do you find?" he inquires. "Sir," replies Marplay, "there is nothing in it that pleases me, so I am sure there is nothing in it that will please the town."[18] The criticism by an anonymous author in the *Grub-street Journal* for 8 March 1732 is addressed from the same angle of vision: the theater managers lack taste, literary judgment, and are after the easy guinea.[19] On the other hand, the translator Thomas Cooke defended the same management, in a somewhat backhanded manner. "If some few Objections may be made to the present Management of our Theatres, is it reasonable that dramatic Performances should be entirely prohibited? We may with as much Justice prefer a Petition to the King to pull down the Church, because disloyal, impudent, and most scandalous, Sermons have been delivered from the Pulpit; and because many Clergymen disgrace their holy Function."[20] Casting Wilks and the Cibbers by analogy as priests at the temple of drama would, and doubtless did, elicit snorts of amusement from Cooke's London readers but, as will be seen, there existed a considerable body of opinion in support of the theory that the theater could take and was taking the place of the church in certain categories of moral instruction.

If the cause of authorial reform in the early eighteenth century often amounted to a call on the part of the authors for the reform of theater management or theatrical practice, it sometimes involved a demand for better playwrights. The versifying parson

who exhorted Charles Fleetwood to clean up Drury Lane complained of the drama's debasement by "Low venal Bards, inspir'd
by Want of Bread," and Pope's presentation in *The Dunciad* of
dramatists at work emphasizes their ignorance and lack of
originality:

> How, with less reading than makes felons scape,
> Less human genius than God gives an ape,
> Small thanks to France and none to Rome or Greece,
> A past, vamp'd, future, old, reviv'd, new piece,
> 'Twixt Plautus, Fletcher, Congreve, and Corneille,
> Can make a Cibber, Johnson, or Ozell.[21]

Here the strand of the controversy which has been termed
authorial reform will be seen to be very near the third strand,
theatrical reform, which includes the reform of dramatic literature. This is of course the target Jeremy Collier aimed at when
he wrote, and is what the hasty student believes is referred to
by "theater reform" wherever he encounters the term in an
eighteenth-century context: the exclusion from stage performances of bawdy language, obscene stage business, and uncom-
plimentary references to the clergy. There were indeed those who
followed Collier's line of attack, root-and-branch reformers of
whom Arthur Bedford and William Law were perhaps the most
skillful and aggressive. Many others, varying widely in learning
and sophistication, entered the fray at one time or another, from
the formidable Reverend George Anderson, minister of the
Tron Kirk in Edinburgh to the anonymous author of *A Prelude
to the Plays* . . . who instanced disastrous fires at performances as
examples of the Almighty's vengeance on theater-goers, including
in his survey the well-known fire at Burwell, Cambridgeshire
in 1727 in which seventy-eight persons died:

> Could you never think that there was a Rebuke of divine
> Providence upon those that attended these Plays, when in
> *Ipswich*, and other Places, their Building fell down, to the
> Hurt of many, and the Fright of many more? Or the burning
> so many at *Burwell?* Shall we attribute these to Luck and
> Fortune, or meer Chance? . . . O what an awful Stroke of
> divine Sovereignty was that at *Burwell*, where the Persons
> perished in the very Act![22]

It was not mere good luck that trapped the playgoers in the
burning barn but a direct instance of God's judgment.

Opposed to these root-and-branch reformers, and constituting a very interesting group were those who picked up the other end of the stick as it were, and urged theater reform in the interest of moral training. The new group profited in a sense from the zeal of those who portrayed the theaters as so many sewers, drawing young Englishmen downward. If the theaters were influential to that extent, the new reformers asked, why could they not be turned into arenas for moral training? Although classical precedent could be cited for such statements and although the arguments of its advocates were sometimes cloaked in religious terminology, this movement was fundamentally secular. It was directed toward replacing the church with the theater as an instrument of moral instruction.

Many of the proponents of exemplary drama would have been horrified, or would have professed themselves horrified, if they had been confronted with so bald a conclusion but there were others—on both sides of the controversy—who recognized the drift of things. Some of William Law's vehemence in *The Absolute Unlawfulness of the Stage-Entertainment* derives, I think, from this penetrating mind's realization of what was implied by those who defended the drama: "All therefore that I desire," Law writes with sarcasm worthy of Swift, "is only a little *Free-thinking* upon this Subject. . . . For to talk of the *Lawfulness* and *Usefulness* of the *Stage* is full as absurd, as contrary to the plain Nature of things, as to talk of the Unlawfulness and Mischief of the Service of the Church."[23] Readers of his day would not need to be reminded that Law's association of the defenders of the stage with religious free-thinkers was not intended as a compliment. It was, however, on the whole accurate.

From the point of view of those who envisioned the stage as a possible instrument for moral training, a large part of its attractiveness had to do with the supposed psychological immediacy of the drama. This is what Richard Steele was thinking of when he wrote in the preface to *The Conscious Lovers*: "For the greatest effect of a play in reading [i.e., in reading a play] is to excite the reader to go see it; and when he does so, it is then a play has the effect of example and precept."[24] Thomas Cooke, whose charitable views were perhaps influenced by the fact that Drury Lane had recently produced his *The Triumphs of Love and Honour*, found the stage abounding in opportunities for instruction and more effective than formal religious training: "Virtue is the inexhaustible Fountain of Joy, and Vice of Misery; and this Lesson the Stage more effectually teaches than a Sermon; because the Spectators have before their Eyes the Actions, and the Causes of them . . . and we cannot suppose that they will soon enter on any Action like what they were just before instructed to behold with Horror and Detestation; and which is attended with inevitable Woe."[25]

The Jesuit Charles Porée, in an interesting oration presented in Paris in 1733, a translation of which was published in London the following year, also emphasizes the potential psychological impact of the drama: The dramatist, he writes, "fashions our Manners in a hidden, artful Way. We are like Children. . . ." Drama of the present day, he admits, is corrupt but it could be made a guide to virtuous conduct if the audience insisted on it.

> 'Tis therefore chiefly your Duty, ye Spectators, since 'tis in your Power to make both the Poet and Actor virtuous on the Stage, to endeavour at its Reformation. The Depravity of the Theatre is owing to your Indulgence, let therefore your Severity reform it. By your Care, that School may form the Mind to Virtue, which by your Connivance is become a School of Vice.[26]

That poetical clergyman who cajoled Charles Fleetwood in vain to reform Drury Lane likewise somewhat ruefully admitted the superior power of the drama, whether used rightly or abused:

> But while such Numbers Vice and Folly arms,
> Our Pulpit Eloquence but faintly warms;
> . . . .
> The Muses's Charms resistless Force impart,
> And drive the moral Precept to the Heart.[27]

The Scottish controversialists of the period are especially interesting on this matter, perhaps because Scots were by disposition and training so alert in recognizing the theological implications of a given proposition. The Reverend George Anderson would have nothing to do with jesuitical arguments that treated the stage as a necessary training ground for virtue. "For the Recommendation of Virtue the GOSPEL doth not want the Assistance of the Stage. . . . And as for their ridiculing of Vice, it is in itself sinful. The Sins of the World call for Rivers of Tears, and not for Laughter."[28] Anderson's anonymous opponent admitted that the stage had been corrupted but contended that true comedy and tragedy were proper modes of instruction: "Thus, where they are well intended, Tragedy and Comedy work to one Purpose: The one *manages* us as Children, and the other *convinces* us as Men."[29] Again, the emphasis on the psychological effectiveness of the stage is clear enough. It will be noted that both the Jesuit Porée and the anonymous Scot employ the metaphor of childrearing in this context. Anderson was quick to reply, asserting that his opponent's position was one that "is extreamly dangerous, and hath led the Way into much *Infidelity* and *Atheism*." He scorns the theaters as agents of moral rectification: "I can never persuade my self that a Play-house Performance can take away one single Sin out of the Heart of Man."[30] This was potentially a damaging argument against the claims of exemplary drama and one, incidentally, which was used many years later in America by Timothy Dwight in his *An Essay on the Stage*: If the stage is such a powerful molder of character, he asked, where is one verifiable instance of its having had a beneficent effect upon any person? Point to the man whose character has been improved by going to the theater.

In the eighteenth century, however, with the spread of those secularizing influences which we group together as the Enlightenment for want of a more precise term, the notion of the stage as an agent of instruction and social amelioration acquired many advocates. The training of the moral sentiments was held to be a desirable, indeed an essential part of the individual's education and the theater was envisioned as an appropriate means for such training because of the popularity and psychological intensity of stage drama. Four examples, one each from Scotland, England, America, and France, must suffice here to illustrate a common attitude.

During the controversy in Edinburgh over Home's *Douglas* (around 1757), the pioneering sociologist Adam Ferguson came to the defense of his friend's play and of the theater in general. The stage may be turned to improper uses but that is not a valid argument for condemning it, Ferguson contends; it is a better pastime for youth than "gaming and riot." He goes on to defend the exemplary nature of the theater: "When we see an audience therefore in tears for an object of compassion, when we find them affected with the generous sentiments which come from a virtuous character, deeply engaged in wishes for the success of the good, and for the disappointment of the wicked; it would scarcely occur that such an audience could be better employed in an hour of leisure."[31]

In England the novelist Samuel Richardson voiced similar beliefs through his character Pamela. Pamela, safely married at last to Mr. B., has leisure to go to Drury Lane, where she is sorely disappointed by the fare:

> Nothing more convinces one of the truth of the common observation, that the best things, corrupted, prove the worst, than these representations. The terror and compunction for evil deeds, the compassion for a just distress, and the general beneficence which those lively exhibitions are so capable of raising in the human mind, might be of great service, when directed to right ends, and induced by proper motives . . . where instruction is kept in view all the way, and where vice is punished, and virtue rewarded. (vol. II, letters LIII–LV)

Pamela, it is true, also objected to the "lewd and even senseless *double entendre*" of the epilogue; some who recommended exemplary drama were also theater reformers of Collier's school. But by no means all or even most of them were. In Virginia, Thomas Jefferson, who was no special friend of reforming clergymen, addressed a long letter of advice to his young acquaintance Robert Skipwith, in which he spoke at length of the power of literature, including the drama, to influence man's conduct. It will be noticed that Jefferson speaks specifically of modern rather than classical literature:

> But wherein is [literature's] utility, asks the reverend sage, big with the notion that nothing can be useful but the learned lumber of Greek and Roman reading with which his head is stored? I answer, every thing is useful which contributes to fix us in the principles and practice of virtue. When any signal act of charity or of gratitude, for instance, is presented either to our sight or imagination, we are deeply impressed with it's beauty and feel a strong desire in ourselves of doing charitable and grateful acts. . . . Now every emotion of this kind is an exercise of our virtuous dispositions; and dispositions of the mind, like limbs of the body, acquire strength by exercise. . . . I appeal to every reader of feeling and sentiment whether the fictitious murther of Duncan by Macbeth in Shakespeare does not excite in him as great horror of villainy, as the real one of Henry IV by Ravaillac as related by Davila?[32]

In prerevolutionary France Denis Diderot expressed opinions much like those of Jefferson, writing of actors:

> Si l'on considère le but de nos spectacles, & les talens nécessaires dans celui qui sait y faire un rôle avec succès, l'état de *comédien* prendra nécessairement dans tout bon esprit le degré de considération qui lui est dû. Il s'agit maintenant, sur notre théâtre François particulièrement, d'exciter à la vertu, d'inspirer l'horreur du vice, & d'exposer les ridicules. . . . [33]

The unanimity with which this odd theater party—Adam Ferguson, Samuel Richardson, Thomas Jefferson, and Denis Diderot—accept the stage as being capable of effecting change in the audience is significant. We are looking at the problem from the wrong direction if we say that they were all proponents of "sentimental drama." Rather they were spokesmen for important elements in the age which saw the drama as augmenting or replacing the church in the capacity of moral instructor. However mistaken they may have been about the application of their principles in theatrical practice, these were four minds of the very first order of intelligence and the principles were important ones, as the controversy in recent times about the role of television in the instruction of preschool children serves to remind one. Is there a relationship, Ferguson and the others were asking in effect, between the theater and the moral life and if so, what is it? *Mutatis mutandis*, the same questions are being asked today. [34]

Many voices were calling for theater reform in the first half of the eighteenth century: theater managers, politicians, dramatic authors, critics, even members of the audience. The relationship among reformers was often complex. As has been demonstrated, there is no reason to assume a priori that someone advocating reform of the stage was also in favor of sentimentalism in the drama. Some reformers looked to the classical past for models, some to the future, some were looking to the main chance. Perhaps the ones with the most enduring legacy were those reformers who envisioned the stage as a means of training the sentiments, as an agent of social change.

Notes

1. John Harold Wilson, *Six Eighteenth-Century Plays* (Boston, 1963), p. vii. This paper in abbreviated form was delivered at the English 14 section of the Modern Language Association meeting in December, 1968. Further research was made possible by a short-term fellowship at the Folger Shakespeare Library, for which I am most grateful.   2. See for example Arthur Sherbo, *English Sentimental Drama* (East Lansing, Mich., 1957) and review thereof by John Loftis, *MLN*, LXXIV (1959), 447–450; as well as B. R. S. Fone, "*Love's Last Shift* and Sentimental Comedy," *Restoration and Eighteenth-Century Theatre Research*, IX (1970), 11–23.   3. Fone, p. 11.   4. Sister Rose Anthony traces the Collier reform tradition in *The Jeremy Collier Stage Controversy, 1698–1726* (New York, 1966), though, as will be seen, I am in disagreement with some points of her interpretation.   5. As printed by Steele in *Town-Talk* no. 6 (20 January 1715/16), see *Richard Steele's Periodical Journalism 1714–16*, ed. Rae Blanchard (Oxford, 1959), pp. 231–232.   6. *The Fears of the Pretender Turn'd into the Fears of Debauchery* (1715), pp. 24–25.   7. *The Occasional Paper*, III, no. 9 (1719), 5–6.   8. Middlesex Record Office, Middlesex Court of Sessions records, Sessions Book 791 (Sessions of April 1721), ff. 118–120.   9. Pages 3–4.

10. Page 8.   11. *A Prelude to the Plays: or, A few Serious Questions proposed to the Gentlemen, Ladies, and others, that frequent the Play-House; Which they are desired to answer deliberately, to themselves, before they go again to those Diversions* (1729), p. 19.   12. *Of the Use and Improvement of the Stage. An Epistle to Charles Fleetwood, Esq;* (1737), lines 259–260. Identified in line 5: "Fl—w—d! for once a Parson deign to hear."   13. 1756, p. 21.   14. See John Loftis, "Introduction," *Richard Steele's The Theatre 1720* (Oxford, 1962); and the present writer's *Sir Richard Steele, M.P.* (Baltimore, 1970), pp. 169–177. Pamphlets, it is true, appeared during the course of the controversy arguing other issues but the dispute between the principals was not concerned with literature.   15. See *Sir Richard Steele, M.P.*, pp. 174–175.   16. *Town-Talk* no. 2, reprinted in *Richard Steele's Periodical Journalism 1714–16*, p. 195. See also John Loftis, *Steele at Drury Lane* (Berkeley, 1952), pp. 84–92.   17. *The Critical Writings of John Dennis*, ed. Edward N. Hooker (Baltimore, 1939–1943), II, 163, 164.   18. Act II, sc. i., *The Author's Farce*, ed. Charles B. Woods (Lincoln, Nebr., 1966), p. 25.   19. *Essays on the Theatre from Eighteenth-Century Periodicals*, ed. John Loftis for the Augustan Reprint Society, Publication nos. 85–86 (Los Angeles, 1960), pp. 35–39.

20. *The Triumphs of Love and Honour, a Play . . . To which are added, Considerations on the Stage, and on the Advantages which arise to a Nation from the Encouragement of Arts* (1731), pp. 69–70.   21. *The Dunciad*, ed. James

Sutherland (London, 1953), pp. 90–91. Pope is of course here treating Cibber as a dramatic author rather than theater manager.   22. 1729, pp. 19–20.   23. Law, pp. 2, 12.   24. *The Conscious Lovers*, ed. Shirley Strum Kenny (Lincoln, Nebr., 1968), p. 5.   25. *The Triumphs of Love and Honour*, pp. 56–57.   26. *An Oration, In which an Enquiry is made Whether the Stage Is, or can be made a School For forming the Mind to Virtue . . . Spoke March 13, 1733, in the Jesuits College at Paris . . .* , trans. J. Lockman (1734), pp. 22, 110.   27. *An Epistle to Charles Fleetwood*, lines 25–30.   28. *The Use and Abuse of Diversions* (1733), pp. 58, 59. I am indebted to my colleague Professor Ross Roy for guidance on the controversy in Scotland.   29. *Some Remarks upon the Rev*d. *Mr. Anderson's Positions Concerning the Unlawfulness of Stage-Plays. In a Letter to the Author* (1733), p. 11.

30. *A Reinforcement of the Reasons Proving that the Stage is an Unchristian Diversion . . . In Answer to the Remarks of an Anonymous Author* (1733), pp. 7, 115.   31. *The Morality of Stage-Plays Seriously Considered* (1757), p. 18.   32. *Papers*, ed. Julian P. Boyd (Princeton, 1950–), 1, 76–77 (letter of 3 August 1771).   33. *Encyclopédie ou Dictionnaire Raisonné des Sciences, des Arts et des Métiers, par une Société de Gens de Lettres*, III (1753), s.v. "Comédien."   34. A well-known instance is Harley Granville-Barker, *The Exemplary Theatre* (London, 1922).

SIR FRETFUL PLAGIARY AND GOLDSMITH'S "AN ESSAY ON THE THEATRE"
The Background of Richard Cumberland's "Dedication to Detraction"

Oliver W. Ferguson

> *Sir Fretful.* The newspapers! Sir, they are the most villainous —licentious—abominable—infernal.—Not that I ever read them—no—I make it a rule never to look into a newspaper.
>
> (R. B. Sheridan, *The Critic*, I, i)

AT the end of his biography of Richard Cumberland, Stanley Williams exclaims, "What the talent and industry of Cumberland could not effect in fifty years of effort, the careless genius of Sheridan won for him in a few hours. Sir Fretful Plagiary!"[1] Allowing for the exaggeration that is burlesque's due, Sheridan's portrayal of Cumberland as Sir Fretful Plagiary in *The Critic* (1779) is accurate. Cumberland's borrowings—usually under-scored by his sturdy assertions of originality—were notorious.[2] Equally so were the traits of personality that inform Sheridan's caricature: Cumberland's insatiable vanity and his contentious responses to adverse criticism. Williams termed him, of all the playwrights of his day "the most thievish, the most sensitive, the most proud, and the most pilloried."[3]

In the course of a full career Cumberland had and took advantage of numerous opportunities to reveal this side of his personality to his contemporaries, but nowhere did he do so more clearly and at greater length than in the essay entitled "Dedication to Detraction," which he wrote on the occasion of the publication in 1775 of his comedy *The Choleric Man*. The play had opened at Drury Lane on 19 December 1774. It was a moderate success, but its reception did not answer Cumberland's high expectations. And though the reviewers were by no means uniformly hostile, they were unfavorable. In particular, there was widespread agreement that the playwright had failed to live up to the excellence of his acknowledged model, Terence's *Adelphi*, and that he had failed to acknowledge an even more helpful predecessor, Shadwell's *Squire of Alsatia.*[4] When Cumberland arranged for the publication of *The Choleric Man*, he replied to these objections, personifying the reviewers collectively as "Detraction," to whom he "dedicated" the published version of his play.

The mock dedication embarrasses as much by its heavy and obvious sarcasm as by the various tones—aggrieved patience, indifference, righteous anger, self-pity—in which Cumberland addresses his adversary:

> High and Mighty Sir,
> The attention, with which you have been pleased to distinguish this inconsiderable production, makes it a duty with me to lay it at your feet. The applauses of the Theatre gave me assurance of its success, but it was your testimony alone, which could inspire me with any opinion of its merit: Nor is it on this occasion only I am to thank you; in whatever proportion I have been happy enough to attract the regards of the public, in the same degree I have never failed being honoured with your's.
>
> How I have merited these marks of your partiality I am not able to guess: I can take my conscience to witness, I have paid you no sacrifice, devoted no time or study to your service, nor am a man in any respect qualified to repay your favours: Give me credit, therefore, when I tell you, that your liberality oppresses me. Was I apt to rate my pretensions highly, and presume upon the indulgence of the public, I might have some claim to your favor; but 'till you hear me complain that my reward is not equal to my merit, I pray you let me enjoy my content and my obscurity.[5]

The Monthly Review for January 1775 remarked on the unintentional appropriateness of Cumberland's diatribe as a preface to a play called *The Choleric Man:* "In a long dedication worthy the pen of *Scriblerus*, the Author of this comedy has, in his own person, given a very lively image of *the Choleric Man*. This prince of the *genus irritabile* will allow no man's dog to bark in his presence; although he courts applause, he will not consider himself as liable to censure; and he proscribes the whole generation of *annotators, remarkers, observers*, &c. from the minor critic of a newspaper, to the grave *Aristarchus* of a Review." This last remark

—which refers to Cumberland's assertion that Londoners owe to Detraction "the great encrease of *news-papers* (not to mention *magazines, reviews,* &c)"—is suggestive. Cumberland does indeed "proscribe the whole generation" of reviewers. As one reads the "Dedication," he realizes that the personified dedicatee is more than a rhetorical flourish: "Detraction" is for the playwright the composite of every unfavorable review he has ever received, the sum of all the anonymous critics who have persecuted him from the outset of his career to the present.

The extreme bitterness—and the imprudence—of the "Dedication to Detraction" can only be understood in terms of this wider context. The reception accorded his latest play was the immediate occasion for Cumberland's essay. But from the cumulative injuries which he fancied had been done him, Cumberland chose to cite one specifically and to elaborate on it in remarkable detail. Halfway through the "Dedication," he says to "Detraction," "But there remains a word to be said on some learned animadversions of your's, entitled *An Essay on the Theatre,* in which you profess to draw a *Comparison between Laughing* and *Sentimental Comedy;* and in which you are pleased evidently to point some observations at my comedy of the *Fashionable Lover*" (p. ix). Cumberland's comedy had been produced in January 1772; the "animadversions" are, of course, Oliver Goldsmith's. "An Essay on the Theatre," which appeared in the *Westminster Magazine* for January, 1773, is the *locus classicus* for his objections to sentimental comedy.

It has commonly been assumed that Goldsmith's authorship of "An Essay on the Theatre" was recognized during his lifetime. The editors of *Boswell for the Defence,* for example, say that Boswell sought to flatter Goldsmith in his letter of congratulation on the successful opening of *She Stoops to Conquer* by playing "variations on the theme" of "An Essay on the Theatre," despite the fact that Boswell was in Edinburgh at the time and had been there when the essay was published; and a recent study of Goldsmith observes that "many of Goldsmith's contemporaries were unable to accept his antisentimental attitudes . . . even though there was unmistakable evidence elsewhere ('An Essay on the Theatre')."[6] Because of this assumption scholars have failed to comprehend how Cumberland could have been unaware that the attack which he singled out for rebuttal in the "Dedication to Detraction" was Goldsmith's. In his study of sentimental comedy Ernest Bernbaum expressed amazement at Cumberland's ignorance. More recently Ricardo

Quintana has marveled that Cumberland nowhere indicated "that he had the remotest idea that the 'Essay' in question was Goldsmith's," a fact which in his opinion adds to "the difficulty of determining the precise relationship" between the two men.[7] Cumberland's ignorance, however, appears surprising only from our vantage point. We have no doubt that Goldsmith wrote "An Essay on the Theatre," but we should remember that he never acknowledged the essay and that it was first attributed to him in 1798, when it was printed in *Essays and Criticisms, by Dr. Goldsmith*, on the authority of Thomas Wright, the printer of the *Westminster Magazine*.[8] Wright is a qualified witness, and the case for Goldsmith's authorship is supported by internal evidence, but these points should not obscure the fact that the "Essay on the Theatre" appeared as an unsigned essay in the first number of a new periodical. Not only is there no evidence that any of Goldsmith's friends knew of his authorship of the piece (or, indeed, that any of them even knew of its existence at the time of its publication); there is explicit and firsthand testimony—testimony that has not heretofore been recognized—that a member of Goldsmith's circle who might be supposed to have been better informed ascribed it to someone else.

On 12 January 1775, the day the "Dedication to Detraction" was published, George Steevens inquired of David Garrick, "To what Essay on the Theatre does Mr. C. refer at the top of p. 9 of his dedication?" The following day Garrick answered Steevens: "the Choleric Man came in just as I had receiv'd yr letter—the *Essay on ye Theatre*, was anonymous, & printed in the Morning Chron^e against Sentimental Comedy & written (as he has been told) by our Lincoln's Inn friend—It was a Stroke at ye fashionable Lover."[9] "Our Lincoln's Inn friend" is the lawyer-playwright, Arthur Murphy; and Cumberland's error is altogether understandable: Murphy's opposition to sentimental comedy was as well known as Goldsmith's, and he and Cumberland openly disliked each other.[10] Cumberland's mistaken attribution, then, is not remarkable. Nor is the fact that he had forgotten, two years after the event, where "An Essay on the Theatre" had been published.[11] His lapse of memory emphasizes the obvious fact that the essay appeared in a notoriously ephemeral medium. And his ignorance of the essay's authorship—an ignorance shared by such knowledgeable men of the theater as Steevens and Garrick— serves to remind us that had it not been for Thomas Wright, the best-known contemporary criticism of sentimental comedy in eighteenth-century England could very well have remained out of the Goldsmith canon.

If Cumberland's misapprehensions about the authorship of "An Essay on the Theatre" are not surprising, his reading of the piece is. "An Essay on the Theatre" neither refers to *The Fashionable Lover* by name nor alludes to any episodes or characters that could be associated exclusively with Cumberland's comedy. The only possible echo is in Goldsmith's remark that as the hero of a typical sentimental comedy is "but a tradesman, it is indifferent to me whether he be turned out of his Counting-house on Fish-street Hill, since he will still have enough left to open shop in St. Giles's" (*Works*, III, 213). Bridgemore, the unscrupulous merchant in *The Fashionable Lover*, lives on Fish-street Hill, and the name occurs several times throughout the play; but he is not turned out of his shop, and his role in the play is anything but heroic. That Cumberland should have built on so tenuous a base is extraordinary (and that Garrick should have tacitly accepted his reading suggests that he was not familiar with Goldsmith's essay). Even had he known that Goldsmith was the author of "An Essay on the Theatre," he would have had no grounds to regard his comedy as the particular object of Goldsmith's scorn. The essay, after all, was written a full year after the production of *The Fashionable Lover*; and it objected to the ubiquity of the type rather than to a specific sentimental comedy—indeed, one of its chief criticisms is that all sentimental comedies were alike!

The explanation for Cumberland's error must lie in Cumberland's vanity—a vanity that almost defies successful caricature. To read the playwright's *Memoirs* is to appreciate fully Sheridan's art: Sir Fretful is funny; there is little mirth to be got from Cumberland's evaluation of his dramatic career. Interestingly, he is most nearly modest (or he affects to be) about the best of his comedies, *The West Indian*: "Such was the good fortune of an author, who happened to strike upon a popular and taking plan." Of *The Brothers*, a thoroughly meretricious piece, he boasts, "I believe I may say that it brought some advantage to the theatre as well as some reputation to its author." *The Fashionable Lover* was in his judgment superior to his previous comedies: "I verily believe if The Fashionable Lover was not my composition, and I were called upon to give my opinion of it . . . I could not deny it a preference to the West-Indian in a moral light, and perhaps, if I were in very good humour with its author, I might be tempted to say that in point of diction it approached very nearly to what I conceived to be the true style of comedy." And to bring our survey up to the time of *The Choleric Man*, of that play Cumberland declares, "If ever there shall be found an editor of my dramatic works as an entire collection, this comedy will stand forward as one of the most prominent among them."[12] When one reads such passages as these, Cumberland's misapplication of "An Essay on the Theatre" to *The Fashionable Lover* is somewhat more understandable: the essay derided sentimental comedy, and Cumberland was the most popular author of sentimental comedies; therefore, *The Fashionable Lover*, his most recent contribution to the genre (and the play that in his considered opinion "approached very nearly to . . . the true style of comedy"), had to be the example the anonymous critic had in mind.

"An Essay on the Theatre" had appeared in 1773; the "Dedication to Detraction" followed in 1775. For two years Cumberland had brooded over what he construed as an attack on *The Fashionable Lover;* and when his next comedy provoked adverse criticism, he not only responded to this but also reverted to his earlier grievance, devoting approximately half of the "Dedication to Detraction" to a querulous and pedantic vindication of sentimental comedy. It is easy to see why Sheridan emphasized Sir Fretful's morbid sensitivity: "He is the sorest man alive, and shrinks like scorched parchment from the fiery ordeal of true criticism."

Cumberland remained convinced that "An Essay on the Theatre" had singled out *The Fashionable Lover* for attack. In his *Memoirs* (begun in 1804 and published in 1807) he reiterated the charge and now asserted that "the chief object" of the "Dedication to Detraction" had been to refute the essay (I, 379–380). He also remained ignorant of the identity of his supposed assailant. In fact, in his *Memoirs* he had nothing but kind words (delivered in the most condescending of tones) for Goldsmith. He was especially proud of the lines with which he is portrayed in "Retaliation," the poem of mock epitaphs which Goldsmith had written shortly before his death and which was published in April of 1774. Here is the portrait that excited Cumberland's gratitude:

> Here Cumberland lies having acted his parts,
> The Terence of England, the mender of hearts;
> A flattering painter, who made it his care
> To draw men as they ought to be, not as they are.
> His gallants are all faultless, his women divine,
> And comedy wonders at being so fine;

> Like a tragedy queen he has dizen'd her out,
> Or rather like tragedy giving a rout.
> His fools have their follies so lost in a croud
> Of virtues and feelings, that folly grows proud,
> And coxcombs alike in their failings alone,
> Adopting his portraits are pleas'd with their own.
> Say, where has our poet this malady caught,
> Or wherefore his characters thus without fault?
> Say was it that vainly directing his view,
> To find out mens virtues and finding them few,
> Quite sick of pursuing each troublesome elf,
> He grew lazy at last and drew from himself?
>   (lines 61–78, *Works*, IV, 355–356)

Cumberland's self-esteem not only led him to miss altogether the delicate ambiguity of Goldsmith's portrait; it also blinded him to strictures on sentimental comedy that had enraged him when he had read them in the "Essay on the Theatre." The description of his comic muse as "dizen'd out" with the trappings of tragedy parallels the essay's assertion that classical comic playwrights never exalted their characters into "buskined pomp" or created "a Tradesman's Tragedy" (*Works*, III, 211). The account of Cumberland's perfect characters and the moral laxity of his comedy that allows folly to escape punishment under cover of "virtues and feelings" is a compressed version of a similar criticism in the essay: "In these Plays almost all the Characters are good. . . . If they happen to have Faults or Foibles, the Spectator is taught not only to pardon, but to applaud them, in consideration of the goodness of their hearts; so that Folly, instead of being ridiculed, is commended" (p. 212). Even the sobriquet "Terence" which Goldsmith bestows on Cumberland echoes the essay, in which that playwright is cited as the ancient who went furthest in mixing comedy and tragedy (p. 211).

Had Cumberland read these lines with his usual hypersensitivity, he would surely have been aware of the subtle irony of Goldsmith's portrait. He might even have recognized the parallels between the portrait and the anonymous essay that had so angered him the previous year, and he might then have taken the next step and guessed at Goldsmith's authorship of the essay. But Goldsmith's solemn observation that Cumberland himself was the model for all his perfect characters was irresistible, and for once Sir Fretful's paranoia was lulled. Vanity does not always leave its subject vulnerable. Sometimes it can protect him.

Notes

1. *Richard Cumberland* (New Haven, 1917), p. 301.   2. Williams's book is the most convenient source for examples of Cumberland's plagiarisms. See especially his comments on Cumberland's first four comedies, *The Brothers, The West Indian, The Fashionable Lover*, and *The Choleric Man*, and on his tragedy, *The Battle of Hastings*. This last appeared in 1778, the year before Sheridan's creation of Sir Fretful Plagiary.   3. "The English Sentimental Drama from Steele to Cumberland," *Sewanee Review*, XXXIII (1925), 422.   4. Williams, pp. 111–113.   5. *The Choleric Man*, 3rd ed. (1775), p. iii.   6. William K. Wimsatt, Jr., and Frederick A. Pottle, eds., *Boswell for the Defence* (New York, 1959), p. 151; Robert H. Hopkins, *The True Genius of Oliver Goldsmith* (Baltimore, 1969), p. 11.   7. Ernest Bernbaum, *The Drama of Sensibility* (1915; rpt. Gloucester, Mass., 1958), p. 251 n 1; Ricardo Quintana, "Oliver Goldsmith as a Critic of the Drama," *SEL*, V (1965), 452–453.   8. Arthur Friedman, ed., *Collected Works of Oliver Goldsmith* (Oxford, 1966), III, 205. Hereafter cited as *Works*.   9. *The Letters of David Garrick*, ed. David M. Little and George M. Kahrl (Cambridge, Mass., 1963), III, 985 and n. 3.

10. Howard H. Dunbar, *The Dramatic Career of Arthur Murphy* (New York, 1946), p. 225.   11. In his *Memoirs* (1807), Cumberland described the essay as "a tract then in some degree of circulation" (I, 379).   12. Ibid., I, 296–297, 264–265, 346–347, 381.

DEFOE, SWIFT, AND FIELDING
Notes on the Retirement Theme

A. S. Knowles, Jr.

> Indeed you judge rightly, in thinking there is commonly
> something extraordinary in the fortunes of those who fly
> from society; for however it may seem a paradox, or even
> a contradiction, certain it is that great philanthropy chiefly
> inclines us to avoid and detest mankind; not on account so
> much of their private and selfish vices, but for those of a
> relative kind; such as envy, malice, treachery, cruelty,
> with every other species or malevolence.
>
> $\qquad\qquad$ (*Tom Jones*, Book VIII, chapter 10)

IN *Some Mythical Elements in English Literature* E. M. W. Tillyard
devotes a characteristically penetrating chapter to the theme of
retirement. After discussing some poetic examples of the genre,
he turns to the novel that he considers to be the "culminating
embodiment"[1] of the tradition, *Robinson Crusoe*. To the reader
familiar only with the first part of Defoe's novel, Tillyard's choice
may seem strange, since the first part of it seems like nothing
other than a remarkably realistic account of the triumph of a
rugged, level-headed, middle-class Englishman over the adver-
sities of enforced solitude. It does not recommend withdrawal
from the world; it is, in fact, very nearly a manual of survival for
anyone who has the misfortune to be cut off, by a capricious fate,
from the society of civilized men. Crusoe is no more a willing
retreater from the "busy crowd of men" than that favorite of
cartoonists, the English hunter who pitches his tent in darkest
Africa and dons black tie for dinner. Both know how to "make
do"; both are determined to take civilization with them, not to
flee it.

In the second part of his adventures, however, Crusoe finds
himself marooned by winter in Siberia, where he converses with
an exiled Russian prince. Crusoe tells the prince of his own
circumstantial exile, and the prince replies, saying

that he found more felicity in the retirement he seemed to be banished to there, than ever he found in the highest authority he enjoyed in the court of his master the czar; that the height of human wisdom was to bring our tempers down to our circumstances, and to make a calm within, under the weight of the greatest storms without . . . and though the greatness, the authority, the riches, and the pleasures which some enjoyed in the world, had much in them that was agreeable to us, yet all those things chiefly gratified the coarsest of our affections, such as our ambition, our particular pride, avarice, vanity, and sensuality; . . . Nor, sir, says he, do I bring my mind to this politically, by the necessity of my circumstances, which some call miserable; but, if I know anything of myself, I would not now go back, though the czar my master should call me, and reinstate me in all my former grandeur; I say, I would no more go back to it than I believe my soul, when it shall be delivered from the prison of my body, and has had a taste of the glorious state beyond life, would come back to the gaol of flesh and blood it is now enclosed in, and leave heaven, to deal in the dirt and crime of human affairs.[2]

This renunciatory theme is echoed by Crusoe's final statement in the novel: "Here [in London] I resolved to prepare for a longer journey . . . having lived a life of infinite variety seventy-two years and learned sufficiently to know the value of retirement, and the blessing of ending our days in peace."[3] In both statements there is an echo, conscious or otherwise, of one of Crusoe's real-life counterparts, Alexander Selkirk, who was reported by Steele to have "frequently bewailed his Return to the world, which could not, he said, with all its Enjoyments, restore to him the Tranquillity of his Solitude."[4]

The two aspects of *Robinson Crusoe* shown here are, obviously, a fitting reflection of the personality of Defoe, who was enough the man of the world to regard being stranded on a remote island as an interesting predicament for a civilized man, and enough the Puritan to regard retirement, however it might be effected, as a wholesome opportunity to put aside the vanities of this life and prepare for the next. The speech of the prince, quoted above, suggests how the Horatian-Augustan ideal of escape from the raging passions, so prevalent in poetry of the period, can merge with Puritan sermonizing on the "pride, avarice, vanity, and sensuality" of the world of affairs.

Tillyard's statement that Defoe's novel of 1719 is the "culmination" of retirement literature, nevertheless, needs qualification. The ample use of the retirement theme in later works would suggest that *Robinson Crusoe* stands somewhat nearer the middle of a tradition that continues to develop through the eighteenth century. Is not Book IV of *Gulliver's Travels*, for instance, also an example of that form of retirement literature that advocates an escape from the raging passions?[5] The basic assumption needed to accept this view is, of course, that Book IV is to be taken at face value, that the Houyhnhnms are to be admired and are not to be considered some subtle form of satire on cold rationalism. The arguments on both sides of this long-standing critical argument are persuasive, but, if the Houyhnhnms are placed against the folly-stricken beings—including Gulliver himself—who populate the pages of the other voyages, it seems likely that Gulliver's admiration of them is a rare example of his good judgment. Consider Swift's apology for his intemperateness in his early "Ode to Doctor William Sancroft":

> Forgive (Original Mildness) this ill govern'd zeal,
>   'Tis all the angry slighted Muse can do
>   In the pollution of these days;
>   No province now is left her but to rail,
>   And Poetry has lost the art to praise,
>   Alas, the occasions are so few:
>   None e'er but you,
>   And your Almighty Master, knew
>   With heavenly peace of mind to bear
> (Free from our tyrant-passions, anger, scorn, or fear)
>   The giddy turns of pop'lar rage,
> And all the contradictions of a poison'd age;[6]

"Heavenly peace of mind," and freedom from "tyrant-passions," virtues of both God and Dr. Sancroft, are also attributes of the Houyhnhnms; they are above anger and fear, and even their scorn is reserved for those who lack reason. In a famous passage Gulliver finds:

> I had no Occasion of bribing, flattering or pimping to procure the Favour of any great Man or of his Minion. I wanted no Fence against Fraud or Oppression: Here was neither Physician to destroy my Body, nor Lawyer to ruin my Fortune: No Informer to watch my Words and Actions, or forge Accusations against me for Hire: Here

were no Gibers, Censurers, Backbiters, Pickpockets, High-
waymen, House-breakers, Attorneys, Bawds, Buffoons,
Gamesters, Politicians, Wits, Spleneticks, tedious Talkers,
Controvertists, Ravishers, Murderers, Robbers, Virtuoso's;
no Leaders or Followers of Party and Faction; no Encouragers
to Vice, by Seducement or Examples: No Dungeon,
Axes, Gibbets, Whipping-posts, or Pillories; No cheating
Shopkeepers or Mechanicks: No Pride, Vanity, or Affecta-
tion: No Fops, Bullies, Drunkards, strolling Whores, or
Poxes: No ranting, lewd, expensive Wives: No stupid,
proud Pedants: No importunate, over-bearing, quarrelsome,
noisy, roaring, empty, conceited, swearing Companions:
No Scoundrels, raised from the Dust upon the merit of
their Vices; or Nobility thrown into it on account of their
Virtues: No Lords, Fidlers, Judges or Dancing-masters.[7]

Among the Houyhnhnms, in short, Gulliver finds a refuge
from the ills that came in the eighteenth century to be identified
with urban society. The only blemish upon his life among the
horses is his resemblance to the loathsome Yahoo. In the Yahoo,
Swift is simply reminding the reader again that, stripped of the
veneer of civilization, man is an animal. The vices of the bestial
Yahoo—greed, lasciviousness, uncleanliness, contentiousness, and
so on—are the vices of men seen in their most basic form. At one
point Swift suggests that the Yahoos are a product of atavistic
forces that are released when men are deprived of all social
restraint: "He . . . affirmed, that the two Yahoos said to be first
seen among them, had been driven thither over the Sea; that
coming to Land, and being forsaken by their Companions, they
retired to the Mountains, and degenerating by Degrees, became
in Process of Time, much more savage than those of their own
Species in the Country from whence these two Originals came."[8]

The Yahoos, then, are the savages that lie just beneath the skins
of all men; the distance between the London miser and the Yahoo
scrabbling in the earth for "shining stones of several colors" can
be measured in terms of a few easily abandoned rules of social
behavior. The fate of the first Yahoos could have been Gulliver's,
had not the Houyhnhnms been there to receive him into their
tranquil and rational life. Nevertheless, Gulliver, upon learning
that he must leave the society of the Houyhnhnms, chooses
retirement and the perils of isolation rather than return to civilization: "My Design was, if possible, to discover some small Island
uninhabited, yet sufficient by my Labour to furnish me with

Necessaries of Life, which I would have thought a greater Happiness than to be first Minister in the politest Court of *Europe*; so horrible was the Idea I conceived of returning to live in the Society and under the Government of *Yahoos*."[9]

Gulliver is frustrated in this wish to become another Robinson Crusoe and is forced, instead, to endure living among his own kind. If this seems a cruel fate, however, we might also wonder whether Gulliver had forgotten what happens to Yahoos who live isolated from any form of society.

Unlike the Defoe who speaks through Robinson Crusoe, the Swift who speaks through the pages of *Gulliver* clearly feels that man without society is imperiled. Nevertheless Book IV of the *Travels* seems to rest within the broad limits of the retirement tradition. If we take Gulliver's observations at face value, rejecting the idea that the Houyhnhnms are a satire upon rationalism or deism, we receive a strong impression of an ideal pastoral society. The Houyhnhnms have every virtue that the Lilliputians and Laputans lacked. They are rational, compassionate, free from the vice of over-sophistication. They are untouched by lust or fear. "Noble and courteous" of disposition they impart to Gulliver "all the little Knowledge I have of any Value." This knowledge, needless to say, is not the pseudo-science of the Laputans but consists rather of observations "on Friendship and Benevolence; on Order and Oeconomy; . . . the Bounds and Limits of Virtue; . . . the Rules of Reason; . . . and . . . the various Excellencies of *Poetry*." It is little wonder that Gulliver, the creation of an author who despised false learning, found his retirement among the Houyhnhnms to be so fortunate an experience that he would rather die than be forced to leave them. While Swift's Utopia may seem a little cold to us, a little lacking in the variety that the extremes of human behavior impart to life, it seems questionable that Swift was here reversing his satire to imply that an overly rational existence is as unsatisfactory as one based upon folly. Viewed in the context of Augustan retirement poetry, there is nothing unusual in his presentation of an ideal, and undoubtedly unattainable, mode of life far from the world of human affairs.

The voyage to the Houyhnhnms, then, may be thought to have two purposes: to provide a vision of Utopian retirement and to find yet another posture in which to criticize society as it exists. That the episode does so in a striking way, however, need not conceal the likelihood that Swift is working well within the premises of a tradition that reaches back to the Sabine farm of

Horace. Any literature that is in any measure Utopian will have this double purpose, and the eighteenth century can provide numerous examples. An interesting variation is furnished in Johnson's *Rasselas*, however, which in its depiction of the vanity of nearly all human wishes observes that the desire for Utopian retirement is as foredoomed as any other: the peasant, that timeless symbol of simple happiness, is "cankered with discontent"; the hermit, forced to admit that escaping temptations to vice had also meant "retiring from the exercise of virtue," leaves his retreat for the city, "on which, as he approached, he gazed with rapture." Yet Johnson's relegation of retirement to the category of folly represents no real evolution of the theme. If the idea had its many advocates, it was bound to have opponents who simply rejected the idea without altering it. In any event Johnson was a realist; the wryness of his response to an essentially idealistic philosophy is perfectly characteristic.[10]

It was in other hands that the theme would evolve. In the novels of Fielding, for example, the idea of retirement is not only consistently present, but between *Joseph Andrews* and *Tom Jones* changes considerably in the manner and the implications of its presentation. The Mr. Wilson episode in *Joseph Andrews* rests firmly enough within the Horatian tradition.

Wilson, who turns out to be Joseph's father, is an example of a man who in retirement has found the door to the Golden Mean. The story of his early life is, however, an exposé of the vanities of London society. Mr. Wilson was born a gentleman and given a liberal education at a public school. Left fatherless at the age of sixteen, he unwisely decided to leave school and find his place in the great world of London. There he became immersed in all the vain pursuits of a fine gentleman, including that which was to be both his weakness and his undoing, the pursuit of woman.

Having slandered the character of a young lady of quality and been brought to the verge of a duel with a guards officer, Wilson found it desirable to change social circles. He moved to the Temple and became a frequenter of Covent Garden, "where I shone forth in the balconies at the playhouses, visited whores, made love to orange-wenches, and damned plays." This phase of his career was brought to a stop by the contraction of a social disease and a month's "forced retirement" from the pursuit of pleasure.

Despite this momentary setback, Wilson's passion for women remained unabated. Upon recovering, he took a mistress, who soon left him after seeing to it that her lover required the services of his surgeon once again. Undaunted, he then debauched a poor girl of gentle birth who lived with him for some months, until he tired of her and began to seek other company. The effect of this upon the girl was to drive her into the company of rakes and finally into robbing and deserting Wilson, who found himself once again on the path to his surgeon's door. His next affair was with a married woman, and it ended in a lawsuit, divorce, and the death of his conquest.

Wilson then "bade adieu to love, and resolved to pursue other less dangerous and expensive pleasures." He joined a society of young sophists:

> These gentlemen were engaged in a search after truth, in the pursuit of which they threw aside all the prejudices of education, and governed themselves only by the infallible guide of human reason. This great guide, after having shown them the falsehood of that very ancient but simple tenet, that there is such a being as a Deity in the universe, helped them to establish in his stead a certain rule of right, by adhering to which they all arrived at the utmost purity of morals. Reflection made me as much delighted with this society, as it had taught me to despise and detest the former. I began now to esteem myself a being of a higher order than I had ever before conceived; and was the more charmed with this rule of right, as I really found in my own nature nothing repugnant to it. I held in utter contempt all persons who wanted any other inducement to virtue, besides her intrinsic beauty and excellence; and had so high an opinion of my present companions with regard to their morality, that I would have entrusted them with whatever was nearest and dearest to me.[11]

But this paradise of deists and Hobbesians had its disillusionments: one of the group ran off with another man's wife; another left the club "without remembering to take leave of his bail"; yet another borrowed money from Wilson and denied the debt. These apparent failures of "rule of right" were explained by one of the members, who told the perplexed Wilson:

> there was nothing absolutely good or evil in itself; that actions were denominated good or bad by the circumstances of the agent. That possibly the man who ran away with his neighbour's wife, might be one of very good inclinations, but over-prevailed on by the violence of an unruly passion,

and, in other particulars, might be a very worthy member of society: that, if the beauty of any woman created in him an uneasiness, he had a right from nature to relieve himself.[12]

But Wilson had not taken complete leave of his senses, and so took leave of the club. At this stage of his career, he had followed two of the several courses that wound through the maze of urban vanity: sexual and intellectual depravity. Both had failed him, and so he turned to a third, gambling. "This," he relates, "opened scenes of life hitherto unknown; poverty and distress, with their horrid train of duns, attorneys, bailiffs, haunted me day and night." His subsequent career as a playwright placed him at the mercy of unscrupulous managers and booksellers, and led finally to a debtor's prison from which he was saved, through a series of circumstances involving a lottery ticket, by "not only the best, but the handsomest creature in the universe," Harriet Hearty.

Having married Harriet, and seen "that the pleasures of the world are chiefly folly," Wilson entered into a retired life: "from a world full of bustle, noise, hatred, envy, and ingratitude, to ease, quiet, and love." His story is perfectly in keeping with that prevalent literature which represented London as the center of the raging passions. His retirement, in the Horatian-Augustan tradition, is a retirement to the Sabine farm. Wilson's "little garden" is without affectations:

> Its only ornament was a short walk, shaded on each side by a filbert-hedge, with a small alcove at one end, whither in hot weather the gentleman and his wife used to retire and divert themselves with their children, who played in the walk before them: but tho' vanity had no votary in this little spot, here was a variety of fruit, and every thing useful for the kitchen, which was abundantly sufficient to catch the admiration of Adams, who told the gentleman he had certainly a good gardener. Sir, answered he, that gardener is now before you; whatever you see here, is the work solely of my own hands. Whilst I am providing necessaries for my table, I likewise procure myself an appetite for them. In fair seasons, I seldom pass less than six hours of the twenty-four in this place, where I am not idle; and by these means I have been able to preserve my health ever since my arrival here without assistance from physic.[13]

Mr. Wilson has come to terms with life by achieving a simple and harmonious routine in the shelter of rural life. While he is mainly free from the evils of the world outside, however, there are from time to time reminders of the brutality he has fled: near the end of the episode, a little dog loved by the Wilsons' eldest daughter is shot and killed by a vicious young squire, the son of a wealthy lord of the district.

In the manner of Mr. Wilson, Heartfree in *Jonathan Wild* affirms the vanity of human wishes. His soliloquy in Book III, chapter 2 expresses in conventional terms the desirability of retirement for those of "elevated and refined temper": "how empty do they soon find the world of enjoyments worth their desire or attaining! How soon do they retreat to solitude and contemplation, to gardening and planting, and such rural amusements, where their trees and they enjoy the air and sun in common, and both vegetate with very little difference between them."[14]

Neither Heartfree nor Wilson, obviously, represents a departure from the Horatian-Augustan tradition. Both echo, in their modest aims, that prime contemporary source of the tradition, Anne Finch:

> Let the fair, the gay, the vain
> Courtship and applause obtain;
> Let th' ambitious rule the earth;
> Let the giddy fool have mirth;
> Give the epicure his dish,
> Ev'ryone their sev'ral wish;
> Whilst my transports I employ
> On that more extensive joy,
> When all Heav'n shall be survey'd
> From those windings and that shade.[15]

With *Tom Jones* and the Old Man of the Hill, however, we catch something more than a glimpse of the way in which the retirement tradition will be absorbed into certain states of thought and feeling that lie beyond the Enlightenment. The Old Man appears in the midst of those chapters touching upon the second Jacobite uprising of 1745. It is perhaps significant that his memoir will recall the abortive plot of the Duke of Monmouth in 1685. The Old Man's past and present, one might say, are related in greater or lesser degree to the passionate atmosphere of political revolution.

There is some suggestion at the beginning of the episode that the Old Man of the Hill is not going to be treated with complete sympathy. After Tom has rescued him from two ruffians who set upon the old gentleman outside his house, Partridge notices the Man of the Hill for the first time and is terrified by his appearance: "To say the truth, it was an appearance which might have affected a more constant mind than that of Mr. Partridge. This person was of the tallest size, with a long beard as white as snow. His body was clothed with the skin of an ass, made something into the form of a coat. He wore likewise boots on his legs, and a cap on his head, both composed of the skin of some other animals."[16]

The suit of skins is reminiscent of Robinson Crusoe, and while it may be proper attire for a castaway, or a hermit living in a remote corner of England, it seems hardly appropriate for a gentleman living with his housekeeper on the road between Gloucester and Worcester. This hint of some flaw in the character of the Man of the Hill reinforces an impression gained earlier from the housekeeper's fear that her master will discover the strangers in his house. It is obvious that the Old Man is not a simple and benevolent hermit, but someone whose behavior is decidedly odd. He is, in fact, a misanthrope who has retired out of detestation of mankind.

The Man of the Hill's story is an account of a rake's progress. Born the younger son of a "prudent and industrious" father and an "arrant vixen" of a mother, the Old Man was a promising youth until he fell in with evil companions at Oxford. Under the tutelage of the profligate Sir George Gresham, the youth became addicted to "loose pleasure" and spent all the meager allowance his father could send him. He considered suicide, but rejected that idea in favor of one "more shameful, though perhaps less sinful." Having stolen forty guineas from a friend, he fled to London in the company of a young lady who became his mistress.

There he was betrayed by his mistress and thrown into jail. But at his trial no witnesses appeared against him and he was released, returning shortly after to London. As the Old Man describes it, London can also be a place of retreat for those in special circumstances:

> I hastened, therefore, back to London, the best retirement of either grief or shame, unless for persons of a very public character; for here you have the advantage of solitude without its disadvantage, since you may be alone and in company at the same time; and while you walk or sit unobserved, noise, hurry, and a constant succession of objects, entertain the mind, and prevent the spirits from preying on themselves, or rather on grief or shame, which

are the most unwholesome diet in the world; and on which (though there are many who never taste either but in public) there are some who can feed very plentifully and very fatally when alone.[17]

Here is a variation on retirement—in this case the retirement of the guilty into an urban setting so chaotic that it precludes the opportunity for contemplation and introspection that the country offers, and that those carrying some shame are anxious to avoid.

In London the Man of the Hill fell in with another former Oxonian, Watson, who led him to the gaming tables and "the whole fraternity of sharpers." Consonant with the nature of his new profession, the Man of the Hill's fortunes rose and fell rapidly, leaving him "today wallowing in luxury, and to-morrow reduced to the coarsest and most homely fare." But one day observing a commotion in the street, he found his father lying wounded after an encounter with robbers. The effect of this reunion was to bring about a temporary reform in the character of the Man of the Hill, and he returned home with his parent despite Watson's admonitions against "burying" himself in the country.

In his new life the Man of the Hill returned to his studies, learning from the works of Aristotle and Plato to despise both "riches" and "worldly power," and developing the misanthropy which marks his later character. The Man of the Hill's description of this interlude of retirement makes interesting implications about the idea of a "philosophical retreat" found in the poetry of the period:

> Being now provided with all the necessaries of life, I betook myself once again to study, and that with a more inordinate application than I had ever done formerly. . . .
>
> These authors . . . not only instruct in the knowledge of Wisdom, but confirm men in her habits, and demonstrate plainly that this must be our guide, if we propose ever to arrive at the greatest worldly happiness, or to defend ourselves with any tolerable security against the misery which everywhere surrounds and invests us.
>
> To this I added another study, compared to which, all the philosophy taught by the wisest heathens is little better than a dream, and is indeed as full of vanity as the silliest jester ever pleased to represent it. This is that Divine wisdom which is alone to be found in the Holy Scriptures: for they impart to us the knowledge and assurance of things much more worthy our attention, than all which this world

can offer to our acceptance, of things which Heaven itself hath condescended to reveal to us, and to the smallest knowledge of which the highest human wit could unassisted never ascend. I began now to think all the time I had spent with the best heathen writers was little more than labour lost: for, however pleasant and delightful their lessons may be, or however adequate to the right regulation of our conduct with respect to this world only; yet, when compared with the glory revealed in Scripture, their highest documents will appear as trifling, and of as little consequence, as the rules by which children regulate their childish little games and pastime. True it is, that philosophy makes us wiser, but Christianity makes us better men. Philosophy elevates and steels the mind, Christianity softens and sweetens it. The former makes us the objects of human admiration, the latter of Divine love. That ensures us a temporal, but this an eternal happiness. [18]

While the attack upon riches and power, and upon the pervading misery of life, is perfectly in keeping with the Horatian tradition and its conventional outbursts against urban vanity and vice, the Man of the Hill implies an attack upon the Horatian ideal as well. Clearly he is saying that retirement based upon pagan philosophy is not enough, that only when retirement leads to an acceptance of Christian belief, of "the glory of the Scriptures," is it of real value. Pagan philosophy, he seems to imply, is another species of worldly vanity, giving comfort but having no power of salvation. The Man of the Hill's conception of retirement as the path to Christian enlightenment at first seems prophetic of the role that rural life is to play in such a later writer as Cowper, but there is an important difference. In the Old Man's contemplation of God's glory there is no peace, no reconciliation with experience. His brand of Christianity only reinforces his detestation of man.

Continuing his story, the Man of the Hill tells of the sudden death of his father and the end of this phase of his retirement. Driven out of his home by his brother's taste for the companionship of empty-headed sportsmen, he went to Bath to drink the waters. There he saved from suicide a man who turned out to be his old nemesis, Watson. The Man of the Hill tried to reform the gambler, but was interrupted in this enterprise by the news that the Duke of Monmouth had landed in the west. The two set off to join the forces of the Duke, took part in the battle at Sedgemore, and found refuge in the house of a woman near Exeter.

Watson then betrayed his companion to the soldiers of King James, but the Man of the Hill managed to escape and wandered until he found his present home, "where the solitude and wildness of the country invited me to fix my abode."

In the years since, the Man of the Hill has traveled through Europe, but what he has seen has only sharpened his contempt for the society of men:

> those who travel in order to acquaint themselves with the different manners of men might spare themselves much pains by going to a carnival at Venice; for there they will see at once all which they can discover in the several courts of Europe. The same hypocrisy, the same fraud; in short, the same follies and vices dressed in different habits. In Spain, these are equipped with much gravity; and in Italy, with vast splendour. In France, a knave is dressed like a fop; and in the northern countries, like a sloven. But human nature is everywhere the same, everywhere the object of detestation and scorn.[19]

Now the Man of the Hill lives in isolation, having rejected mankind completely:

> The retirement has been so complete, that I could hardly have enjoyed a more absolute in the deserts of the Thebias than here in the midst of this populous kingdom. As I have no estate, I am plagued with no tenants or stewards: my annuity is paid me pretty regularly, as indeed it ought to be; for it is much less than what I might have expected in return for what I gave up. Visits I admit none; and the old woman who keeps my house knows that her place entirely depends upon her saving all the trouble of buying the things I want, keeping off all solicitation or business from me, and holding her tongue whenever I am within hearing. As my walks are all by night, I am pretty secure in this wild, unfrequented place from meeting any company. Some few persons I have met by chance, and sent them home heartily frighted, as from the oddness of my dress and figure they took me for a ghost or a hobgoblin. But what has happened to-night shows that even here I cannot be safe from the villainy of men; for without your assistance I had not only been robbed, but very probably murdered.[20]

How are we to accept this view of retirement? The answer lies partly in Tom's reaction to the Man of the Hill's misanthropy.

"The abhorrence which you express for mankind," Tom protests, "is much too general, . . . [an error] committed by those who, from want of proper caution in the choice of their friends and acquaintance, have suffered injuries from bad and worthless men." Here, probably, Fielding is speaking, for Tom is right; the Man of the Hill's misanthropy has sprung from his associations. But the latter is not to be moved by Tom's plea for a more balanced view, and the argument ends with neither side persuaded.

While Fielding appears to reject the Man of the Hill's cynicism toward mankind, however, we must note again that in this recluse's attitudes there is much that is prophetic. Not only has he turned his back upon the vanities of urban life in the approved manner of contemporary Horatianism, he has also consciously sought out nature as the site for his contemplation of the majesty of God's creation. When Tom suggests that the recluse's solitude must want variety, the latter replies:

> I am not at all surprised that to one whose affections and thoughts are fixed on the world my hours should appear to have wanted employment in this place: but there is one single act, for which the whole life of man is infinitely too short: what time can suffice for the contemplation and worship of that glorious, immortal, and eternal Being, among the works of whose stupendous creation not only this globe, but even those numberless luminaries which we may here behold spangling the sky, though they should many of them be suns lighting different systems of worlds, may possibly appear but as a few atoms apposed to the whole earth which we inhabit? Can a man who by divine meditations is admitted as it were into the conversation of this ineffable, incomprehensible Majesty, think days, or years, or ages, too long for the continuance of so ravishing an honour? Shall the trifling amusements, the palling plea-sures, the silly business of the world, roll away our hours too swiftly from us; and shall the pace of time seem sluggish to a mind exercised in studies so high, so important, and so glorious? . . . There is not an insect, not a vegetable, of so low an order in the creation as not to be honoured with bearing marks of the attributes of its great Creator; marks not only of His power, but of His wisdom and goodness.[21]

Were it not for his detestation of mankind, the Man of the Hill's panegyric on the physical universe might label him a Deist; but his attitude toward man is a crucial flaw, for the Deist must believe in the essential goodness of all of creation, including man. What we have instead is a species of nature worship that is marred by pride, based upon the recluse's conviction that he has been "admitted . . . into the conversation" of the mysteries of creation, and therefore stands outside, and superior to, the mass of men. Whatever hesitation one may feel about using the term Romantic must give way to the feeling that there is something peculiarly Romantic in the Man of the Hill's belief in his own singularity.

Interpretations of this episode in *Tom Jones* are bound to vary, for Fielding's intentions are not entirely clear. Ernest Baker, for instance, calls attention to the fact that the Man of Hill's misfortunes came from "squandering his affections on one who afterwards betrayed him," and he sees the whole tale-within-a-tale as "a parable to Jones, who for his part finds that natural sagacity and regard for the lessons of experience are a better guide than credulous reliance on the goodness of others."[22] Martin Battestin, on the other hand, speaks of the "antithetical attitudes we are meant to hold toward the different solutions of the benevolent Mr. Wilson [of *Joseph Andrews*] and the misanthropic Man of the Hill,"[23] implying that we are to view the latter with disapproval not only for what he was but for what he has become: a man without charity, without a sense of duty to society. In any event the Man of the Hill episode suggests that Fielding found the retired misanthrope repugnant, and may have been using the incident as a way of striking out at certain attitudes that prefigure the Romantic pose.

These two episodes from Fielding's novels have several points of interest. First, they show in brief form the development of his art. The Wilson and Heartfree episodes from the novels of 1742 and 1743 are effective but lacking in originality. Fielding appears simply to have taken over, uncritically, a well-established literary motif and placed it in the form of exemplary tales in the midst of his novels. Take Hogarth's "The Rake's Progress," add the standard poetic portrait of the city as a den of iniquity and a whirlpool of raging passions, bring the protagonist finally to his senses and to the peacefulness of the Horatian farm, and the result is the tale of Mr. Wilson. All that is left unclear, perhaps, is why Fielding, the supreme ironist and a writer with little patience for fashionable sentimentality, treated this material straightforwardly; the possibilities for parody might have seemed irresistible. The fact that he did not choose to parody the genre, however, may be a tribute to the hold that the retirement theme, in this form, exercised over the period. The Richardsonian novel was a safe target, but the moralistic rejection of urban society was not. The Man of the Hill episode, seven years later, shows Fielding handling the retirement myth in a more complex manner. While it is perfectly possible that the author was himself unaware of all the resonances in the episode, he was obviously writing with more originality. There is much that is enigmatic about the Man of the Hill. Christian, nature-worshiper, misanthrope, he has found no joy, only relief, in retirement. No Horatian farm figures in his life, no faithful wife and adoring children. Give him sixty-five or seventy years and he will be Manfred or Melmoth the Wanderer.

Notes

1. E. M. W. Tillyard, *Some Mythical Elements in English Literature* (London, 1961), p. 95.   2. Daniel Defoe, *Robinson Crusoe* (New York, 1931), pp. 524–525.   3. Ibid., p. 538.   4. Richard Steele, *The Englishman*, ed. Rae Blanchard (Oxford, 1955), p. 109.   5. See W. B. Carnochan, "The Complexity of Swift: Gulliver's Fourth Voyage," *SP*, LX (1963), 23–44. 6. Harold Williams, ed., *The Poems of Jonathan Swift* (Oxford, 1937), I, 38. 7. Jonathan Swift, *Gulliver's Travels*, ed. Herbert Davis (Oxford, 1959), pp. 276–277.   8. Ibid., p. 272.   9. Ibid., p. 283.

10. Johnson's views on retirement are well reflected in *Idler*, no. 16 (29 July 1758), in the character of Ned Drugget, who when old and rich retires to the country only to spend his time at a window watching the carriages as they go back and forth; and in a burlesque poem recalled by Mrs. Piozzi: Hermit hoar, in solemn cell, / Wearing out life's evening gray; / Strike thy bosom, sage! and tell / What is bliss and which the way? / Thus I spoke, and speaking sigh'd, / Scarce repress'd the starting tear, / When the hoary Sage reply'd, / Come, my lad, and drink some beer. (G. B. Hill, *Johnsonian Miscellanies*, I, 193.)   11. Henry Fielding, *The History of the Adventures of Joseph Andrews* (Oxford, 1926), II, 32–33.   12. Ibid., pp. 33–34.   13. Ibid., p. 49.   14. Henry Fielding, *The History of the Life of the Late Mr. Jonathan Wild the Great* (London, 1947), p. 106.   15. "The Petition for an Absolute Retreat," lines 284–293 (1713).   16. Henry Fielding, *The History of Tom Jones a Foundling* (New York, 1943), p. 376.   17. Ibid., pp. 388–389.   18. Ibid., pp. 397–398.   19. Ibid., p. 408.

20. Ibid., p. 409.   21. Ibid., pp. 409–410.   22. Ernest A. Baker, *The History of the English Novel* (New York, 1957), IV, 132.   23. Martin C. Battestin, *The Moral Basis of Fielding's Art* (Middletown, Conn., 1959), p. 48.

LANGUAGE, DIALOGUE, AND POINT OF VIEW IN FIELDING
Some Considerations

C. J. Rawson

THE dialogues in Fielding's novels are often highly stylized and tend, like many other elements in his writings, towards the self-enclosed autonomy of the set piece.[1] At the same time such highlighting of authorial "artifice" exists in piquant interplay with an extremely authentic (or "realistic") sense of the emotional and social overtones of speech, and the dialogues reveal in particular that Fielding had a remarkably sharp ear for the cadences and vocabulary of the actual spoken language.[2] As we might expect, however, it is an ear that specializes in normal usage, the readily recognizable social idiom,[3] including cant phrases and accredited polite slang as well as (in *Shamela*) certain aspects at least of coarse demotic speech. It does not extend to those singular or coined usages in expressive common speech which come from the need to express a particular feeling more exactly, or from a linguistically creative awkwardness, or from an individual's freedom (whether subliterate or sophisticated) from the inhibitions of standard usage. The existence of such "singular" idiom is normal in the common speech of any social milieu (though there were pressures against it, as against any singularity, in the gentlemanly code of Fielding's day), and it is one of the factors which makes languages develop. But many individual singularities would in themselves seem too remote from normal (let alone "correct") speech to be acceptable to an author like Fielding for serious literary notation.

The master among eighteenth-century novelists of this more adventurous and subtle linguistic field was of course Richardson. His coinages (whether they are inspired singularities of his own imagining, or current usages caught at an early stage of their career in the actual spoken language) offended many contemporaries, one of whom feared that they might "become current in common Conversation, be imitated by other writers, or by the laborious industry of some future compiler, transferred into a Dictionary"—in other words, improperly made standard by Richardson's authority.[4] *Meditatingly* and *scrupulosities* are two examples which this critic disliked, but such phrases have the living accent of colloquial speech and several have in fact passed into normal current usage.[5] Chesterfield perceptively recognized that Richardson's coinages admirably expressed the "little secret movements" of the heart, but this was coupled in his mind with the feeling (also and more viciously expressed by Lady Mary Wortley Montagu, Horace Walpole, and others) that, when Richardson deals with "high life, he grossly mistakes the modes."[6]

The gentlemanly avoidance of singularity in all things, preached by Chesterfield and other courtesy-writers, naturally extended to language: "In *Words*, as *Fashions*, the same Rule will hold; Alike Fantastick, if *too New*, or *Old*."[7] Gentlemanly decorum and a neoclassic centrality blend in Pope's couplet and underlie a severe linguistic self-consciousness among many writers of the period. Defensive phrases like "as they call it" or "as they say" occur remarkably often, accompanying usages which (however widely accepted) savored remotely of neologism or of any other form of oddity. Richardson's Sir Charles Grandison, speaking to Sir Hargrave Pollexfen and other gentlemen, says that his father let him go abroad on "the Grand Tour, as it is called."[8] The phrase "Grand Tour" had in fact been in use since the seventeenth century, and one would not expect Sir Charles's friends to be unfamiliar with it or with the fashionable activity which it described. It would be oversimple, however, to take this as an example of Richardson mistaking "the modes" of "high life." Fielding, writing of the squire in *Joseph Andrews* (III, vii), says: "He made in three years the tour of Europe, as they term it." The defensive phrase is used frequently by both Fielding and Richardson, in essays and personal letters as well as by narrators and characters in their novels.[9] Perhaps the very self-consciousness which this denoted might be thought ungentlemanly by a purist like Chesterfield, for he includes the phrase in an amusing mimicry of typical trite usages of a "vulgar man": "If anybody attempts being *smart*, as he calls it, upon him, he gives them *tit for tat*, ay, that he does."[10]

Thus a phrase used to soften or to excuse singularity is pilloried for its "commonness," and a gentleman might not want to distinguish too precisely between the excessively singular and the excessively common, singularity being itself a typical symptom of vulgarity. Chesterfield's letters are full of monitory lists of trite phrases, proverbs, vulgarisms, and it is an amusing fact that Richardson's Pamela happens to use many of these. Since the speaker in this case is a servant-girl, an obvious justification can be made on "dramatic" grounds. But in such matters, there would not always be a readiness to distinguish too precisely between an author's speech and that of his characters.

"Singularity" and trite vulgarisms were almost equally "low." "Lowness" also meant indecorous or gross language. And the literary decorum which prescribed " 'accommodation' of style to subject" might well come into conflict with another decorum, which shied from "low" subjects as such. John Lawlor has written well that such stylistic congruences were felt to have their limits, and that " 'lowness' of style . . . offers difficulties to a sensibility that cherishes the ideal of 'correctness.' " [11] This easily implied in some cases not only that a writer must not use "low" language, but that his "low" characters should not use it either, or even that he should not deal in such characters at all. [12] By Fielding's time gentlemanly standards and the centralizing, normative predilections of neoclassicism came to be partly reinforced, and also partly undermined, by an increasingly vocal element of middle-class squeamishness. This created a piquant situation in which the bourgeois Richardson, and the gentleman novelist Fielding, could each think of the other as "low," Richardson being so taken for his pseudo-genteel awkwardness and his use of idioms both "singular" and "common," and Fielding for his interest in a coarser, more popular kind of "lowness." Richardson said patronizingly to Sarah Fielding: "Had your brother . . . been born in a stable, or been a runner at a sponging-house, we should have thought him a genius, and wished he had had the advantage of a liberal education, and of being admitted into better company." [13] It is a coincidence which Fielding would have relished that in the letter of the following year (1753) in which Chesterfield noted Richardson's genius and his ignorance of "high life," he also said that Richardson "would well have deserved a higher education than he has had"! [14]

Fielding's notation of the coarser kind of "low" speech has considerable vigor, although it occurs most freely, perhaps, in *Shamela* and in those places in the novels where it can claim the excuse of parody or of a special comic or satiric need; and

Fielding always tends in any case to distance it by various means. Even so, critics not only of Richardson's persuasion accused him of lowness in both matter and manner. Fielding's limited but hearty freedoms with "low" matter and language doubtless sprang from natural gusto combined with a pointed superiority to the straight-laced middle-class form which the objection (as he would see it in Richardson) sometimes took. His fondness for a popular entertainment like the puppet show, and his dislike of the contemporary tendency to soften popular entertainments by the extrusion of "low stuff," [15] suggests an element of that patrician readiness to assert itself on the side of genuine demotic vitality against more bourgeois forms of genteelism. [16] Moreover the coarse "lowness," in certain literary kinds, could be defended by an appeal to time-honored comic tradition (Aristophanes, Lucian, Rabelais). This would satisfy some neo-classical objections, since precedents of such distinction and antiquity in themselves supplied a kind of norm. Fielding was not, however, altogether easy on this whole question, and came, later in life, to repudiate Aristophanes and Rabelais, though not Lucian, for their indecency. [17]

Fielding's dialogue may at times be "low" (whether coarsely or otherwise) in ways which reproduce actual widespread usage, but it has little or no singularity in the Richardsonian sense. Fielding's interest in spoken language, particularly in the cant phrases which reveal moral and social attitudes, is, on the other hand, enormous; and *this* interest (in the expressive clichés of current informal idiom—of whatever class, though not fully received as part of the polite *standard*) does in fact overlap with Richardson's. But where Richardson treats such "typical" idiom as part of the vivid flow of spontaneous speech, Fielding stylizes it, standing outside, isolating it by some act of ironic distancing, implying that it is regrettably "normal" (i.e., in general use) rather than mainly "natural" to the particular, immediate situation. Characteristically he is given to anthologizing such usages, in oddly exuberant lists which occur from time to time in the novels.

The fantasticating "dissertation" on high people and low people in *Joseph Andrews*, for example, notes the refusal of these two orders "to regard each other as of the same species" and immediately launches into a linguistic list for proof of this: "This, the terms 'strange persons, people one does not know, the creature, wretches, beasts, brutes,' and many other appellations evidently demonstrate."[18] One recognizes here the language of many a dialogue from Fielding's works, but also the sense of sheer generalizing pleasure which the list communicates, as if an infinity of particular snobberies were being triumphantly boiled down to their verbal essentials. The point about these phrases is that they are the normal vacuous currency of snobbish contempt. There is not one among them which is original or fresh in itself, yet they kindle into a wittily disembodied life in this abstract catalogue. A more remarkable example of such cataloguing occurs in *Jonathan Wild*, when it is announced that Theodosia Snap has given birth to an illegitimate child. For here there is no frankly generalizing "dissertation," and the list occurs as sheer narrative of a specific event:

> At this time an accident happened, which, though it did not immediately affect our hero, we cannot avoid relating, as it occasioned great confusion in his family, as well as in the family of Snap. It is indeed a calamity highly to be lamented, when it stains untainted blood, and happens to an honourable house—an injury never to be repaired—a blot never to be wiped out—a sore never to be healed. To detain my reader no longer, Miss Theodosia Snap was now safely delivered of a male infant, the product of an amour which that beautiful (O that I could say virtuous!) creature had with the count. (III, xiii)

The cant of moral outrage is catalogued with a similar routine comprehensiveness, comically suggesting that, whenever such things happen, the same phrases all come up. We observe Fielding's familiar procedure of interweaving particular narration with a generalizing awareness of the world's ways. The Snap household is in fact rather disreputable, which is part of the joke, but the phrases specifically anticipate the reactions of Theodosia's extremely dissolute sister Laetitia, who, in the next paragraph, expresses shock at this "dishonour" to her "chaste family" and "affront to her virtue." To this extent, Fielding's amusingly generalized mimicry is partly a projection of the mind of a main character. For while Fielding addresses the reader and proclaims his own share of the joke, he is also entering into Laetitia's outlook, presenting the situation through mental processes which Laetitia is about to adopt in her own name. It would be going much too far to see in this any proto-Jamesian manipulation of "point of view," but the passage exists, in this as in other respects, in an amusing twilight zone where signposted typicality and the highly specific interpenetrate.

A good modern parallel might be the scene in *Ulysses* where Stephen looks over Mr. Deasy's cliché-ridden letter to the press:

> May I trespass on your valuable space. That doctrine of *laissez faire* which so often in our history. Our cattle trade. The way of all our old industries. Liverpool ring which jockeyed the Galway harbour scheme. European conflagration. Grain supplies through the narrow waters of the channel. The pluterperfect imperturbability of the department of agriculture. Pardoned a classical allusion. Cassandra. By a woman who was no better than she should be. To come to the point at issue.[19]

This is presumably how Stephen's mind selects and reacts to what he is reading. But, as in Fielding, the passage conveys a teasing two-way traffic between witty authorial summary and the mental processes of the character; and as in Fielding, a typifying and anthologizing satire interpenetrates with the very specific episode in the novel's action.

Such interpenetration occurs also, in a different way, in the more frankly abstract list from *Joseph Andrews*. The list comes in the middle of a lengthy digression on snobbery, whose ostensible purpose in the narrative is to explain why, in the previous chapter, Mrs. Slipslop ignored the greeting of Fanny, whom she knew well, pretending to wonder "who the creature was." The digression, which proves "that Mrs. Slipslop did not in the least deviate from the common road in this behaviour," is nevertheless a humorous essay in its own right, frankly labelled a "dissertation" in the chapter heading. Its relation to the story is formally gone into only at the beginning and end. But at the point where the catalogue occurs, Fielding flashes Mrs. Slipslop back into the picture, allowing a quick glimpse of her individual part in the mazy dance of universal snobbery:

> The people of fashion [and] . . . the people of no fashion . . . seem scarce to regard each other as of the same species. This, the terms "strange persons, people one does not know, the creature, wretches, beasts, brutes," and many other appellations evidently demonstrate; which Mrs. Slipslop, having often heard her mistress use, thought she had also a right to use in her turn; and perhaps she was not

> mistaken; for these two parties, especially those bordering nearly on each other, to wit, the lowest of the high, and the highest of the low, often change their parties according to place and time; for those who are people of fashion in one place are often people of no fashion in another.

This brief sight of Mrs. Slipslop consciously deciding that the entire repertoire of contemptuous phrases is at her disposal shows the snobbery being mechanized to a further degree of clockwork absurdity. It is, as we can see from the quotation, part of a protracted escalation of absurdities which is otherwise conducted in general terms until the formal return, several sentences later, to the story proper. But her momentary emergence in this sea of jargon adds a further reciprocal vitality to both her and the catalogue.

These catalogues of standard usages testify not merely to a generalizing temperament, but to a positive creative delight in viewing specific events through generalizing arrangements. They show Fielding not only capturing those cliché phrases which typically reveal certain attitudes, but collecting them in the abstract—that is, outside actual conversations. In such lists vacuous banalities come alive through the sheer enumeration, as well as entering into lively relationships with the individual incidents. This kind of generalizing abstraction helps to make the particular typical, but it highlights instead of ironing-out the vividness of the particular itself. Several of Fielding's great set pieces of *actual* dialogue have a similar air of being stylized anthologies of cant phrases, too exactly and exclusively drawn from standard social jargon to be quite credible as realistic rendering, yet preserving in this stylized form both the rhythms of actual speech and the authentic play of disreputable attitudes. The famous quarrel between Mrs. Western's maid and Mrs. Honour shows phrases like "their betters," "hoity! toity!," "madam is in her airs," "marry, as good as yourself, I hope," "creature! you are below my anger," in a self-absorbed ballet of highly vivid but formalized absurdity.[20] The dialogue between Mrs. Slipslop and Miss Grave-airs about admitting Joseph into the stagecoach likewise concentrates a mass of emotionally charged but utterly commonplace banalities, to a degree almost of ritual: "Miss Grave-airs said, 'Some folks might sometimes give their tongues a liberty, to some people that were their betters, which did not become them: for her part, she was not used to converse with servants.' Slipslop

returned, 'Some people kept no servants to converse with'"
(JA :ii, v). The barbed phrases, the pointed use of the third person, are the standard usage of haughty pique. They convincingly
suggest low people giving themselves the airs of high people,
and they are charged with the crude emotions of the quarreling
women. But sheer ritual concentration makes the dialogue move
by way of this realistic-typical notation to a world beyond realism,
which derives its moral authenticity, as well as the proper pointing
of ridicule, from a brilliant stylization of the actual. Like other
passages considered in this essay, the "smart dialogue between
some people and some folks"[21] is something of a set piece, con-
spicuously holding the center of the stage for its appointed length,
and halted only by further narrative developments when it has
fulfilled itself.[22] Fielding's exploitation of typical spoken usage
has much the same function as his other stylizations, modifying
the realism, giving the scene a certain air of authorial performance,
suffusing it with comic life, yet making it vulnerable to a special
kind of moral exposure. The tendency of such passages to the
self-sufficiency of the set piece, like the self-feeding absurdity of
the characters, gives the snobbery a motiveless, disembodied air,
as of an irrepressible moral pedantry existing *in vacuo*.

The "smart dialogue" is further formalized by being partly
in a form of semi-indirect speech which Fielding was fond of
exploiting. A more elaborate example is the dialogue between
Joseph Andrews and Parson Barnabas (i, xiii). Joseph, after being
robbed and beaten, is lying at an inn, where Parson Barnabas
visits him:

> Mr. Barnabas was again sent for, and with much difficulty
> prevailed on to make another visit. As soon as he entered
> the room, he told Joseph, "He was come to pray by him,
> and to prepare him for another world: in the first place,
> therefore, he hoped he had repented of all his sins." Joseph
> answered, "He hoped he had; but there was one thing
> which he knew not whether he should call a sin; if it was,
> he feared he should die in the commission of it; and that
> was, the regret of parting with a young woman whom he
> loved as tenderly as he did his heartstrings." Barnabas
> bade him be assured, "That any repining at the Divine
> will was one of the greatest sins he could commit; that he
> ought to forget all carnal affections, and think of better
> things." Joseph said, "That neither in this world nor the
> next could he forget his Fanny; and that the thought,

however grievous, of parting from her for ever, was not half so tormenting as the fear of what she would suffer when she knew his misfortune." Barnabas said, "That such fears argued a diffidence and despondence very criminal; that he must divest himself of all human passions, and fix his heart above." Joseph answered, "That was what he desired to do, and should be obliged to him if he would enable him to accomplish it." Barnabas replied, "That must be done by grace." Joseph besought him to discover how he might attain it. Barnabas answered, "By prayer and faith." He then questioned him concerning his forgiveness of the thieves. Joseph answered, "He feared that was more than he could do: for nothing would give him more pleasure than to hear they were taken." "That," cries Barnabas, "is for the sake of justice." "Yes," said Joseph, "but if I was to meet them again, I am afraid I should attack them, and kill them too, if I could." "Doubtless," answered Barnabas, "it is lawful to kill a thief; but can you say you forgive them as a Christian ought?" Joseph desired to know what that forgiveness was. "That is," answered Barnabas, "to forgive them as—as—it is to forgive them as—in short, it is to forgive them as a Christian." Joseph replied, "He forgave them as much as he could." "Well, well," said Barnabas, "that will do." He then demanded of him, "If he remembered any more sins unrepented of; and if he did, he desired him to make haste and repent of them as fast as he could, that they might repeat over a few prayers together." Joseph answered, "He could not recollect any great crimes he had been guilty of, and that those he had committed he was sincerely sorry for." Barnabas said that was enough, and then proceeded to prayer with all the expedition he was master of, some company then waiting for him below in the parlour, where the ingredients for punch were all in readiness; but no one would squeeze the oranges till he came. (I, xiii)

This pseudo-"death bed" dialogue with a bibulous parson may usefully be compared with the scene between Moll Flanders and the Ordinary of Newgate:

> The Ordinary of *Newgate* came to me, and talk'd a little in his way, but all his Divinity run upon Confessing my Crime, as he call'd it, (tho' he knew not what I was in for) making a full Discovery, and the like, without which he told me God would never forgive me; and he said so little to the Purpose that I had no manner of Consolation from

him; and then to observe the poor Creature preaching
Confession and Repentance to me in the Morning, and
find him drunk with Brandy by Noon; this had something
in it so shocking, that I began to nauseate the Man, and his
Work too by Degrees, for the sake of the Man; so that I
desired him to trouble me no more. [23]

Moll's reporting of the chaplain's speech, brisk with indigna-
tion at its worthlessness, comes in the context of a state of mind
so taken up with urgent fears of hanging and of hell that this
worthlessness would be bound to strike her forcibly. Immediately
before, she had described "how I was harrass'd, between the
dreadful Apprehensions of Death, and the Terror of my Conscience reproaching me with my past horrible Life." In such a
state of mind, the routine pieties of a disreputable parson might
well be dismissed with a terse distaste such as the summarizing
account in indirect speech conveys. There is nothing of the set
piece about Moll's paragraph. It describes a shabby episode as
something that comes and goes, an event among others in a full
factual and emotional context, and its feeling develops from the
preceding mood with a complete and self-authenticating inner
logic. The emotional charge in her account does not lead to anything resembling Fielding's externalizing procedures: the facts
remain naked, unclothed by any stylistic business, and intimately
near.

When Mrs. Barbauld spoke of Defoe's "minuteness" as being
"more employed about things" than, like Richardson's, "about
persons and sentiments," she was speaking about *Robinson Crusoe*
and the *Family Instructor*, not having read the novels proper. [24]
But this description of Defoe's manner has sometimes been extended to the novels, and (despite the rough justice of the comparison with Richardson) it seems worth stressing that the entire
Newgate sequence in *Moll Flanders* is more vividly concerned
with the feelings of Moll than with the mere recording of what
she sees and hears. [25] Fielding is normally and correctly described
as much less interested in detailed particularities than Defoe. But
it is arguable that more "facts" about the Newgate scene, and
especially about the people there, may be acquired from the
Newgate chapters of *Amelia* than from *Moll Flanders*, even
though Fielding is concerned to present these facts as moral or
sociological "examples," rather than as realistic detail for its own
sake. [26] Similarly, as between the two dialogues, we learn a great

deal more about what was said in Fielding's than in Defoe's, even though the initimacy with which we enter into the feelings of Fielding's characters and narrator is much less. That our sense of Fielding's implied "presence" is much greater will surprise no one; but it is interesting to find him more "particular."

Thus, where Moll Flanders skimps the details of her parson's preachings because they are "so little to the Purpose" and her anxious feelings leave little time for him, Fielding opens up Barnabas's preachings into an animated ritual of vacuous self-revelation. The energetic particularity with which everything is put down becomes a pointed exposure of the moral nullity. Fielding's use of indirect speech is part of the piquancy of this contrast. Where Moll frankly summarizes to get the account over quickly, Fielding dwells on the unabridged entirety of what is said, so that the summarizing tendency of indirect speech makes the particularity seem especially absurd and mechanical. Fielding, unlike Moll, is not really, but "artificially," in a hurry, and the indirect reporting, while preserving all the content of a more direct quotation, speeds the dialogue up just beyond its natural pace to the brisk tempo of a comic routine. The automatic regularity of the dialogue's narrative links, "Joseph said," "Barnabas said," "Joseph answered," "Barnabas replied," and so on, contributes to the clockwork effect.[27] Authorial domination and a sharp efficient wisdom are strongly established. The automatism conveys a quick and knowing grasp. As with the "smart dialogue between some people and some folks," we are made to understand that in similar situations similar persons can invariably be relied upon to go on thus. Barnabas and Joseph, like the quarrelling ladies, become actors in a wildly extravagant collection of stock responses, and the very circumstantial report is edged with a feeling of endless recurrence, of perpetual re-enactment "these [last] four thousand years; and I hope . . . as many yet to come."[28]

Fielding's use of the past tense paradoxically supports this feeling. Neither Moll nor Fielding is much given to "writing in the present tense," like Pamela.[29] But Moll's past tense is merely part of the normal idiom of her chronicle and places the incident (however typical it may or may not be of Newgate parsons) as a single event in her story. As the syntax of *oratio obliqua* obviously requires, Fielding's past tense highlights itself by entering into the very fabric of what is said in the dialogue: "he told Joseph, 'He was come to pray by him, and to prepare him for another world:

in the first place, therefore, he hoped he had repented of all his sins.'" But the point about this is not so much that it introduces further layers of remoteness in time, as that (unlike Moll's or Pamela's normally quite unselfconscious use of indirect speech) it reinforces the feeling of mechanical repetition. Fielding's particularity aims neither at the immediacy of present reality, nor at a scrupulous reconstruction of the past. It is a particularity of the typical, celebrated not by the "naked" truth but with the full honors of authorial "performance."

This suggests that the correlation sometimes implied by critics of the early English novel, between a "naked" or unstylized notation, and circumstantial particularity or even prolixity, is not always justified. The Royal Society scientists had many years before claimed that a "naked, natural way of speaking" would tend on the contrary to be very concise.[30] Scientific conciseness is not of course the same thing as a detailed novelistic recording of events and feelings; but it does share with the often prolix styles of Defoe and Richardson a readiness (absent in Fielding) to treat facts "nakedly," without the distancing veil of stylized interference. "Nakedness" and "prolixity" were thought of as going together from an early date. An amusing illustration is Lady Mary Wortley Montagu's famous complaint about Clarissa's habit "of declaring all she thinks to all the people she sees, without reflecting that in this Mortal state of Imperfection Fig leaves are as necessary for our Minds as our Bodies, and tis as indecent to shew all we think as all we have."[31] The real point of the "Fig leaves" is not of course that Clarissa (or Richardson) gave many details that were indecent, but that it was indecent of them to give so many details. Involved in it is a recoil, both gentlemanly and neoclassic, from, as Fielding put it in the preface to the *Voyage to Lisbon*, "recording things and facts of so common a kind, that they challenge no other right of being remembered, than as they had the honour of having happened to the author, to whom nothing seems trivial that in any manner happens to himself." This point is often made by courtesy-writers, in their prescription of conversational good manners, and is often thus extended to literary styles. Fielding's preface says that the only small incidents which his journal records are those which "naturally" give rise to "some observations and reflections."

This distaste for the "naked" immediacy of fact also motivates many procedures of "style," which was, after all, the *dress* of thought: procedures of decorous distancing, ironic indirection, and generalizing implication (which makes a fact more than a *mere* fact). Provided the stylistic protections were sufficiently firm, the particular and the specific could be allowed a good deal of play. Fielding can turn certain kinds of circumstantiality in themselves into signs of an expansive stylization. In the dialogue between Joseph and Barnabas the strongly rendered implications of typicality give an edge to the specific exchange, without significantly blurring its individual force. It is remarkable how exactly this style of brisk summarizing dispatch captures Barnabas's very special kind of lazy patness, the readiness with which his pedantic legalism peters out in a muddled get-it-over-with laxity when Joseph agrees to forgive "as much as he could," and the Pickwickian conviviality with which he hurries back to the parlor to "squeeze the oranges" for punch.

This delightful detail about squeezing the oranges is obviously more circumstantial than Moll Flanders's bare remark that her parson was "drunk with Brandy by Noon." But the real difference is that it is flecked with Fielding's sharp but companionable irony. The small detail adds its own animation to the portrait, but not so much because it contributes to a full record, as because of a selective vividness which conveys Fielding's mixed feelings of affection and censure, and his fun. The detail adds to our knowledge of Barnabas, but convivially (that is, at a social distance) rather than intimately. Contrast the closeness of emotional hostility in Moll Flanders's remark; and a fortiori in one of Pamela's comments about Mrs. Jewkes, "I dare say she drinks," which puts Pamela *and* us as it were breath to breath with the woman.[32]

Fielding's special use of indirect or semi-indirect speech, and of the past tense, in this dialogue emphasizes a controlling and externalizing authorial "presence," and helps, in Ian Watt's language, to make his "realism" a "realism of assessment" rather than of "presentation." It is not, however, the mere grammatical forms but a certain witty manipulation that differentiates Fielding from Richardson or Defoe. Richardson's or Defoe's narrators both, after all, use indirect speech and the past tense[33] and can indeed make them convey ironic or indignant commentary rather than mere neutral reporting. But they seldom use it to convey a feeling of distance or superiority in the narrator or author, whereas Fielding is very fond of playing with forms of indirect speech for exactly this and related purposes. When Mrs. Western tries to get her brother the squire, as a magistrate, to punish Mrs. Honour for having cast aspersions on her beauty, the magistrate's clerk feels compelled to warn that "you cannot legally commit anyone to Bridewell only for ill-breeding." Western knows that a magistrate nevertheless has considerable discretionary powers, but since the offense, not being against the laws of hunting, is of limited gravity, he is prepared to take his clerk's advice. "The squire, therefore, putting on a most wise and significant countenance, after a preface of several hum's and ha's, told his sister, that upon mature deliberation, he was of opinion that 'as there was no breaking up of the peace, such as the law,' says he, 'calls breaking open a door, or breaking a hedge, or breaking a head; or any such sort of breaking; the matter did not amount to a felonious kind of thing, nor trespasses nor damages, and, therefore, there was no punishment in the law for it'" (*TJ*: VII, ix).

The narrator, in such high spirits, is here almost a raconteur, and any incredulity at Western's headlong absurdity is disarmed by our willingness to share the raconteur's fun rather than question his truth; straight dialogue, unless hedged with other stylizations which we have seen Fielding use, would more readily tend to strain belief. This indirect speech purports to record as completely as any straight dialogue, but does not emulate its impartiality or self-effacement. If the narrator is straight-faced, it is so as to bring out the squire in his full comic splendor. If he is aloof, it is to establish himself as a superior presence.

It may indeed be that, despite the example of Defoe and Richardson, certain kinds of indirect reporting of speech or thought tend toward an effect of authorial superiority, whether intended or not. In Fielding this superiority often emerges as that of the comic artist over a predictably erring humanity, or again that of an urbane and gentlemanly Augustan sage. There is no doubt that Fielding is consciously committed to these attitudes and tones. But compare this passage from Ford Madox Ford, who set such great store by authorial self-effacement and who complained of Fielding's gentlemanly posturing:[34]

> Sergeant-Major Cowley, his form blocking the doorway, surveyed the stars. He found it difficult to realize that the same pinpricks of light through black manifolding paper as he looked at, looked down also on his villa and his elderly wife at Isleworth beside the Thames above London. He knew it to be the fact, yet it was difficult to realize. He imagined the trams going along the High Street, his missus in one of them with her supper in a string bag on her stout knees. The trams lit up and shining. He imagined

her having kippers for supper: ten to one it would be
kippers. Her favourites. His daughter was at the w.a.a.c.'s by
now. She had been cashier to Parks's, the big butchers in
Brentford, and pretty she had used to look in the glass case.
Like as if it might have been the British Museum where
they had Pharoahs and others in glass cases. . . . There were
threshing machines droning away all over the night. He
always said they were like threshing machines. . . . Crikey,
if only they were! . . . But they might be our own planes,
of course. A good welsh rarebit he had had for tea. [35]

Ford's narrator in *No More Parades*, unlike Dowell in *The
Good Soldier*, is omniscient and unnamed, and it would take an
unnatural and pedantic purism to distinguish him, in the reading,
from an authorial presence—whether his feelings are biographi-
cally Ford's or not. He is very much what Ford called an "official
Author,"[36] and certainly not to be confused with the hero
Tietjens. Nevertheless he is clearly impregnated with some of
Tietjens's romanticized squirearchical outlook, and he has for
this sergeant-major in Tietjens's command something of Tietjens's
own affectionate paternalism. The effect is probably unintentional,
but this superiority is partly suggested by the attempt to enter
into the sergeant's thoughts, while keeping the sergeant's idiom
slightly at bay through the narrator's reporting voice. Ford's effort
is to create a sober particularized illusion of the sergeant's consciousness, and in such a context of apparent neutrality the
intrusive superiority cannot help appearing patronizing. The
awkwardness of "and pretty she had used to look," "like as if
it might have been the British Museum," and "a good welsh
rarebit he had had for tea" suggests nothing so much as an
embarrassed class-consciousness in the authorial voice. The passage is by no means representative of Ford's distinguished best.
But Ford often rebuked Fielding for supercilious intrusion, and
it is open to us to prefer Fielding's undisguised and morally
generous presence to the somewhat mealy-mouthed uppishness
of Ford's passage. Fielding does not involve us in illusions of
actuality, and thus does not run Ford's particular risks. The
mimicry of Western's subliterate demotics belongs so much to
fantasticating comedy that any offensiveness is unlikely to arise:
nor does this particular scene involve *social* superiority. But it
can be said for Fielding's patrician *hauteurs* that they not only
have the chance to declare themselves frankly, but that they are
at their most stinging when directed at snobs.

When Fielding says that "Mrs. Western's maid claimed great superiority over Mrs. Honour" because "her birth was higher: for her great grandmother by the mother's side was a cousin, not far removed, to an Irish peer,"[37] he is, in a rudimentary way, purporting to render her state of mind. What is irony from him is her sober thinking, rather as, in the passage from *Jonathan Wild* about Theodosia Snap, Fielding's irony entered into the mind of canting hypocrites like Laetitia. The irony is in both cases very obvious, because the states of mind are rendered in their full moral outrageousness rather than their realistic form. There is no serious invitation to enter into the characters' consciousness, and every invitation to share Fielding's implied comment. If illusion is lacking, there is no lack either of narrative vitality or of a humanly attractive and centrally relevant moral viewpoint. Ford's passage suggests that a thoroughgoing formal practice of self-effacement does not, on the other hand, necessarily guard against intrusive impressions of actual authorial attitude; that a high degree of illusion may even intensify such impressions where they occur; and that there may indeed be a special risk of unguarded, unintentionally damaging self-projections from the author's sheer security in his formal self-effacement. An example from Richardson, whom Ford admired, will illustrate this. Pamela is talking about Mrs. Jewkes: "I was sadly teazed with her impertinence and bold way; but no wonder; she was an inn-keeper's house-keeper, before she came to my master; and those sort of creatures don't want confidence, you know."[38]

This comes from one of the most brilliant scenes in *Pamela*, showing Mrs. Jewkes wielding power over Pamela in her repellently ingratiating way and combining a bullying pandarism with a vividly rendered element of archly hearty Lesbianism. Pamela's words are a masterly, *unstylized* notation of actual speech, without witty interference or any formal shapeliness of sentence or phrase. Even the neatness of "an inn-keeper's house-keeper" is not a sign of conscious verbal craftsmanship, but an idiomatic form of verbal play, in very common use. The phrase "gentleman's gentleman" (for a footman or valet) occurs in Steele in 1703, twenty-two years earlier than the *OED*'s first example (from Defoe).[39] Trapwit in Fielding's *Pasquin* speaks of the Mayoress in his play as having "been woman to a woman of quality";[40] and Mrs. Western's maid haughtily tells Mrs. Honour that "in town I visit none but the women of women of quality." [41]

Pamela speaks as a maidservant might well have spoken, and Richardson's genius to render this with great authenticity and vividness is something Fielding cannot normally match. Only, in order to speak thus, the maidservant would need, whatever her other virtues, to be arrogant, complacent, and mealy-mouthed, like Mrs. Western's maid, or more especially perhaps like the sort of person Fielding read into *Pamela* and Richardson never meant. [42] Thus, despite the masterly rendering in a narrow sense, the words reflect a Pamela somewhat other than the one which the novel as a whole invites us to see, and by that fact creates an illusion-breaking shock that diverts attention momentarily to the author. It seems a sign not merely of a technical lapse but of a certain moral obtuseness that Richardson should take such remarks for granted as raising no moral problems and leaving his heroine unscathed. The notion that this is simply dramatic notation without any participation by the author cannot be entertained. Unlike Ford, Richardson did not have a rigorous theory of self-effacement, and the entire novel invites us to endorse virtually everything the heroine says or does. It also induces in us the habit of expecting that anything meant to be taken as reprehensible will be voluminously pointed out. (Pamela is virtually the only narrator, but she quotes what people write and say to her, and plenty of openings for corrective views exist). On a matter like this, an absence of authorial disengagement, however lightly hinted, turns in such a context into an uncomfortable sense of authorial presence. And the personality which imposes itself unavoidably at such moments, however unconsciously and with whatever actual relation to the biographical Richardson, is one which has understandably repelled so many of Richardson's readers. The point is not that Fielding would have been incapable of sentiments like Pamela's, but that he would normally have felt compelled to see through them. No character of his can get away unscathed with saying "those sort of creatures" of anyone, and, if intrusion is the price to pay for this, it may be felt not to be too high.

Notes

1. In the notes to this essay W. E. Henley's *Complete Works of Henry Fielding*, 16 vols. (London, 1903) is referred to as *Works*. I use R. P. C. Mutter's edition of *Tom Jones* (Harmondsworth, 1966), and Martin C. Battestin's Riverside edition of *Joseph Andrews* (Boston, 1961). Battestin's major Wesleyan edition of *Joseph Andrews* (Oxford, 1967) has been consulted throughout, but I have preferred to quote from the modern-spelling Riverside text because no authoritative old-spelling editions exist as yet for the other novels.   2. A more detailed discussion of this interplay between stylization and "realism" in several dialogues from the novels is given in my essay, "Some Considerations on Authorial Intrusion and Dialogue in Fielding's Novels and Plays," *Durham University Journal*, n.s. XXXIII (1971), 32–44.   3. For some special aspects of Fielding's pleasure in the habitual phrase, see Sheridan Baker, "Henry Fielding and the Cliché," *Criticism*, 1 (1959), 354–361. A good recent treatment of Fielding's interest in language and in the social uses and abuses of language in his day is Glenn W. Hatfield, *Henry Fielding and the Language of Irony* (Chicago, 1968).   4. *Critical Remarks on Sir Charles Grandison, Clarissa and Pamela* (1754), p. 4. See Ian Watt, *The Rise of the Novel* (London, 1957), p. 195. For praise of Richardson's coinages, see *A Candid Examination of the History of Sir Charles Grandison*, 3rd ed. (1755), pp. 38–39.   5. The OED credits Richardson with the first use of *meditatingly*, but *scrupulosity* goes back at least as far as 1526 in the singular and 1600 in the plural.   6. Chesterfield to David Mallet, 5 November 1753, cited in A. D. McKillop, *Samuel Richardson, Printer and Novelist* (Hamden, Conn., 1960), p. 220. Lady Mary Wortley Montagu to Lady Bute, 20 October 1755, in *Complete Letters*, ed. Robert Halsband (Oxford, 1965–1967), III, 96–97. Walpole to Sir Horace Mann, 20 December 1764, in *Letters*, ed. Mrs. Paget Toynbee (Oxford, 1903–1904), VI, 163.   7. Pope, *Essay on Criticism*, lines 333–334.   8. *Sir Charles Grandison* (Oxford, 1931), I, 404.   9. *Champion*, 13 March 1739–1740, in *Works*, XV, 242; *Amelia*, X, ix; *Pamela* (London, 1955), I, 91; Richardson to Astraea and Minerva Hill, 4 August 1749, in *Selected Letters of Samuel Richardson*, ed. John Carroll (Oxford, 1964), p. 128.

10. Chesterfield, *Letters*, ed. B. Dobrée (London, 1932), IV, 1407, 27 September 1749. For a fuller survey of notions of "correctness," and their relation to gentlemanly standards of usage, see S. A. Leonard, *The Doctrine of Correctness in English Usage, 1700–1800* (New York, 1962), esp. chap. 10; and see Hatfield, pp. 109ff.   11. John Lawlor, "Radical Satire and the Realistic Novel," *Essays and Studies*, n.s. VIII (1955), 59.   12. The author of *An Essay on the New Species of Writing Founded by Mr. Fielding* (1751), p. 29, described a crude form of this: "these very kind of Books I am treating of fall into the Hands of a Set of People who are apt to cry out, on the Sight

of any Thing that gives a lively Representation of the Manners of the common People,—Oh! that's cursed low, intolerably vulgar, &c." Even Richardson was censured for "not altogether unexceptionable" language (see A. D. McKillop, *Samuel Richardson*, p. 48).   13. Richardson to Lady Bradshaigh, 23 February 1752, in *Selected Letters*, p. 198.   14. McKillop, *Samuel Richardson*, p. 220.   15. *Tom Jones*, XII, v. On the anti-low in the theater, see also *Tom Jones*, V, i and VII, i.   16. The canting puppet-master in *Tom Jones*, XII, v, prides himself on having resisted the wishes of "some of the quality at Bath, two or three years ago, [who] wanted mightily to bring Punch again upon the stage." For some discussion of this passage, see Martin C. Battestin, "Fielding and 'Master Punch' in Panton Street," *PQ*, XLV (1966), 194.   17. *Covent-Garden Journal*, ed. G. E. Jensen (New Haven, 1915), no. 10 (4 February 1752) I, 194; no. 52 (30 June 1752) II, 47–48.   18. *Joseph Andrews*, II, xiii. See also the list in *Champion*, 26 February 1739–1740, in *Works*, XV, 218. Fielding dealt, in several other essays, with the jargon of various social classes: *Champion*, 17 January 1739–1740, in *Works*, XV, 157–161; *Covent-Garden Journal*, no. 4 (14 January 1752), in Jensen, I, 153–157; no. 27 (4 April 1752), in Jensen, I, 293–298; no. 37 (9 May 1752), in Jensen, I, 344–449.   19. *Ulysses* (London, 1955), p. 30.

20. *Tom Jones*, VII, viii.   21. *Smart* as mockingly used here seems to have been a current pseudo-genteel vulgarism; the term is mentioned in Chesterfield's admonitory list, *Letters*, IV, 1407 (27 September 1749).   22. Contrast the scene on the waggon and at the inn in *Roderick Random*, chap. 11, which contains satire of similar haughty usages ("some people," "better folks," "creature!"), and which may have been partly inspired by the scene from *Joseph Andrews*. Smollett's action shows much less tendency to crystallize momentarily into self-enclosing set pieces, and flows instead with a boisterous continuity. In chap. 53, Smollett's Roderick gives "A smart Dialogue between my Mistress and the Captain," but this label is only part of a long chapter-heading, and the dialogue itself (also in a stagecoach, as it happens) once again has no special tendency to self-enclosure. For a snobbish exchange, archly conveyed in indirect speech, see chap. 54; and for "*some people* and *some folks*," see chap. 19.   23. *Moll Flanders* (Oxford, 1927), II, 103.   24. "Life" prefixed to Richardson's *Correspondence* (1804), I, xx.   25. *Moll Flanders*, II, 98ff.   26. I discuss more fully these scenes in *Amelia*, and compare them with Defoe, Smollett, and others in my book, *Henry Fielding and the Augustan Ideal under Stress* (London, 1972), chap. 3.   27. This method of reporting speech is superficially commonplace, and occurs in Defoe and others, but the special *effect* is Fielding's. Contrast the neutral and unmodified factuality of Moll's lively narration: "After some very kind Expressions, he ask'd me, if I would be very honest to him, and give a sincere Answer to one thing he would desire of me: After some little Cavil with him at the word *Sincere*, and asking him if I had ever given him any Answers which were not Sincere, I promis'd him I would; why then his Request was, *he said*, to let him see my Purse; I immediately put my Hand into my Pocket, *and laughing at him*, pull'd it out, and there was in it three Guineas and a Half; *then he ask'd me*, if there was all the Money I had? I told him no, *laughing again*, not by a great deal" (*Moll Flanders*, I, 115–116).   28. *Joseph Andrews*, III, i.   29. *Shamela*, letter VI.

30. Thomas Sprat, *History of the Royal-Society of London* (1667), Part II, sec. xx, in *Critical Essays of the Seventeenth Century*, ed. J. E. Spingarn (Oxford, 1908), II, 118.   31. To Lady Bute, 20 October [1755], *Complete Letters*, ed. Robert Halsband (Oxford, 1965–1967), III, 97. See also Robert Halsband, "Lady Mary Wortley Montagu and Eighteenth-Century Fiction," *PQ*, XLV (1966), 153: "The fig-leaf metaphor occurs elsewhere in Lady Mary's letters; it was a decorum which she, with stoic reticence, generally observed herself."   32. *Pamela*, I, 97.   33. E.g., *Moll Flanders*, I, 86; *Pamela*, I, 90, 319. See also the example in n. 27 above.   34. Ford's major attack on Fielding occurs in *The March of Literature* (London, 1947), pp. 522–540. See also his *The English Novel* (London, 1930), pp. 89ff.   35. Ford Madox Ford, *No More Parades* (London, 1948), pp. 13–14.   36. See Ford's description of the "official Author," who must limit "himself to presenting without comment or moralization," in his article, "Techniques," *Southern Review*, o.s. 1 (1935–1936), 33. See also the remarks on authorial neutrality in the dedicatory letter to William Bird prefixed to *No More Parades*. Nevertheless Ford has an interesting letter of October 1900 to Galsworthy suggesting the desirability of a certain authorial superiority to one's characters and even of letting it "peep out" on occasion (*Letters of Ford Madox Ford*, ed. Richard M. Ludwig, Princeton, 1965, p. 12).   37. *Tom Jones*, VII, viii.   38. *Pamela*, I, 91.   39. See Tuvia Bloch, "'Gentleman's Gentleman,'" *N&Q*, CCXII (1967), 405.

40. *Pasquin*, II, i, in *Works*, XI, 179. Trapwit is trying to explain how it is that in his play a "country mayoress" is said, "out of character," to have been at a ridotto. Her previous occupation is supposed to account for this, but the main reason for the improbability is that polite conversation in a comedy "cannot be carried on without these helps" of uncharacteristic speech.   41. *Tom Jones*, VII, viii.   42. Leslie Fiedler notes in a different connection that Richardson "knows really what Pamela is after . . . though he does not quite know how he knows it; this happy state of quasi-insight (he never falsifies the hidden motivations of his protagonists) he shares with his heroines and the readers who identify with them" (*Love and Death in the American Novel*, London, 1970, p. 60). There are weaknesses as well as strengths in this.

THE LESSON OF *AMELIA*

J. Paul Hunter

THE recent harvest of excellent scholarship and criticism suggests that Fielding, once undervalued if not neglected, is now at the crest of a wave of good feeling about early English fiction. Since 1959, there have been more books about Fielding than in the previous two hundred years, and each new year brings scores of dissertations, monographs, essays, and notes. For the most part recent studies have been of very high quality, offering us more contextual facts and better interpretations than any previous age has had available.[1] But I am not sure we yet see Fielding whole, with accomplishments and limitations in proper perspective. The sheer number of studies seems destined to overwhelm us and inflate Fielding's reputation, rather than give us perspective. If the last generation undervalued Fielding, we seem more likely to reverse than reform its judgment. Like many another segment of literary history and criticism, Fielding scholarship seems now to need time and judgment to absorb and evaluate the new information and make judicious use of the better interpretive tools and stances. If once we focused from too far, now we seem too close. We need desperately a sharpening of lines that will show Fielding clear and that will suggest his size in relation to the landscape beyond him.[2] The wealth of recent learning needs to become a basis for discriminating what Fielding can do from what he cannot, not simply a quantitative index of Fielding's current rating.

Perhaps the ultimate guarantee that Fielding will not be overrated is *Amelia*. The lesson of *Amelia* derives not so much from a failure within itself as from the fact that this last novel (1751) points backward toward some limitations in Fielding's art which are not plainly to be seen in the earlier novels. In *Joseph Andrews* (1742) and *Tom Jones* (1749) Fielding had used a number of strategies which were brilliant in those self-defined worlds, but which in other worlds—including the larger context of the Fielding canon—show some things which Fielding could not do. His limitations stand forth boldly in *Amelia*, and—unlike in the earlier novels—he does not turn out the lights and let us marvel at the timely darkness.

Amelia is not without pleasures, adornments, and triumphs of its own. Sometimes Fielding's accomplishments here are beyond those elsewhere. The seduction of Booth by Miss Matthews, for example, is brilliant, even though one might be forgiven for wondering if—outside the prison of space and time —either participant would have been patient enough to get the job done. But the prison setting, besides its allusive richness, provides a timeless world of the moment where past and future can be temporarily construed as meaningless and where a grim pastoral (derived perhaps from a hint by Gay) may sponsor the tedium of a past divided morally between virtues and vices. Even the slowness and boredom become here a value as we watch the inverted pursuit work with vengeance and wit. Had Lady Booby been so clever in engineering a setting, one despairs for the virtue of Joseph; Fielding's treatment in *Joseph Andrews* is more rollicking and ridiculous (in keeping with the local parodic purposes and with the larger aims of preserving perfection against the onslaught of bothersome folly), but in *Amelia* the treatment is more sardonic, reflective of a world where vice is more subtle and relentless, willing to risk boredom to demonstrate its macabre point. Booth here is a disarmed hero, a victim of deceived self-value and his own inflated paragraphs, and evil is flexible enough to adjust its shape to the bumbling garrulousness of good intentions. Set against the insistent time of the later books, the walled-in prison books define the relationship of holiday to reality, and they argue, by context, the grim insistence of endurance, obligation, consequence, implication.

A second accomplishment resides in the frequent narrative stasis which reflects the inability of characters to cope with the forces of oppression. Taken singly, some of these incidents are simply tedious and slow, but cumulatively they achieve a certain pathos because passivity is shown to be not a chosen course but rather a condition thrust upon characters by difficult situations and unsympathetic forces. Booth's seemingly endless petitions to great men, his furtive routine calculated to avoid the eternal pursuit of creditors, the pointless circularity of the masquerade, the silliness and failure of the wine-basket device to gain Booth access to Amelia—all these incidents and actions linger beyond meaning to demonstrate the absurdity of trying to cope in a world where evil is relentless and goodness has few allies. The Booths' powerlessness is sometimes boring to read about (the imitative fallacy), but Fielding's portrayal of it achieves, at times, a certain claustrophobic, smothering sense of frustration, panic, and doom.

Also admirable is the occasional glimpse inside characters, at the tortured battle which even the virtuous face against temptation. I cannot fully agree with Aurélien Digeon's defense of *Amelia* as a psychological novel.[3] The telling glimpses are not sustained, nor is the depiction of human motivation very complex or interesting, even if it does suggest a fairly successful imitation of Richardsonian character-analysis. In *Shamela* especially, and more irregularly thereafter, Fielding had shown himself a shrewd exposer of the not wholly conscious devices of the wicked, but he had been kinder to the desires of those who passed his test of virtue, as if he were unwilling to examine their darker corners. But *Amelia* does admit those corners, if it does not probe them, so that its portrait of virtue rewarded suggests a real trial. Amelia remains steadfast, not because of supernatural control or some mystical election, but because, aware of human weakness, she is careful. Fielding shows us, briefly and hesitantly, a tempted woman. I take Amelia's scrupulous avoidance of the masquerade as awareness of her frailty, though I admit that her discussion of the matter admits other possible interpretations. But I think the most remarkable account of fallibility occurs when Joseph Atkinson confesses his childhood theft of her picture and reveals his passion for her:

> "I can truly say [says Joseph] it was not the gold nor the diamonds which I stole—it was that face; which, if I had been the emperor of the world——"
> "I must not hear any more of this," said she. "Comfort yourself, Joe, and think no more of this matter. Be assured, I freely and heartily forgive you—But pray compose yourself; come, let me call in your wife."
> "First, madam, let me beg one favour," cried he: "consider it is the last, and then I shall die in peace—let me kiss that hand before I die."
> "Well, nay," says she, "I don't know what I am doing—well—there." She then carelessly gave him her hand, which

he put gently to his lips, and then presently let it drop, and fell back in the bed.

Amelia now summoned Mrs. Atkinson, who was indeed no farther off than just without the door. She then hastened down stairs, and called for a great glass of water, which having drank off, she threw herself into a chair, and the tears ran plentifully from her eyes with compassion for the poor wretch she had just left in his bed.

To say the truth, without any injury to her chastity, that heart, which had stood firm as a rock to all the attacks of title and equipage, of finery and flattery, and which all the treasures of the universe could not have purchased, was yet a little softened by the plain, honest, modest, involuntary, delicate, heroic passion of this poor and humble swain; for whom, in spite of herself, she felt a momentary tenderness and complaisance, at which Booth, if he had known it, would perhaps have been displeased.

Having staid some time in the parlour, and not finding Mrs. Atkinson come down, (for indeed her husband was then so bad she could not quit him,) Amelia left a message with the maid of the house for her mistress, purporting that she should be ready to do anything in her power to serve her, and then left the house with a confusion on her mind that she had never felt before, and which any chastity that is not hewn out of marble must feel on so tender and delicate an occasion.[4]

Fielding does not dwell on ambivalence nor detail her physiological reactions as, say, Milton might have, but he makes it clear that a virtuous woman of nearly pure good nature has impulses that frighten her. Surely we are here meant to recall the early seduction scene in *Joseph Andrews*[5] and spy not only the reinversion of aggressor / aggressed but also the shift in seductive method, the presence here of real trial, the change in Fielding's tone, the refusal to push seriousness aside. Sometimes in the scenes involving the "noble lord" and Colonel James a reader may be tempted to offer his own Shamelian account of vanity and opportunistic, sadistic teasing, but scenes like this one suggest that Fielding knew the limits of perfection, even if he was sometimes fearful of portraying them. Given the guarded portrayals of feminine weakness in the earlier novels, *Amelia* is for Fielding something of a risk, something of a challenge to his own double standard of morality and his own personal frets and fears.

The reason for the risk here is probably not a desire to follow or surpass Richardson, but rather a theological implication of Fielding's choice of motif. Throughout *Amelia* Fielding contrasts his hero and heroine sharply, but the difference is not simply between good nature and bad, or between active and passive virtue. Instead the major difference stems from distinctive attitudes toward temptation—Booth continually placing himself in harm's way and Amelia doing her level best to avoid unnecessary trial. This distinction is more than a recognition of human fallibility; it derives from the orthodox view that human beings are responsible for avoiding potential temptation and God is responsible for providing grace when temptation comes unasked. The distinction is discussed, for example, by Bishop South in the second of his seven sermons on temptation; a person, he says, may meet temptation "purely by his own free choice, no necessary business or circumstance of his life engaging him in it, by unhappily casting the matter of a temptation before him in the course of his lawful occasions," or he may be tempted "in the pursuit of his honest calling or profession, or in such a condition as he is unavoidably brought into by an overruling hand of Providence." In the former case, because the person puts himself "upon needless, adventurous trials . . . [and] leads himself into temptation . . . [he] has no cause to rely upon God for a deliverance out of it"; in the latter, he "may comfortably and warrantably hope for such assistances from God, as shall carry him safe and successfully through the temptation be it what it will."[6] Except for his first temptation at the hands of Miss Matthews, Booth engineers his own trials (although some of them are cumulative, so that he does not specifically choose to be tempted on each separate occasion); Amelia, by contrast, does all in her power to avoid trial, though it takes a good bit of doing because her beauty and her virtue make not only an attractive but a challenging target.

Once Amelia becomes the center of the novel's attention (that is to say, once Booth's trial and fall take place, and once Amelia's entrance is prepared by the traditional promissory stories about her) Fielding shapes most of the narrative from her trials and tribulations, following the orthodox reading of the "three temptations."[7] The various assaults upon her follow the traditional pattern of virtue successfully defended because the temptations were imposed and not sought. Amelia is able to withstand the trials not because she is perfect and infallible, but because she gets all sorts of divine aids—Mrs. Bennett's "history" as a guard against the lord, Joseph's dream about the plot of Colonel James, and the accumulated brotherly feelings toward Joseph which help to control Amelia's passion on the one occasion when she faces real sexual attraction.

The psychological glimpses into a tempted woman are made possible by such theology. Associated by means of the three temptations motif with Christ's wilderness experiences, her tried virtue becomes exemplary; the force of her example depends upon recognition that she is human and fallible, and that the power of her virtue stems from grace offered to those beset by temptation not of their own making. The lord (the temptation of avarice or ambition) is something of a threat largely by situation; the Booths' stark poverty gives dramatic appeal to the children's trinkets and the potential wealth and power which Amelia might purchase. His is the weakest, though the most drawn out, of the temptations, but still Amelia is shrewd enough to avoid the masquerade where loss of public identity might easily offer additional incentive to fall (as Mrs. Atkinson's behavior there later reminds us). Fielding does not really exploit Amelia's avoidance here, leaving it implicit in the situation of lost identities and masked substitutions, but he is more explicit about the other temptations. The climax of the temptation of Colonel James (vainglory or presumption) comes in his long visit with Amelia while Booth is in prison. The unsuspecting Amelia soaks up his flattery "till it was very late, the colonel never offering to stir from his chair before the clock had struck one." Amelia is not on guard and her vanity is flattered far more than she wishes to admit, even when Mrs. Atkinson prompts her to face the truth after the visit is over. Amelia repeatedly insists that the colonel is only concerned for Booth, but Mrs. Atkinson makes it clear that Amelia had listened attentively to insistent praise of herself:

> "Did he not then," said Mrs. Atkinson, "repeat the words *the finest woman in the world*, more than once? did he not make use of an expression which might have become the mouth of Oroöndates himself? If I remember, the words were these—that, had he been Alexander the Great, he should have thought it more glory to have wiped off a tear from the bright eyes of Statira than to have conquered fifty worlds."

"Did he say so?" cried Amelia—"I think he did say
something like it; but my thoughts were so full of my
husband that I took little notice. But what would you infer
from what he said? I hope you don't think he is in love
with me?"

"I hope he doth not think so himself," answered Mrs.
Atkinson; "though, when he mentioned the bright eyes
of Statira, he fixed his own eyes on yours with the most
languishing air I ever beheld."

Amelia was going to answer, when the serjeant arrived,
and then she immediately fell to inquiring after her husband,
and received such satisfactory answers to all her many
questions concerning him, that she expressed great pleasure.
These ideas so possessed her mind, that, without once
casting her thoughts on any other matters, she took her
leave of the serjeant and his lady, and repaired to bed to her
children, in a room which Mrs. Atkinson had provided
her in the same house; where we will at present wish her
a good night. (II, 87)

I am not sure how much irony to assume in such a phrase as
"without once casting her thoughts on any other matters,"
but Fielding's stress on Amelia's refusal to admit what she has
heard, and how it has affected her, suggests that he may here
be parodying Amelia's version of her mind. Such strategy also
carries over to the beginning of the next chapter, where Amelia's
insistently blind version gives her exaggerated repose: "While
innocence and chearful hope, in spite of the malice of fortune,
closed the eyes of the gentle Amelia on her homely bed, and
she enjoyed a sweet and profound sleep, the colonel lay restless
all night on his down." The third temptation (carnal appetite)
is represented only by the scene with Joseph that I have already
quoted. Interestingly enough, Fielding places this temptation
last, violating the biblical sequence.[8] Given Fielding's aims
(and his protective view of woman) lust is the climactic temptation
for Amelia, overshadowing the other temptations which, while
sexual, never really involved physical attraction and in fact
never even forced Amelia to admit any kind of fleshly appetite.
The portrait of Amelia as a new Eve, a model of human perfection,
makes the temptation of carnal appetite the logical dramatic
climax for Fielding, whose age tended to view all sin as sexual
and whose personal vision of women elevated them to such a
point that lust was the ultimate test of their mortality.

The pattern of the three temptations and their allusive basis underscores Amelia's fallibility and her strength in the face of it, as well as the providential protection available to those whose temptations are not self-inflicted. Amelia is no more diminished by these demonstrations that she is human than is Christ; rather she becomes a more viable alternative to the weakness of Booth, though perhaps not enough so for most readers, who are likely to find tempted failures more interesting and convincing than successes. Her fallibility, though introduced, is not emphasized; three temptations may be sufficient for a biblical account of a messiah or even for a hagiographic description of a Samson or a Job in a heroic age, but they seem almost trifles in the age of lead which *Amelia* presents us for twelve long books.

The temptation theme that I have described—in its distinction between active and passive pursuit of trial and in its traditional motif as the "triple equation"—merges with many other biblical motifs in *Amelia*. There are, for example, the forged Jacobean birthright (with probable political overtones), the dream of Joseph, the allusions to Job's tribulations and suffering, and the silver cup in Murphy's possession which points to the theme of famine, plague, oppression, and bondage. All of these operate in tension with the parallels to the *Aeneid* and other classical motifs and allusions, and the tension underscores the opposition between Christian and classical-pagan values, isolated in its most simplified form in the stoicism of Booth and the Christianity of Amelia, though why the classical tradition is made masculine and the Christian tradition feminine I will not presume to say.

One might elaborate tediously how the Christian / classical antithesis is established and borne; such elaboration would reinforce the notion of Fielding's aims and intentions that I am here assuming, and it might clarify the reasons for certain troublesome incidents and devices, but I do not think it would make *Amelia* seem a better novel. Intricate and elaborate though Fielding's strategy may be here, it doesn't make *Amelia* interesting enough, and its failure seems instructive about Fielding's talents as well as his limitations.

George Sherburn once assured us that *Amelia* is not necessarily duller than Fielding's other novels, but not many critics have found that concept of necessity attractive.[9] Except for a few defenses of *Amelia* as an "experiment" or innovation in something (Alter, Digeon, e.g.) and some neutral accounts of its genealogy

(Sherburn, Powers, Johnson), criticism has been generally hostile to *Amelia's* "shift" from earlier Fielding strategies.[10] Even more revealing is the lack of attention to *Amelia* by Fielding's most vigorous proponents. In summarizing here some of the most frequent and telling charges, I mean to indicate the extent of this shift and explore some possible reasons for it, so that I may suggest what I think *Amelia* tells us about the nature and limits of Fielding's vision and art.

The earliest charge against *Amelia*, and still the most overpowering, is that of dullness; Fielding's famous 1752 defense of *Amelia* and renunciation of its muse was primarily a response to that charge.[11] Unless the term is elevated to metaphysical status and allowed to stand for the powers of creative darkness (a familiar eighteenth-century elevation), the charge cannot really be answered in any objective way. Modern criticism is better equipped to explain meanings and justify methods than it is to persuade away boredom. No amount or kind of explanation will much affect a reader bored by *Amelia;* heightened sensitivity toward intention and accomplishment may increase a reader's profit, but it does not necessarily induce much more pleasure. Unlike Fielding's earlier books *Amelia* is at least as interesting a book in summary as it is page by page and scene by scene. To trim the digressive garrulousness from *Tom Jones* would be to cut at its very life, but the briefer description and commentary of *Amelia* seems longer and less an integral part. Even such a staunch and learned admirer as Digeon confesses that he feels "a certain indulgence towards those who, in spite of all its qualities, have found this book a little long."[12] There is a sense in which this charge sums up all the others and operates as a cumulative affective description of the problem of *Amelia*. I shall have more to say about why this is so when we have considered the expectations created by Fielding's earlier novels and the moderation or frustration of them in *Amelia*.

A second charge is that its plot is too intricately contrived, too dependent on coincidence to be convincing or probable. The visibility of the contrivance is hard to dispute, but I think that the complaint about plot in *Amelia* is usually phrased in the wrong terms. Were Fielding's mode realistic, then contrivance would indeed be a serious matter, but the frequency of contrivance is as great in *Joseph Andrews* or *Tom Jones*, especially in the form of coincidence where the Author takes the brunt of the blame for arranging the action and manipulating the timing. Looked at realistically, the big inn scene in *Tom Jones* (as well as its counter-part in *Joseph Andrews*) is incredible, fully as incredible as the arrival of Amelia at precisely the time when Miss Matthews is about to make off with Booth at the prison door. Both involve the providential devices of melodrama; there is throughout Fielding a great deal of withheld information, mistaken identity, and miraculous confrontation which, viewed realistically, is not very successful. But the question is whether it ought to be viewed realistically.

Finding coincidence in *Tom Jones* successful and in *Amelia* absurd testifies not to distinctions within the strategy itself, but rather to the varied context from which it springs and the tone it produces. In *Tom Jones* the narrator encourages us to laugh along with Fielding; if we find the coincidence absurd, we are invited to think that Fielding finds it so too. Further, we are encouraged to think that its absurdity has philosophical impli-cations: in "real life" things may not contrive so well for good, but in comic art we fortunately have an Author who may induce poetic justice. We are not asked to think that life is a comedy, but only that a clever author may turn art into one. But in *Amelia*, because of the novel's basic tone, we have no such "out"; here is pretense of showing some of life's sordid realities, and avoidance by coincidence seems cheap and meretricious. The problem is not in plot contrivance per se, but rather in how the contrivance is handled tonally, and what it is made to represent in terms of the relationship of art to life. The strategy is subject to the mode which supplies its context.

Coincidence in *Amelia* may also seem more striking than in the earlier books because the main action of the novel is kept more consistently in the forefront of attention. In *Joseph Andrews* and *Tom Jones*, digressive commentaries or scenes centered on minor characters continually vie for attention with the main plot; in fact one of the major appeals of these novels is the tension between the ongoing main action and the various narrative devices used to slow the action down, shift our attention else-where, or question the interpretive perspective which is to be exercised on that action. *Amelia* still contains digressions, but they are fewer, and Fielding is apologetic about them. Chapter 2 of Book v, unusual in its almost total disregard of plot, recounts a debate between an apothecary and a physician about how to treat a sick Booth child. The scene is reminiscent of the Dr. Y–Dr. Z debate in *Tom Jones* (II.ix), but the chapter in *Amelia* ends with a lengthy apology: "Some readers will, perhaps, think this whole chapter might have been ommitted [*sic*]; but though it contains no great matter of amusement, it may at least serve to inform posterity concerning the present state of physic" (I, 212–215). After the first edition, Fielding did omit the chapter.[13] Such omission seems strange in Fielding, for we have become accustomed to his characteristic panorama which stresses breadth of presentation, at the willing expense of depth or concentration. The lessening of digression in *Amelia* (and the concomitant refusal to dilute concentration) may be an intrinsic loss to Fielding's art; certainly it focuses greater attention on the main action, so that any avoidance of probability (in the context of pretended realism) is emphatic indeed.

A third charge is equally about cheapness, but of another kind. The sentimentality of *Amelia* is not simply a matter of describing emotional excess; the passion and tears which present such a high temperature-humidity index might be justified representationally if they were not an equivalent for *Amelia*'s affective intentions. The mid-century flow of taste toward men, and works, of sentiment may indicate the climate which produced *Amelia*, but it does not justify *Amelia*'s method. Much of the extreme emotion derives easily from the subjects and incidents Fielding engages: unjust imprisonment, disinheritance, adulterous passion, abject poverty, frustrated promises. One could hardly treat such matters lightly (when they provide the dominant context), and the characters involved might well be expected to respond passionately. But Fielding seems to ask that readers respond with similar feelings; often that seems to be asking a bit much, especially since the language is not always rhetorically convincing, even in scenes which give extraordinary representational satisfaction. In a passage I have already cited, for example, Amelia turns away Joseph's passion as she gives him her hand to kiss: "'Well, nay,' says she, 'I don't know what I am doing—well—there'" (II, 252). The scene allows us to believe in Amelia's action in spite of inept linguistic control, but her line is worthy of Shamela or Lady Booby—in fact it "echoes" the latter. And elsewhere, especially when the narrator talks us toward serious sentiment, the scene overrules less well. Readers might be inclined to be more charitable had not Fielding himself attacked similar attitudes and strategies in other writers, especially Richardson and the authors of contemporary romances. Fielding often seems uncertain in the depiction of the private or humble;

Richardson's condemnation of *Amelia* as "low" would be fair enough if applied to Fielding's handling of certain subjects, not their mere presence. When potentially affecting subjects and scenes appear in Fielding we are accustomed to seeing the narrator back off and relieve the feeling, often with a nervous laugh. But *Amelia* offers no such relief. Consider, for example, Amelia's catechism of her children just after Booth has received Dr. Harrison's rigid misinformed letter asking for payment of the loan:

> [Booth] was no sooner departed than his little boy, not quite six years old, said to Amelia, "La! mamma, what is the matter with poor papa, what makes him look as if he was going to cry? he is not half so merry as he used to be in the country." Amelia answered, "Oh my dear, your papa is only a little thoughtful, he will be merry again soon." —Then looking fondly on her children, she burst into an agony of tears, and cried, "Oh Heavens; what have these poor little infants done? why will the barbarous world endeavour to starve them, by depriving us of our only friend?—O my dear, your father is ruined, and we are undone."—The children presently accompanied their mother's tears, and the daughter cried—"Why will anybody hurt poor papa? hath he done any harm to anybody?"— "No, my dear child," said the mother; "he is the best man in the world, and therefore they hate him." Upon which the boy, who was extremely sensible at his years, answered, "Nay, mamma, how can that be? have not you often told me that if I was good everybody would love me?" "All good people will," answered she. "Why don't they love papa then?" replied the child, "for I am sure he is very good." "So they do, my dear," said the mother," but there are more bad people in the world, and they will hate you for your goodness." "Why then, bad people," cries the child, "are loved by more than the good."—"No matter for that, my dear," said she; "The love of one good person is more worth having than that of a thousand wicked ones; nay, if there was no such person in the world, still you must be a good boy; for there is One in Heaven who will love you, and His love is better for you than that of all mankind."

This little dialogue, we are apprehensive, will be read with contempt by many; indeed, we should not have thought it worth recording, was it not for the excellent example which Amelia here gives to all mothers. This admirable woman never let a day pass without instructing her children in some lesson of religion and morality. By which means she had, in their tender minds, so strongly annexed the ideas of fear and shame to every idea of evil of which they were susceptible, that it must require great pains and length of habit to separate them. Though she was the tenderest of mothers, she never suffered any symptom of malevolence to show itself in their most trifling actions without discouragement, without rebuke, and, if it broke forth with any rancour, without punishment. In which she had such success, that not the least marks of pride, envy, malice, or spite discovered itself in any of their little words or deeds. (I, 174–175)

However much we may admire historically this early fumbling attempt to treat children sympathetically (or at all) in a serious work of literature, we are not likely to stay for adoration of the whole episode. The practiced reader of Fielding—urged by such phrases as "excellent examples"—waits impatiently for some retreat from the intense moral lesson, but instead of gently backing off and apologizing for the mimetic necessity of presenting such a scene, as earlier Fielding narrators would have done, the narrator here "fears" for the scene's reception, then wades in with even more intense moralizing. We have come to expect something different from Fielding, and perhaps we feel ourselves betrayed when he does not relieve excess feeling by turning our attention elsewhere. A reader who has admired *Joseph Andrews* and *Tom Jones* probably would rather briefly admit and view from a distance deep feelings of sadness than bathe in them; Fielding had spent too many pages drying us off for him now to change his mind. The indulgence in sentimental portrayal is not, in itself, so offensive as the betrayal we feel of heightened expectations.

A fourth complaint against *Amelia* involves its lack of irony; this, too, is the complaint of the betrayed, for the characteristic irony of *Joseph Andrews* and *Tom Jones* is not only the style but often the center of meaning as well, providing not only a way of keeping simplicity at a distance, but also making the books' major points about the uses of words and the relationship between various levels of experience. Such a method induces empathy and involvement in a specific way, for instead of sympathy and transference—instead of reading character and plot as surrogates for oneself and one's own situation—there is a minimum of feeling and a maximum of distanced thought. Fielding's irony is so complex and so thick that it is continually turning us back on ourselves, then adding new convolutions, often even bringing us out where we began, but giving full value of experience for the round trip.[14] Those earlier books seldom simply "tell" us anything or offer a picture with simple lines and straightforward connections; *Amelia* is stark by contrast, the more so because it seems to promise the same cast of mind and style. The chapter headings seem to continue the teasing tradition of *Tom Jones*, and *Amelia*'s narrative voice pretends at the beginning to continue an established Fielding character.[15]

Such signs make the straightness of the commentary even more emphatic. But irony is not so totally missing that we can comfortably dismiss *Amelia* as a work of Fielding's senility, demonstrating his loss of creative power; the chapter headings, the occasional facetiousness of the narrator, and the constant awareness that characters (all of them, including Amelia and Dr. Harrison) have more going on in their heads than they care to admit—all these strategies remind us that the cast of mind in *Amelia* is still recognizably Fielding's, and they suggest that the soft-pedaling of irony was a conscious choice.

Another complaint involves characterization. I have already indicated some subtleties in the conception of Amelia; Fielding also makes conscious efforts to humanize Dr. Harrison and to prevent humors characters like the Lord, Colonel Bath, and Colonel James from seeming totally unattractive and absurd. Still, of course, it is easy to tell the good guys from the bad guys, and the world here may seem to be conceived in a rather Manichean fashion. But the relevant thing, it seems to me, is that this is the same divided world we find in *Joseph Andrews* and *Tom Jones*. Still there are the righteous who are not good (the old and young clergymen), and the unrighteous who have good hearts; still the dividing line is provided by "good nature" and still good nature needs additional qualities (such as prudence, generosity, religion, honor) to become viable and capable of inspiring full admiration. Fielding's ethic stays relatively constant and so does his notion of what people's motives are like. The difference in *Amelia* lies in the sense of evil and oppression generated by groups of people. It is not always an individual whose cruelty or selfishness or thoughtlessness brings about complication and unhappiness; sometimes the guilt seems to belong as much to a class or institution as to an individual, and evil characters are thus relieved of a certain amount of responsibility for their actions. But such a change does not make the characters substantially "thinner" or "flatter," and in *Amelia* the characters generally are as fully realized as in earlier Fielding novels. Only Tom Jones himself is more satisfying all around, and he lacks the occasional psychological subtleties present in Amelia. But Fielding's strength in the earlier novels was not really in conception of character, except in his own broad sense of providing a feast of "Nature." The elegance of that feast rests in its variety and splendid affluence, not in the subtle seasoning of a single dish. If there is a disappointment about "character" in *Amelia*, it is in the relative spareness of digressive scenes which present humors characters to fill out the panorama. *Amelia*'s increased attention to the main plot and main characters sacrifices not depth but some of the breadth we associate with the earlier novels. The canvas of *Amelia* does not have inferior texture, but it is a narrower canvas than that of *Tom Jones*.

A sixth charge involves the simplicity of moral in *Amelia*. The reward of virtue in earthly life and on worldly terms is not easy for most readers to accept as a realistic summary of the world they live in; such a solution and the optimistic moral that it implies seem rather to belong to the world of wish-fulfillment and fantasy in the genre of romance than to the recognizable patterns of events in the genre of "history" that pretends to describe life as it is. Fielding's ruthless exposure of this moral in *Pamela* makes its presence in *Amelia* seem even more surprising—unless we remember that the moral might also serve as an accurate precis of action in *Joseph Andrews* and *Tom Jones*. Yet the rewards of Joseph's chastity, Fanny's constancy, Parson Adams's faithfulness, Tom's spirit and good heart, and Sophia's modesty and pluck are not disturbing in the worlds of *Joseph Andrews* and *Tom Jones* because the "comic history" of which they are a part promises a happy ending as a generic given, and admits from the start that the events are fictionally contrived to bring one about. No promise is made that virtue will be rewarded outside the book's covers. One is therefore not likely to think of a precis of what happens in *Tom Jones* as a "moral," at least not in the same sense as one does in *Pamela*—or in *Amelia*. *Amelia* does not claim to be a comic history; in fact, its title page makes no generic claim at all. The pretense of coping with suffering and evil seems to me the relevant consideration for *Amelia*. We are tempted by Fielding's subject, and his handling of it, to apply "realistic" criteria; it is not the in-the-novel pattern of events which gives us trouble, but rather the prevailing tone and the context from which we approach that pattern.

Another charge is that in spite of all the satiric representation and social comment, Fielding does not always keep the enemy clearly in focus. I have already said that in *Amelia* Fielding is as prone to find institutional or class causes for evil as to rest blame solely on individuals. His earlier Augustan faith in institutions as a check on human depravity seems very much shaken; such potential solutions to immoral behavior now seem to him a major continuing source of the problem. One dramatic indication of Fielding's shift is in the satire on the clergy in Book IX. The old and young clergymen here are not necessarily more despicable than Parson Trulliber or Thwackum, but their brazen condoning of evil becomes a metaphor for the corruption of the whole profession, not just of individuals within it. Dr. Harrison's presence reminds us that goodness is possible, but the prevailing standard is shown to be so deteriorated that, to use Pope's phrase, "Not to be corrupted is the Shame." Dr. Harrison is fairly gentle in his disapprobation of the present state of his profession. Discussing the growing disrespect for the clergy, he suggests that "some little share of the fault is, I am afraid, to be imputed to the clergy themselves" (II, 158). Fielding is more brutal. He not only portrays the two clergymen as scoundrels and fools, concerned only with their own fortunes, but gives the profession the blame. "How do you expect to rise in the Church," he has the older clergyman ask his son, "if you cannot temporize, and give in to the opinions of your superiors?" (II, 162). Fielding can still imagine a fine man like Dr. Harrison in the profession, but fineness is the exception, untouched by the institutional corruption. Fielding's earlier corrupt clergymen had had themshelves to blame.

Fielding's disenchantment with institutional solutions for human tendencies toward evil, though perhaps induced by his own personal experience as a magistrate, reflects the changing thought of mid-century, when emphasis on natural human depravity was giving way to blame on environment and the social structure. Fielding's conception of innate human nature had never, of course, been as grim as Swift's, nor was it to become as hopeful as Blake's, but his own transition does describe, in little, the eighteenth-century shift from finding causes in the individual will to finding them in external social pressures. One trouble with *Amelia* may be that Fielding never fully made up his mind where he stood, for if there is more harshness toward institutions and classes here, there is also an unwillingness to acquit the individual, on the one hand, and the ultimate order of things, on the other. (We still need a thoroughgoing study of Fielding's metaphysical commitment, for we now presume it—perhaps wrongly—from his ethical formulations and their theological source.) It is ultimately not clear whether the plight of the Booths is due to fate or fortune, the corrupt aristocracy and other institutionalized evils such as the law, or a failure of fiber in the Booths themselves. Such complexity makes *Amelia* in some ways a more interesting book but also a less satisfying one, for it defines uncertainties that perhaps never needed to be defined in the worlds of *Joseph Andrews* and *Tom Jones*, where the fictional creator, at least, was benevolent and could guide whatever creatures he elected past any evils that befell them— in the garden of their hearts, or in the tainted gardens and mazy wildernesses of their worlds.

I have been emphatic about *Amelia's* similarities to the earlier books because it seems to me that *Amelia* is often condemned for the wrong reasons, reasons which in effect deny relationship to the rest of the Fielding canon. The explanations of failure because of Fielding's carelessness, fatigue, or age will not do either; there are too many indications of continuity for us to be content with the alibis of loss, and the changes testify to calculation and conscious artistic choice, however mistaken and unsuccessful. We can finally be precise about the degree and source of *Amelia's* uniqueness only when we are certain, and calm, about its similarities to *Joseph Andrews* and *Tom Jones*.

Amelia is like those novels in using (1) a complex and intricate plot, heavily laden with coincidence; (2) a system of poetic justice in which rewards and punishments are meted out according to a polarized moral world with good nature serving as the basic dividing line; and (3) characters who are subordinated to the plot and are easily identifiable (to the reader, though not necessarily to each other) as good or evil. The major differences between *Amelia* and the earlier novels are thus not for the most part in character, incident, plot resolution, or any aspect of the action described in the novel; the major differences rather are in attitudes toward that action and in the resultant tones. The comic worlds of *Joseph Andrews* and *Tom Jones* are full of complication, but not of irredeemable crises. In *Amelia* Fielding still deals with characters, action, and resolution from the world of comic romance, but he chooses to dwell on grim detail rather than broad comic outlines and on difficulties rather than the surmounting of difficulties. Most important, he creates a narrator who self-consciously conceives himself as an advocate and arbiter—not an actor and stage manager—and who thus feels obliged to stir moral passions and designate rigid commitments. Fielding's earlier narrators had rather sought to disengage the reader from the potential intensity of narrative action so that the reader might thoughtfully form conclusions against the resonances of the book's dialectic between action and commentary.

The uniqueness of *Amelia*, then, consists in its emphasis on grim detail, its darkened tone, its more rigid insistence on stated moral precepts, its straightforwardness in directing judgment, and its refusal to provide a modal frame which insulates the comic resolution of events from their tragic possibilities. The disappointments of *Amelia* lie within this uniqueness. Some differences from the earlier books involve inherent weaknesses that readers perhaps would not tolerate in any book by any writer, but the intensity of our frustration derives from thinking that Fielding has betrayed us by abandoning those strategies which in the earlier novels had succeeded in instructing us even while pretending only to amuse and delight.

If dullness summarizes the standard charges against *Amelia*, the shift in didactic method most nearly suggests, in a single phrase, what changes in Fielding *produced* the disappointment of *Amelia*. The liveliness in Fielding's earlier books derives at least in part from a successful merger of attempts to instruct and delight; Fielding's changed didactic method emphasizes *Amelia*'s anxiety to instruct, willingly abandoning some of the more delightful aspects of his art. The result for most readers is a book without much pleasure or profit.

Fielding's didactic strategies in *Amelia* go against the grain; they try to reverse a rhetorical method he had brilliantly and painstakingly set up in earlier novels. That earlier method—charming the reader off his guard by various strategies of indirection—enables Fielding to be quite definite, even rigid, without ever seeming to be dogmatic; for everywhere is the pretense that the reader is making up his own mind, applying his own discrimination and ethic. That method arose from a sense of human perversity, a belief that a reader is repelled by direct moralizing and can only be turned toward virtue by careful, shrewd ironies which he seems to solve himself. This illusion of the open end—in books that are carefully and totally calculated to portray not only self-contained events, but also self-contained resolutions and moral answers—lures the reader cannily, and lets him seduce himself.

The illusion of the open end embraces three strategies of indirection which had been integral to Fielding's didactic method in *Joseph Andrews* and *Tom Jones*. The first is the strategy of the disappearing exemplar: models of "perfection" are introduced, only to disintegrate and thereby demonstrate that no perfect examples exist. Joseph Andrews talks about Pamela as such an exemplar, the illustrious inspiration for his own chastity, though her Richardsonian heritage guarantees from the first that Fielding will not treat her exemplary status seriously. The beginning of the book is set up as a trial of the "trite but true" observation that men learn by example, and Fielding burlesques the notion by pretending to follow it: he cites such predecessors as Plutarch, Nepos, the Champions of Christendom, and "John the Great . . . the Giant Killer." He goes so far as to claim that a good example "inspires our imitation in an *irresistible* manner" (italics mine). [16] But even the best of Fielding's characters transcend exemplary status quickly. The characters which Sheldon Sacks calls "fallible paragons" seem to me better considered as disappearing exemplars, for it is not their fallibility which distinguishes their peculiar function in Fielding. [17] Rather it is Fielding's rhythmic, rhetorical use of them. No sooner does Parson Adams distinguish himself as virtuous and worthy of emulation than he proves naive, or shortsighted, or gullible. He continues to shift back and forth; the pattern is repeated again and again. Fielding plays with the characters not only to show them fallible (a representational intention), but to illuminate for the reader the constant pattern he faces in life: men who seem exemplars are never entirely so, and emulation of a seeming exemplar is not the road to virtue and wisdom (a rhetorical intention). The weaknesses of Adams and Allworthy are more than humanizing traits; they are part of the rhetoric of drawing in the reader, then pulling the rug out from under him.

The second strategy is complementary; it might be called the comedy of false promises. Here expectation operates in the opposite direction. Joseph, for example, seems to promise at first to be anything but the instance of chastity which he ultimately proves to be. The fact that he is Pamela's brother, and looks to her for advice and power, suggests that Fielding is going to undercut Joseph's pretense, as he had earlier undercut Pamela's (*Shamela*, 1741). Such expectation provides tension for the reader each time Joseph is in a difficult spot; it provides much of the comedy in the scenes with Lady Booby, keeping the reader off balance, guessing ahead and misguessing. As an indirect didactic device it is extremely effective, for it draws the reader in by his own prurience, then keeps him at the author's mercy. It is an especially important device in the early chapters of *Joseph Andrews* and *Tom Jones*, as characters are being introduced and beginning their patterns of action. It relates closely to the third strategy, a refusal of the narrator to take a simple and direct stand.

This strategy seems to leave much to the reader, for the narrator is continually backing away from explicit evaluation or direction of any kind, substituting facetiousness or self-conscious notation of his scrupulous refusal to comment. But the narrator's retreat never signals Fielding's withdrawal of control; the events are still contrived to prove specific things and to comment on themselves. Still Fielding is instructing; his strategy is the homiletics of retreat. When there is commentary, it is usually ironic, but its degree of irony is measurable against the events and the description of them so that there is substantial certainty about what one is to think. Such a strategy involves, of course, some risk and a great deal of basic respect for the reader's intelligence and good will. But for the most part Fielding sticks to it throughout *Joseph Andrews* and *Tom Jones;* seldom does he comment straight or direct a verdict, and never is there sustained haranguing on a point already made clear by the action itself or by the dialectic between action and ironic commentary.

In *Amelia* it is as if Fielding had changed his mind about how reader psychology works. He largely abandons the illusion of the open end and the three strategies I have described. He does not exactly surrender to the exemplar strategy he had earlier attacked, but he allows Mrs. Bennett's "history" to warn Amelia, informing her of her own predicament much more straightforwardly than do the interpolated tales of *Joseph Andrews* and *Tom Jones*.[18] And Amelia herself, though not perfect, is far more an exemplar than any earlier protagonist; plainly Fielding regards her as an object of imitation in a way he had avoided for Joseph Andrews and Tom Jones. He similarly abandons the comedy of false promises, refusing to capitalize on the description of Amelia's peculiar nose[19] or on the enormous potential of introducing her as the "best of women"—something he might well have exploited in the manner of the Joseph introduction and still retired her as a model of chastity. The homiletics of retreat also largely disappears, as in the scene where Amelia catechizes her child; replacing it is frequent and lengthy evaluative summation. For me, at least, the betrayal of expectation is crucial, for such an ironic method does not seem reversible, even when an author turns to a new book and presumes to inject new assumptions. Morality in *Amelia* is no longer very amusing, and the reader is not to be trusted to figure things out for himself. This is no longer the method of the patient, bemused, benevolent teacher, nor of the less jovial, many-faced satirist; it is more like that of a humorless policeman.

Fielding seems either to have decided cynically, in despair, that no clever strategies would really work or to have finally accepted the brutal directness he had once rejected as simplistic and naive. The change in method seems to betray a radical shift in Fielding's view of human nature—from a sense of superficial perversity which goodness could outwit to an overwhelming sense of bad nature prevailing. Of course, one might argue the reverse, that Fielding now optimistically uses simple direct appeals because he no longer thinks it necessary to use the devious, sometimes ambiguous methods of irony. But it seems to me that the general darkness of *Amelia* and the tone of the addresses to the reader suggest less faith and hope in didactic possibility, not more; one wonders whom Fielding expects *Amelia* to reform. But whether Fielding's shift is toward optimism or pessimism, it is a radical, end-of-the-spectrum shift that comes to much the same thing, and the devices he uses are often the ones he pointedly satirized in *Pamela* and rejected from his own earlier work: the simplified use of exemplars, humorless portrayal of virtue in distress, simplified ethical judgments, straight didactic commentary, and dogmatic assertion of rigid evaluations.

The absence in *Amelia* of Fielding's characteristic didactic strategies helps to define their presence and uses in the earlier books. Similarly, *Amelia* clarifies some other Fielding interests and patterns that, while present in the earlier books, are not so prominent or clear there. For example, the concentration of *Amelia* on marriage rather than courtship clarifies Fielding's sexual ethic. And his shift from a male to a female main character raises into prominence his conception of the feminine role. The two matters are very nearly one.

The lessened tolerence for sexual transgression in *Amelia* is partly due to the simple difference of marital commitments. Fielding's harshness with Booth for the Miss Matthews affair derives not from horror at sexual violation per se, but from horror at a betrayal of Amelia. It may be true that in later life Fielding became obsessed with his own youthful indiscretions, [20] and such concern may have influenced the theme of *Amelia*, but the text does not indicate that Fielding had radically changed his mind since *Tom Jones*. Fielding could be charitable toward Tom's falls not because he had a laxer view in 1749 than in 1751, but because of the absence of the marriage bond; the moments that come closest to tragedy in *Tom Jones* involve the impingement of a world of responsibility on Tom's transgressive maturation. But Fielding is not forgiving about adultery; it cannot represent for him a fortunate fall, part of the process of growing up, and it has no place, except as threat, in the comic world of *Tom Jones*.

And Fielding cannot regard a woman's fall cheerfully, whether she is married or not. One reason for the striking power of the bedside incident with Joseph Atkinson is that Amelia is here shown to be human in a way usually reserved for Fielding's men. Fielding seems as unable as Richardson to tolerate the notion that a woman could be tainted and still survive. His heroines are all rigidly chaste, and not entirely, I think, because of their kinship to Charlotte Craddock. Only the minor characters—"bad" women, or old—can violate chastity with any impunity, and this because their humanness is not a serious issue. The most revealing case is the celebrated one of Molly Seagrim. Once Tom has seduced her (or she him), Fielding seems compelled to demonstrate almost immediately that she is already fallen—therefore not to be worried about. One wonders what would have been the effect on Tom had he gotten pregnant the girl he imagined Molly to be—tempting, fallible, but basically innocent and well-intentioned. And one wonders what would have happened to Fielding had he confronted that situation. Surely the comic world of *Tom Jones* would have been shattered; there is no room in it for a Sophia to fall, and for this reason the question of "what if" becomes an irrelevant one, ignoring the mode which Fielding had there chosen and for which his vision and talent had great affinity. Confronting even the possible fall of a good woman darkens the tone of *Amelia*; once Fielding decided to write mostly about a woman and not about a man, his sexual ethic virtually guaranteed a darker book than either *Joseph Andrews* or *Tom Jones*, and perhaps a wholly different mode. *Amelia*'s flirtation with romance on one side and tragedy on the other may well derive partly from the simple choice of centering the book on a woman.

The sentimentality of *Amelia* also tells us something we perhaps had just as soon not know. It seems to me that proximity to sentimentality is always there in the earlier books, that we are continually just one sentence away from tears. But Fielding's sustenance of a comic world keeps sentimentality, as well as disaster, at bay by his refusal to write that one sentence, or by his writing one which retreats or looks another way. I do not wish to denigrate the deftness of this strategy; far from it, for it is brilliantly employed to suggest the fragile tenacity of the comic world of feeling under control. But it does mean that excessive sentiment is ever close in Fielding, that he is attracted to it at the same time that he is repelled by it, so that irony for him is more defense than discovery. One is tempted to think that Richardson offended him so dramatically because of the vigorous appeal of the temptations which he thought Richardson had succumbed to.

One final matter that *Amelia* clarifies is the degree of potential rigidity present in Fielding from the start. The didactic strategies that I have discussed are, in every instance, rhetorical devices introduced to bring the reader to the author's point of view. Ultimately *Joseph Andrews* and *Tom Jones* are not open-minded. If Fielding seems to draw on the romance of the open road for didactic strategies, as well as narrative ones, it is a trick (and a very effective one) to draw the reader in and persuade him without letting him raise defenses. The inn metaphor in *Tom Jones* makes Fielding's position clear. The reader may, of course, refuse the whole journey—meals, lodging, coach, and all—but the vehicle and the places belong to Fielding, and the reader is not really free, once he decides to dine in a particular place, to eat anything he likes, for the menu is a limited one, restricted to human nature dressed in the way that Fielding chooses to dress it. The narrator talks permissively, but the creator has control. When, in *Amelia*, the narrative voice matches the prescribing creator in rigid control, the world of Fielding's art seems dogmatic, contrived, and dull.

The history of literary history suggests that new interpretations inflate evaluations and that one age often manages to overvalue a certain writer only in order to let the next age—in its insistent revolution of taste—undervalue him. Our own specialized age offers particular problems for the next age. Perspective is not our major characteristic; we tend either to explicate and imply value, often too high, or to evaluate subjectively, pronouncing verdicts that are testaments to our taste but which are not earned by sufficient attention to intention, mode, or canon.

In slaying certain dragons, modern criticism often seems to defoliate the forests, leaving them not only safer, but also without life or interest. Any essay that goes beyond explication participates in that risk, and I want to emphasize that my interest here is not to demean Fielding's talent but to provide some notes toward defining his reach. His reputation as England's foremost writer at mid-century—of prose or poetry—is well deserved. His accomplishments in *Joseph Andrews* and *Tom Jones* guarantee his place, and they speak for themselves, especially since critics like Martin Battestin[21] have dispelled some of the muting forces upon them. Fielding's voice there was perfectly suited to his medium. He could leisurely exploit the potential of playful manipulation in a self-consciously factitious world, where there could be no irredeemable crises and where his reluctance to confront certain issues was an asset to maintaining the tenuous comic order—an order which was perhaps to him as well as to us a contrived refuge from the chaos of reality. I think that in the long run we will evaluate even his supreme accomplishments more highly and more justly if we recognize the specific nature of his talents, admit the restricted directions of his power, and allow ourselves to see him fallible and potentially tragic when he journeyed beyond the borders of the comic world, whose order and fragility he knew so well.

Notes

1. Among the foremost recent critics are Martin Battestin, John Preston, Sheridan Baker, Robert Alter, Glenn W. Hatfield, William B. Coley, Sheldon Sacks, Homer Goldberg, Henry Knight Miller, and Leo Braudy.   2. Michael Irwin, *Henry Fielding: The Tentative Realist* (Oxford, 1967) attempts such a broader evaluation, and he asks many of the right questions. But often the answers seem easy and unearned, and the anxiety to cope with recent Fielding enthusiasms results in judgments that seem carping and simply negative.   3. *The Novels of Fielding* (London, 1925), pp. 206ff.   4. *Amelia*, Everyman edition (New York, 1962), II, 251–252. Subsequent citations to this edition are in the text.   5. See Sheridan Baker, "Henry Fielding's Comic Romances," *PMASAL*, XL (1960), 411–419.   6. Robert South, *Sermons Preached upon Several Occasions* (1842), III, 461.   7. My discussion takes its terms from Barbara K. Lewalski's account of the "triple equation" ("Theme and Action in *Paradise Regained*," *Milton's Epic Poetry*, ed. C. A. Patrides, Baltimore, 1967, pp. 322–347).   8. Both New Testament accounts agree in placing the temptation of carnal appetite first, though they differ on the order of the other two temptations, Luke placing avarice/ambition second and Matthew placing it third.   9. See "Fielding's *Amelia*: An Interpretation," *ELH*, III (1936), 2.

10. Alter defends *Amelia* as "an embryonic novel of social protest" (*Fielding and the Nature of the Novel*, Cambridge, Mass., 1968, pp. 141ff.), and Digeon as a modern psychological novel (p. 224); Sherburn suggests *Amelia*'s connection to the *Aeneid* (pp. 3–4), and Lyall H. Powers and Maurice Johnson detail the parallels ("The Influence of the *Aeneid* on Fielding's *Amelia*," *MLN*, LXXI, 1956, 330–336; *Fielding's Art of Fiction*, Philadelphia, 1961, pp. 139–156). Alter's account of *Amelia*, though it leans rather too heavily on anticipations of later fiction and tacitly places a high premium on modernity per se, is an excellent one, the best until C. J. Rawson's brilliant essay, "Nature's Dance of Death," *ECS*, III (1970), 307–338; 491–522.   11. Appearing as Amelia's "father" before the "Court of Censorial Inquiry," Fielding seems deeply hurt by the charge: "I do not think my Child is entirely free from faults. I know nothing human that is so; but surely she doth not deserve the Rancour with which she hath been treated by the public. However, it is not my Intention, at present, to make any Defence; but shall submit to a Compromise, which hath been always allowed in this Court in all Prosecutions for Dulness. I do, therefore, solemnly declare to you, Mr. Censor, that I will trouble the World no more with any Children of mine by the same Muse" (*Covent-Garden Journal*, no. 8, 28 Jan. 1752).   12. Digeon, p. 221.   13. The chapter is designated 1* in the Everyman edition.   14. I find Eleanor Hutchens's definition of irony too polar: "the

sport of bringing about a conclusion by indicating its opposite" (*Irony in Tom Jones*, University, Ala., 1965, p. 13).   15. See Hatfield, *Henry Fielding and the Language of Irony* (Chicago, 1968), pp. 215–217.   16. In *The Champion* for 10 June 1740, Fielding argues that examples are far more powerful than precepts, but the essay is often misapplied. Fielding's point there is that of the Augustan satirist: he is talking about negative examples and the power of evitation.   17. See *Fielding and the Shape of Belief* (Berkeley, 1964), pp. 110ff.   18. For my assumptions about how Fielding's kind of interpolated tale works, see "Response as Reformation: *Tristram Shandy* and the Art of Interruption," *Novel: A Forum on Fiction*, IV (1970), 132–146.   19. The nose has, of course, a biographical basis in Charlotte Craddock, but that need not prevent Fielding from playing with its comic possibilities of expectation as he had done with Sophia's beauty (also based on Charlotte Craddock) when he first introduced her in *Tom Jones*. One can readily think of ways the earlier Fielding might have toyed with Amelia's "nose . . . beat all to pieces" (1, 55); and one may wonder whether Sterne noticed the unexploited possibility.

20. See, e.g., Wilbur L. Cross, *The History of Henry Fielding* (New Haven, 1918), II, 328–335; and Digeon, p. 208.   21. Even more than his seminal *The Moral Basis of Fielding's Art* (Middletown, Conn., 1959), I am thinking of such essays as "*Tom Jones* and 'His Egyptian Majesty,' Fielding's Parable of Government," *PMLA*, LXXXII (1967), 68–77, and "Fielding's Definition of Wisdom: Some Functions of Ambiguity and Emblem in *Tom Jones*," *ELH*, XXXV (1968), 188–217.

UNITY IN EIGHTEENTH-CENTURY EPISODIC NOVELS

H. K. Russell

IN his preface to *The Adventures of David Simple*, Fielding distinguishes between the *Iliad*, in which the action *"is entire and uniform,"* and the *Odyssey*, which *"is rather a Series of Actions, all tending to produce one great End."* *Don Quixote* has this latter construction, and so has Sarah Fielding's novel, *"where the Fable consists of a Series of separate Adventures detached from, and independent on each other, yet all tending to one great End; so that those who should object want of Unity of Action here, may, if they please, or if they dare, fly back with their Objection, in the Face even of the* Odyssey *itself."* Though the adventures are separate and independent, *"every Episode bears a manifest Impression of the principal Design, and chiefly turns on the Perfection or Imperfection of Friendship."* [1]

Despite Fielding's argument for his sister's book, we do not think of *Don Quixote* or *David Simple* as having the unity of action of the *Odyssey*. It is true that Odysseus is a wanderer who undergoes many hardships and finally reaches his home; but the story of his adventures begins in medias res. This organization differs from Cervantes's and Sarah Fielding's and from the characteristic time order in narratives of episodic adventures.

The Adventures of David Simple is described in histories of the novel as episodic (by Cross, Baker, and Stevenson, for example; and by Malcolm Kelsall in his recent edition of the novel). Relying on Fielding's defense of the book, we can say that in this kind of novel each episode is separately developed but is appropriate to the career of the protagonist on his way toward a final, stable situation and contributes to a statement about human conduct.

Our handbooks and dictionaries of critical terms emphasize the separateness, the independence, of the episodes, the lack of consequential relationship among them. A defense of the episodic novel is rare; we can be grateful to Richard M. Eastman for saying, "Loose or episodic plotting, though once judged to betray primitive artistry, can be put to its own sophisticated uses. . . . Loose plotting encourages the reader to focus on important non-plot materials which may offer illustration, commentary, or psychological preparation."[2]

My purpose here is to follow up Fielding's claim and see what kinds of unity can be found in some eighteenth-century episodic novels. The term "plot" cannot properly be used for the structure of an episodic novel. The concept of plot can, however, give us an idea of the sort of unity an episodic novel does not have but may approximate in its own fashion.

Every extended narrative is episodic in the sense that it is made up of episodes. These episodes are presented in a time order which may be chronological or not, and which is established by the point of entrance. With a plot this point is likely to be late, not only for immediate interest, but for compression and emphasis on the consequential relationship among the episodes. With an episodic structure the point of entrance is early, signaling to the reader that his interest will develop gradually, that the narrative will be full rather than compressed, and that the emphasis in organization will be sequential rather than consequential. There is a difference in attitude toward the story and the storyteller, and a difference in attitude toward life and letters. A plot does evoke a more alert and intelligent response. But we need not underrate a narrative organization which encourages a slowly developed concern and a readiness to follow the contingencies of experience.

We are likely to assume that because the plotted novel is artfully constructed the episodic is not. With a plot there is usually an early event which defines the issue that will be developed into the crisis and eventually be resolved with the culminating event. When Clarissa leaves home with Lovelace the situation she must face is defined; the crucial violation confirms her plight, and her death is the culminating event in this chain of cause and effect. Fielding has designed Tom Jones's career so that it hinges on his banishment, on the conjunction of Tom, Mrs. Waters, and Sophia at Upton, and on the discovery of his parentage. In a comic plot the discovery and reversal need to be delayed; after these events there is little more to be done. For tragedy and pathos the crisis is the appropriate place: with the violation Clarissa discovers fully the villainy of Lovelace. In Walpole's Gothic tragicomedy, *The Castle of Otranto*, discoveries are appropriately placed at both the crisis and the culmination. Manfred's attack on Isabella ("Heaven nor hell shall impede my designs") obviously announces his plan; the discovery that Jerome is Theodore's father and Frederic the father of Isabella precipitates the crisis and the reversal of Manfred's designs; the murder of Matilda and the discovery that Theodore is the rightful heir of Otranto make the culmination.

In episodic novels we often find, parallel to these emphatic occasions in plots, events which define the situation of the characters and the kind of response they will meet in the world, act as a confirmation of their predicament or the direction their careers are taking, and provide a culminating discovery and reversal. Moll Flanders at Colchester, betrayed by *"that Cheat call'd,* LOVE," learns that security is valued above affection. Her theft of the bundle in Leadenhall Street has almost the weight of a conventional crisis. Pressed by fear of destitution, she turns from that half of her career in which human relationships and affection have had a part and becomes increasingly obsessed by things. The lesson she has learned earlier is confirmed and she turns toward the culmination of her business as thief and whore—Newgate and hanging. Defoe provides in transportation to the New World a second culmination, appropriate for her life as a woman whose capacity for affection has been almost destroyed by a predatory society. The discovery of her Lancashire husband lifts her "Lethargy of Soul"; she "griev'd Day and Night for him" and "was perfectly chang'd, and become another Body."[3]

Smollett sets up a pattern for Roderick Random's career when Random arrives in London, where, Strap says, the devil has set up his throne. A friendly, "very decent sort of a man" turns out to be a crook; Random loses his money but gets affection and help from Strap (chaps. 14–15). The novel is loosely constructed, yet there is a kind of turn and implication of the outcome: between the brutal navy and army episodes, Smollett introduces Narcissa, who is beautiful, sincere, and affectionate (39–41). Heretofore Random's adventures have been "low"; after Strap rescues him from the army he invades "society," eventually discovers his father,[4] and marries Narcissa (66–68). There are sixty-nine chapters in the novel. I have listed the chapter numbers so as to indicate where these structural events fall in the novel as a whole. Their placing corresponds to the location of the events they parallel in plotted novels: the defining event about one-fourth or one-third from the beginning; the crisis somewhat past the middle; the culminating event in the last chapters.

David Simple's disillusionment with Miss Johnson (Bk. I, chap. 6) establishes the danger from selfish and deceptive people in his search for true friendship in a wife. With his belief that in Camilla he has found what he seeks (Bk. III, chap. 1), he turns toward the solution of his problem; his jealousy of Lord ———(Bk. IV, chap. 6) reveals the depth of his attachment to Camilla, and their marriage follows. (There are four books in the novel; the sequel, Books V–VII, published nine years later, is not properly a part of the structure of the novel as we are examining it.)

Tristram Shandy, an unfinished antiplot novel, is a special case. Yet certain conspicuous events make a fairly satisfactory structure. Tristram's birth and his crushed nose (Bk. III, chap. 23) define his career of misadventures; the accident of the window sash (Bk. V, chap. 17) confirms the course of insults to his manhood that Tristram is subject to; in volume 9 Uncle Toby, in his affair with Mrs. Wadman, and the Shandy bull complete this program of humiliation that we, in one way or another, are liable to between our expectations and our performance in this scurvy world.[5]

These episodic novels do not, naturally, show the precise consequential relationships of a plot. The key events are not so thoroughly prepared for, but when they appear they mark stages in the characters' careers and guide the reader's expectations. Episodes from one stage cannot sensibly be transferred to another; it is not accurate to say that the parts of an episodic novel can be "shuffled" and that the only principle of order is chronology.

The loose organization appears more clearly in the transition from one episode to the next than in the order of the episodes in the story. In a consequentially ordered novel each episode (especially those enclosing the defining event, crisis, and culminating event) narrows the options available to the characters. In episodic novels, on the other hand, the characters are free, not from circumstances but from specific choices. Thus each episode is likely to close with its own culminating event. The characters then face a new situation for which they must improvise appropriate conduct.[6] This sort of structure is inevitable if the novelist is to give the impression of a full representation of life including the varied types of men and social conditions he has chosen for his fictional world.

In discussing *David Simple* Gordon Hall Gerould remarks that "Miss Fielding's sound but uninspired work is one indication the more that the representation of individual personalities had become the dominant theme of fiction in the mid-eighteenth century."[7] An episodic novel provides a natural medium for this representation of personality, and the sustained presence of an individual throughout the narrative is a unifying influence. This character is, for Smollett, the "one particular personage, whose fate must interest the reader, and whose importance must . . . unite the whole concatenation of scenes and adventures."[8] This kind of unity is, it must be admitted, fairly primitive. Nevertheless, when tales about clever foxes are put together as episodes in the adventures of Reynard, a not inconsiderable step has been taken in the progress of prose fiction. A significant arrangement of episodes then becomes possible, paralleling to some extent the structure of a plot, as we have noted. The impression of unity can be strengthened when the protagonist tells his own story: the reader has the unmediated presence of a central character to arouse and sustain his concern.

The customary, though by no means invariable, point of view in episodic fiction is the autobiographical. (Characters tell their own story in epistolary fiction, but the social position of the correspondents limits a broad portrayal of the world, and the need for a manageable time span leads to the close-knit structure of a plot.) *The Life of Lazarillo de Tormes* became a model for the picaresque novel and demonstrated the appropriateness of a protagonist-narrator and an episodic structure for this kind of novel so effectively that the term "picaresque" has been inaccurately used as equivalent to the inclusive term "episodic."[9] The confusion is understandable. Episodic novels in general have picked up much in purpose and technique from their subkind. The novelist has seen a harsh world; men and the institutions they have made for their protection are unjust and hypocritical; a gulf separates poverty and privilege. He wants to entertain, but he also wants his readers to look at life from an unaccustomed angle.

Satire is traditionally a feature of picaresque fiction and is common in episodic novels. A sustained satiric tone can be a unifying force. For this effect an omniscient point of view is more practicable than an autobiographical. Stylistic irony and satiric "characters" come more appropriately from a professional writer than an adventurer, though he may be composing his narrative in the leisure of retirement. It is probable that if the novelist who sits down to write an episodic story has even some modest "literary" schemes in his inkwell, he will choose the omniscient position.[10]

The usual first-person episodic novel shows satiric touches, of course, but we often find overt comments on the social and moral situation. Roderick Random is amazed at the attitude of a soldier in the French army—"the absurdity of a rational being, who thinks himself highly honoured in being permitted to encounter abject poverty, oppression, famine, disease, mutilation, and evident death, merely to gratify the vicious ambition of a prince, by whom his sufferings were disregarded, and his name utterly unknown." Roxana tells her readers,

> I say, I cou'd not but reflect upon the Brutallity and blindness of Mankind; that because Nature had given me a good Skin, and some agreeable Features, should suffer that Beauty to be such a Bait to Appetite, as to do such sordid, unaccountable things, to obtain the Possession of it.
>
> It is for this Reason, that I have so largely set down the Particulars of the Caresses I was treated with by the Jeweller, and also by this Prince; not to make the Story an Incentive to the Vice, which I am now such a sorrowful Penitent for being guilty of, *God forbid any shou'd make so vile a Use of so good a Design*, but to draw the just Picture of a Man enslav'd to the Rage of his vicious Appetite; how he defaces the Image of God in his Soul; dethrones his Reason; causes Conscience to abdicate the Possession, and exalts Sence into the vacant Throne; how he deposes the Man, and exalts the Brute.[11]

Such moralizing passages seem obtrusive and even tiresome. Perhaps we have been too much disturbed by the didactic in eighteenth-century literature, especially in the episodic novel. These people read instructive essays with satisfaction; they seem to have attended divine service oftener than we do; their schools inculcated religion and morality; their poetry admonished as well as pleased. It is unlikely that realistic, particularized prose fiction offended readers by warning against exploiters, criminals, hypocrites, seducers, bribed justices, ill-considered marriages, the waters at Bath, irreligion, and failure of the sympathetic imagination. The detective novel and Ann Landers had not yet been invented.

A more discriminating objection to these didactic passages arises from the traditional first-person point of view in episodic fiction. In the midst of his career, the narrator is presumably more concerned with his adventures than with instruction of the public.[12] The omniscient novelist's position as observer and reporter can make these comments more palatable. But the first-person narrator is writing from the perspective of his final situation; he has made the journey and, in retrospect, might well judge his own and others' conduct. He has, as Alexander A. Parker says, two voices.[13] He recounts his experiences with the immediacy that good storytelling requires; he is also looking back with full knowledge.

Our acceptance of these expressions of the narrator's opinions is influenced by our attitude toward him. At first glance, it would seem that with omniscience the novelist has more freedom to guide the reader's responses than he does if he turns his story over to a character. R. S. Crane has shown how skilfully Fielding in *Tom Jones* managed the "interplay" of the reader's "desires and expectations sequentially in relation to the incidents by which it is produced." When the novelist directs our "emotionalized expectations"[14] in accord with this sort of affective structure, we may well find ourselves as much interested in him as in his personages. This attraction is all right: one of the pleasures of reading is watching the animation and ingenuity of the author.

But an episodic novel—often titled a "history"—is, though fiction, a report on life in the real world. The affective progression here not so much guides the reader's "emotionalized expectations" as leads to acceptance of the basic assumption that the fictional world and the real world are identical. If the novelist is to be persuasive he needs to blur the line between the actual world and his fictional world. An omniscient account lacks the authority rhetorically of a report by a person presumably in our real world.[15]

The reader's acceptance of the autobiographical protagonist sustains the affective progression. Our attachment to him can be heightened if he is introduced in childhood, when he is defenseless and innocent—an innocence that leads to misjudgments of the world. Irony arises naturally from the contrast between his assumptions about life and what he finds. Didactic commentary is not needed: the lost possibilities of reason and benevolence are grounded in the events.[16] Moll Flanders's childish misjudgment of what makes a gentlewoman goes with her through life and gives Defoe his chance for the ironic suggestion that she may indeed be right. Colonel Jack as a boy thinks picking pockets is a trade to which he is apprenticed. Random is usually too irascible to be the innocent: Smollett gives Strap and often Bowling this function. Sarah Fielding, who understood this matter, chose for her protagonist David Simple, a boy "who, as he was too young to have gained much Experience, and never had any ill Designs on others, never thought of their having any upon him." Henry, in *The Fool of Quality*, "will be accounted a mere idiot . . . without some of the fashionable foibles and vices of the age."[17]

The third-person point of view used by Sarah Fielding is likely to be needed when the protagonist's innocence of the world takes the form of idealism. The opinions of other characters and the author's comments can point up the contrast between the idealist with his blind spots and the practical people who get in his way. *Don Quixote* is exemplary for this handling of point of view, its influence appearing not only in books like *The Spiritual Quixote* and *Sir Launcelot Greaves*, but in the later apprenticeship novels like *Wilhelm Meister's Apprenticeship*, *Pendennis*, and *Of Human Bondage*, whose episodes show the often quixotic young man learning by trial and error the nature of the world and his proper place in it.

A loosely inclusive unity for episodic narratives is available in the motif of the exposed infant (Daphnis and Chloe are more appropriate instances here than Oedipus). This motif is commonplace in picaresque fiction and, with modifications, provides situations neatly suited to the construction of episodic novels. The protagonist is on his own in the world, open to the sequence of adventures that the novelist needs to represent the variety of life; and, when we are ready for the culminating event, the discovery of a parent or an inheritance can give security in the final situation. Because of the popularity of this motif or of variations on it, the exposed condition of the protagonist leads the reader to anticipate the culminating discovery; the two circumstances make an enveloping action for the episodes. The regaining of a home after many hardships by Odysseus or Huon of Bordeaux or Tom Jones or David Simple or Roderick Random or Henry Earl of Moreland, the Fool of Quality, makes a completed cycle and suggests, at a respectful distance, that the hero of an episodic novel may in his fashion touch the chord which has been struck by the hero with a thousand faces.[18]

Next to the unity that the protagonist gives to episodic fiction, thematic unity is perhaps the most evident. As we have noted, Fielding claimed for *David Simple* that "*every Episode bears a manifest Impression of the principal Design, and chiefly turns on the Perfection or Imperfection of Friendship.*" In a novel with a plot, the theme is demonstrated by the consequentially related events. This organization would be Kenneth Burke's "syllogistic progression." His "repetitive form" includes the episodic novel: it is "the consistent maintaining of a principle under new guises. It is restatement of the same thing in different ways. . . . Repetitive form, the restatement of a theme by new details, is basic to any work of art, or to any other kind of orientation, for that matter. It is our only method of 'talking on the subject.' " [19]

Smollett wanted to write a novel and to talk on the subject of "the sordid and vicious disposition of the world." He devised episodes of selfish relatives, brutal school teachers, hypocrites, cheats, army, navy, low life, high life. To complete the picture he included episodes about an unfortunate woman, Miss Williams, and an abused poet, Melopoyn. Defoe wanted to show the economic pressures on the unsheltered ("the wise Man's Prayer, *Give me not Poverty least I Steal*") and the excitement and hazards of criminal life, and to show how easily one leads to the other. Tristram tells us that we can best live with the "pitiful misadventures" that come to us in "this scurvy and disasterous world" by benevolence and by learning what we are and accepting the difference between what we comically are and what we think we prodigiously are. The mysterious narrator of *The Man of Feeling* has "observed one ingredient, somewhat necessary in a man's composition towards happiness, which people of feeling would do well to learn; a certain respect for the follies of mankind." The Man of Feeling himself is not free of folly; Harley has faith in his skill in physiognomy, and is cheated by a sharper. But injustice is the cause of most of the suffering he witnesses and tries to relieve. The narrator concludes, as he visits Harley's grave: "every nobler feeling rises within me! every beat of my heart awakens a virtue!—but 'twill make you hate the world—No: there is such an air of gentleness around, that I can hate nothing; but, as to the world—I pity the men of it." The theme of man's folly, the examples of his injustice and suffering, and the narrator's compassion give this sentimental novel a dignity that its extravagance sometimes obscures.

The interpolated narratives in episodic novels usually reinforce the theme, as the histories of Miss Williams and Melopoyn do in *Roderick Random*. The story of Le Fever exemplifies Uncle Toby's philanthropy. The histories of Cynthia, Camilla, and Isabelle contribute to the sequence of events and elaborate the subject of friendship and, more particularly, the hardships caused by selfish and wilful relatives: the tyranny of a father, the machinations of a wicked stepmother, and the violence of illicit passion.[20]

In an extended narrative, thematic unity can be supported by appropriate imagery. The most effective images are those which make a natural part of the events, like Moby-Dick or James's golden bowl or Caddy Compson's muddy drawers. But we hardly expect this artful device in realistic episodic novels; such images, because they would be in the story anyway as part of the circumstantial representation, are difficult to certify. If attention is focused on an image and if it recurs with cumulative significance, we can claim for it the effect if not the full force of a literary symbol. The importance of material objects in Moll Flanders's life has perhaps been overstressed; before she turns thief she is so emotionally attached to Jemmy that she can communicate with him telepathically, and she is genuinely fond of her banker husband. But when she takes a gold watch from a lady's side she becomes, as she says, "a compleat Thief, harden'd." And gold watches appropriately signify both her pride in professional skill, and money and gentility. She lifts a watch from the baronet who picks her up at Bartholomew Fair. Besides other instances a gold watch finally implies her equivocal repentance and a touch of humor Moll has developed in her old age now that she is "easy." The "gentlewoman" gives one to her son in Virginia—"I desir'd he would now and then kiss it for my sake; *I did not indeed tell him* that I had stole it from a Gentlewomans side, at a Meeting-House in *London*, that's by the way."[21]

Roxana's Moorish costume recurs as an impressive image. It is not her most important equipment as a courtesan, but it carries the full significance of her career. Wearing it, she charms her guests at her ball; her dance gets her the name Roxana. Her daughter's description of the costume almost discovers her past and leads to Amy's presumed murder of the girl. Roxana's narrative ends with "a dreadful Course of Calamities . . . the Blast of Heaven seem'd to follow the Injury done the poor Girl . . . and I was brought so low again, that my Repentance seem'd to be the only Consequence of my Misery, as my Misery was of my Crime."[22]

In *Roderick Random*, in addition to Smollett's characteristic animal and physiological imagery,[23] the recurrent term "naked" becomes an epithet-image for the victims of exploitation and injustice. Miss Williams has seen prostitutes, "naked wretches reduced to rags and filth," and she herself has been "turned out helpless and naked into the wide world." In the Marshalsea, Random finds among "a number of naked miserable wretches" the poet Melopoyn, who has been cast "out into the streets naked, friendless, and forlorn."

There are other devices which can help to unify episodic narratives. The writer may forecast an action or situation and thus give an impression of unity, an implication that he has his story under control. These anticipatory devices may be obvious and rather heavy-handed. Roderick Random's mother dreams of giving birth to a tennis ball which the devil bats violently away and which returns and grows into a flourishing tree ("How truly this was foretold, will appear in the sequel"). Roxana's statement about Amy—"yet it was but a bad Coin that she was paid in at last, as will appear in its Place"—is not much more satisfactory. Defoe can prefigure skilfully, however, as he does when young Moll chooses for her model the sort of gentlewoman she later becomes. In Moore's *Zeluco*, the villain-protagonist as a child crushes his pet sparrow in his hand. One of his last criminal acts is the strangling of his own baby; and the author makes him recall the sparrow.

The episodic novel was well suited to the temper and attitudes of the eighteenth century. Of the authors said to have been the "early masters," the men who achieved the "rise" of the novel in this century, Defoe, Smollett, and Sterne wrote episodic fiction, and Fielding included episodic sequences in his plotted novels. They and their readers were concerned for the individual as he seeks a tenable place in society; they recognized the insecurity, the contrast between poverty and wealth, the violence of everyday life.[24] They found in the pace and change of scene in episodic fiction a suitable expression of their "quest . . . for knowledge of actual men and manners, or for knowledge of permanent, common human nature"—a quest which made "the travel book . . . one of the most vigorous of the contemporary kinds" and which, as Paul Fussell adds, "sustained the vogue of the picaresque in the novel."[25]

Readers accepted representation[26] as the appropriate expression of these attitudes in prose fiction, and the shape of the episodic novel was ready in such books as *Lazarillo*, *Guzmán*, *Don Quixote*, *The English Rogue* (ramshackle as it was), and criminal biographies, as well as in the model of life itself. There are badly managed episodic structures just as there are badly managed plots. But a sequential arrangement of events can be unified by legitimate artistic means at the same time that it stays close to the divagations of life.

The eighteenth-century episodic novel offers the most appropriate vehicle for the representation of experience, not obviously manipulated for literary effects, conforming to the uncertainties of life but including the probable, though not necessary, outcome of right and wrong conduct, taking an individual from ignorance to knowledge or to a perspective from which he can assess the pains and minor triumphs of staying alive. It talks about justice and injustice, benevolence and self-love, idealism and policy. Whether as a curate's gun-wadding or the relic of an eccentric tenant or wrappers from a chandler's shop, the episodic novel has a way of getting into the real world to tell us what it is like, to amuse and instruct, and to work in us fear and pity for man's lot.

Notes

1. Quotations from *The Adventures of David Simple* are from Malcolm Kelsall's edition (London, 1969).   2. *A Guide to the Novel* (San Francisco, 1965), p. 15.   3. Quotations from *Moll Flanders* are from J. Paul Hunter's edition (New York, 1970). Defoe usually places a break in his characters' careers at the point where a crisis normally occurs. Captain Singleton, having completed his African journey, comments that he thus ends his first harvest of wild oats and moves on to piracy. Colonel Jack in Virginia decides that he has not yet attained the life of a gentleman and returns to England.   4. Smollett prepared for such a "recognition scene, a plot device of venerable antiquity," in four of his five novels. See Albrecht B. Strauss, "On Smollett's Language: A Paragraph in *Ferdinand Count Fathom*," in *Style in Prose Fiction: English Institute Essays 1958*, ed. Harold C. Martin (New York, 1959), p. 27.   5. Wayne C. Booth, in *The Rhetoric of Fiction* (Chicago, 1961), p. 231, says, "We have, in fact, only two simple story threads: Tristram's conception, birth, naming, circumcision, and breeching, and uncle Toby's courtship of the Widow Wadman." The structure can be unified, I think, if we take both threads as representations of man's predicament.

Other episodic novels, like those discussed above, parallel the events of a plot. Smollett, in *Sir Launcelot Greaves*, motivates and unifies the quixotic adventures of his hero by means of the love affair with Aurelia Darnel, whose uncle opposes the alliance. Greaves rescues Miss Darnel from run-away horses and wounds her uncle in a duel (chap. 6). The lovers are separated but reunited when Sir Launcelot restores a lady's pocketbook and discovers the lady to be Aurelia (chap. 15)—thereafter, his chivalric delusions abate; he and Aurelia are rescued by his friends from a private madhouse (chap. 24) and their union follows. Peregrine Pickle is rude to Emilia (in the seventy-second of 114 chapters) after his stay in France; thus he turns toward the violent attempt he later makes on her virtue. The author of *The Spiritual Quixote* admits that he has "transgressed . . . the strict rules of epopoea." But he develops a turning point in the career of Geoffry Wildgoose at the meeting with Whitfield (Bk. VII of twelve books); after close association with the Methodist leader his "religious phrensy" declines.   6. See, for example, the comment on *Roderick Random* by Rufus Putney in "The Plan of *Peregrine Pickle*," *PMLA*, LX (1945), 1060.   7. *The Patterns of English and American Fiction: A History* (Boston, 1942), p. 100. And Ian Watt, *The Rise of the Novel: Studies in Defoe, Richardson and Fielding* (Berkeley, 1957), pp. 13, 18.   8. Review of *The Peregrinations of Jeremiah Grant, Esq.: The West-Indian*, *Critical Review*, XV (January 1763), 13.   9. Robert B. Heilman cautions against this inaccuracy. See "Variations on Picaresque (*Felix Krull*)," *Sewanee Review*, LXVI (1958), 552. The term "picaresque" itself is in litigation. *Lazarillo*, *Moll Flanders*, *Gil Blas*, and *Roderick Random* have been called picaresque and not picaresque, depending upon the critic and his thesis. And see W. M. Frohock, "The Idea of the Picaresque," *Yearbook of Comparative and General Literature*, no. 16 (1967), pp. 43–52.

    10. Sarah Fielding, I think, is an instance. Smollett could not easily have worked in the sensational, sentimentalized separation and reunion of Renaldo and Monimia in *Ferdinand Count Fathom* with the protagonist as narrator. Ronald Paulson sees as the reason for Smollett's change to omniscience for *Peregrine Pickle* and *Ferdinand Count Fathom* the need to control his protagonist and to provide "a court of appeal above and beyond" the character who is both villain and satirist (*Satire and the Novel in Eighteenth-Century England*, New Haven, 1967, pp. 181, 208). *Zeluco*, by John Moore, is an example of this need for a distanced narrator; the chief character is an unmitigated scoundrel.   11. Quotations from *Roxana: The Fortunate Mistress* are from Jane Jack's edition (London, 1964).   12. The problem is at least as old as *Guzmán de Alfarache*. See Alexander A. Parker, *Literature and the Delinquent: The Picaresque Novel in Spain and Europe, 1599–1753* (Edinburgh, 1967), pp. 23, 33–37.   13. Ibid., p. 36. Bertil Romberg uses the terms "distant perspective" and "near perspective" or, following Leo Spitzer, "narrating 'I'" and "experiencing 'I'" (*Studies in the Narrative Technique of the First-Person Novel*, Stockholm, 1962, p. 95).   14. "The Concept of Plot and the Plot of *Tom Jones*," in *Critics and Criticism: Ancient and Modern*, ed. R. S. Crane (Chicago, 1952), pp. 622, 631.   15. Fielding, though his novels are only incidentally episodic, knew what he was doing when he put the novelist into the novel, getting a copy of a deposition, fearing to offend Sophia's modesty, tracing Mrs. Waters's whereabouts. David Goldknopf reminds us of the implications of the first-person point of view in a remark I wish I could have thought of: "Someone *inside* the novel is talking to someone *outside* the novel. This strikes me as a remarkable, almost hair-raising phenomenon." See "The Confessional Increment: A New Look at the I–Narrator," *Journal of Aesthetics and Art Criticism*, XXVIII (1969), 17.   16. This irony is the effect that Henry and Sarah Fielding and some of their contemporaries found beyond the satiric reading of *Don Quixote*, as Stuart M. Tave has shown in *The Amiable Humorist: A Study in the Comic Theory and Criticism of the Eighteenth and Early Nineteenth Centuries* (Chicago, 1960), pp. 142–145.   17. A

powerful use of the "simple" character, the traditional "wise fool," for ironic criticism of society in the episodic novel distinguishes the seventeenth-century German *Simplicissimus*: "Yet in spite of all, that pure simplicity (in comparison with other men's ways) hath ever clung to me: and therefore did the hermit ... ever call me Simplicissimus," trans. A. T. S. Goodrick (London, 1912). Huck Finn has some of this innocence, shrewd as he is.   18. Joseph Campbell, *The Hero with a Thousand Faces*, Bollingen Series XVII (New York, 1949), pp. 245–246 and passim. I am suggesting merely that, transposed to an everyday level, the episodes of the monomyth may evoke our response to this archetypal experience: the hero's "setting forth," "brother-battle," "dragonbattle," "tests," "helpers," "recognition by the father-creator," and "return" having proved himself against "the powers."   19. *Counter-Statement* (1931; rpt. Chicago, 1957), pp. 124–125.

20. The stories in *Chrysal; or, The Adventures of a Guinea* and *History of Pompey the Little; or, The Life and Adventures of a Lap-Dog* are not interpolated narratives because the sequence of events is merely a frame to justify putting them in one cover. These books are not properly episodic novels.   21. The significance of Moll's watches can be pushed further. Terence Martin, in "The Unity of *Moll Flanders*," *MLQ*, XXII (1961), 117, suggests that she steals watches "to steal back time and to capture the symbolic essence of the business-oriented, clockwork world around her."   22. *Roxana* is generally episodic, but next to *Robinson Crusoe* among Defoe's novels it comes closest to a consequential structure. The defining event, Roxana's first husband's desertion, and the crisis, the question of giving up her liberty by marrying the wealthy merchant, clearly carry the theme of women's subordination in marriage. For this theme, see Jane Jack's introduction to her edition of *Roxana* (London, 1964), p. ix.   23. Strauss, pp. 38–43.   24. M. Dorothy George, *London Life in the Eighteenth Century* (1925; rpt. New York, 1965), chap. vi, "The Uncertainties of Life."   25. *The Rhetorical World of Augustan Humanism: Ethics and Imagery from Swift to Burke* (Oxford, 1965), pp. 262–264. This Lockean statement justifies and almost describes the episodic novel: "Knowledge was assumed to result from the sequential accumulation of sense particulars collected from a multifarious but verifiable objective reality" (p. 263).   26. "It is of the essence of that century in which the novel came into its own that art should be seen as a representation rather than an illustration of life." See Robert Scholes and Robert Kellogg, *The Nature of Narrative* (New York, 1966), p. 87.

VOICES SONOROUS AND CRACKED
Sterne's Pulpit Oratory

Arthur Cash

WHEN Laurence Sterne doffed his cassock to put on motley, stepping down from the pulpit and up to the stage of the mountebank, when he gave up hawking the lessons of religion and morality and began to cry up the human comedy, the change of posture and style was easy for him. The difficulty lay with the audience.

> ——Why, 'tis a strange story! *Tristram.*
> ——Alas! Madam, had it been upon some melancholy lecture of the cross——the peace of meekness, or the contentment of resignation ——I had not been incommoded. . . . But as I never blot any thing out——let us use some honest means to get it out of our heads directly.
> ——Pray reach me my fool's cap——I fear you sit upon it, Madam——'tis under the cushion——I'll put it on——(p. 511)[1]

These dialogues with the auditors, the exhortations and apostrophes, the narrator's lifting and dropping the curtain upon a drama of life which, as he pretends, he did not create himself, are techniques forecast in Sterne's sermons. Shandyism, as Lansing Hammond said, was not born full-blown in 1759, but developed throughout Sterne's long career as writer and preacher of sermons.[2] John Traugott, who analyzed the rhetoric of *Tristram Shandy*, thought that Sterne owed the church a debt for permitting (or forcing) him to develop his personal rhetoric "through the forms of tradition."[3] James Downey suggested that Sterne learned the craft of digression in the pulpit.[4] The sermons even appear to have shaped the prose style of *Tristram Shandy*. At least we now know that Sterne's pretended "conversational" style is really only a facade. Eugene Hnatko points to the high incidence of anticipatory hypotaxis, suspension, and balance. Sterne brilliantly disguised what he was doing, argues Hnatko, but his syntax is oratorical and incantatory.[5] We are not jolted when Sterne, forgetting that he has made Tristram officially, so to speak, a rural squire, allows him to mention "the two bad cassocks I am worth in the world" (p. 179).

Rhetoric, however, was not a key word in Sterne's own mind. He thought about preaching in the terms of drama. Walter Shandy describes Yorick's sermon as "dramatic" (p. 141), and we know from an advertisement[6] that Sterne had originally intended to call his published sermons, *The Dramatick Sermons of Mr. Yorick*. He was fully aware that preaching was, not a literary, but a living art, that a dramatic sermon required a good actor. Late in his life, in Paris, Sterne saw the performance of an ideal pulpit actor, the Abbé Denis-Xavier Clément:

> his matter solid, and to the purpose; his manner, more than theatrical, and greater, both in his action and delivery, than Madame Clairon, who, you must know, is the Garrick of the stage here, . . . his pulpit, oblong, with three seats in it, into which he occasionally casts himself; goes on, then rises, by a gradation of four steps, each of which he profits by, as his discourse inclines him: in short, 'tis a stage, and the variety of his tones would make you imagine there were no less than five or six actors on it together. (*Letters*, 154–155)[7]

Sterne's narrative method in *Tristram Shandy* evolved directly and simply from his notion of a preacher-actor. He only changed the costume and the subject matter. He did add an inner stage and other actors who appear thereon, but he left the preacher-turned-Harlequin at the forefront, lecturing, teasing, and talking with the audience.

Moreover, when the narrator steps aside to lift the curtain of the inner stage, the episode is apt to be one in which the characters are orating—Trim reading a sermon, Squire Shandy's oration upon death, Uncle Toby's apologetical oration on war. The significance of these scenes lies less in dialogue and action than in the nuances of manner—the gesture, the flourish of a stick, the cast of a voice. These scenes came easily to Sterne because the activity of writing drew him back imaginatively into the pulpit. That habit of Sterne's is revealed by two instances of dramatic oratory in the novel when words came into Sterne's mind that he had used years before in his sermons. Walter Shandy has been lying on his bed of pain after hearing that the baby's nose was broken by Dr. Slop's obstetrical forceps. He rises to make a speech, assuming the attitude of Socrates as painted by Raphael, "holding fast his fore-finger betwixt his finger and his thumb": "When I reflect, brother *Toby*, upon MAN; and take a view of that dark side of him" (pp. 277–278), a paraphrase of the opening passages of Sterne's sermon, "Trust in God." Trim hears the news of Bobby's death: "Are we not here now . . . (striking the end of his stick perpendicularly upon the floor, so as to give an idea of health and stability)——and are we not——(dropping his hat upon the ground) gone! in a moment!" (p. 361). "We [are] not stocks and stones," he goes on, and the narrator, expounding upon his words, begins to quote from Sterne's sermon, "Worship" (*Sermons*, II, 345).[8]

I find it impossible to believe that this rhetorical-dramatic novel could have been written by a clergyman who had been a failure as a pulpit orator. That, however, is the prevailing opinion among scholars today. It is surely a mistaken opinion, and my purpose is to correct it.

Sterne's current reputation as a bad pulpit orator is traceable to a comment by that unconscionable anecdotist, John Croft. Croft's notion of historic truth and his sense of justice were distorted by a mean puritanism, and the anecdotes he sent to Caleb Whitefoord in 1795–1796 contain only a few personal recollections of Sterne dredged up from fifty years back. He was away at school most of the time that Sterne served as Vicar of Stillington, where Croft lived. At the age of fifteen he was sent to Portugal to learn the family wine business, and he did not return until shortly before Sterne died. Nevertheless we can hardly ignore his description; for Croft lived with his older brother, Stephen, one of Sterne's closest friends, he surely heard Sterne preach in the country, and he had at least one opportunity to hear him at York Minster—an occasion which probably lies behind his comment: "When it was Sterne's turn to preach at the Minster half of the Congregation usually went out of the Church as soon as he mounted the Pulpit, as his Delivery and Voice were so very disagreeable."[9]

Over against this we must set the recently discovered description of Sterne in the pulpit given by his parishioner of Sutton-on-the-Forest, Richard Greenwood. A humble man who never learned to read or write, Greenwood had nothing to gain or lose from his stories of Sterne except the sixpence he was offered for an interview by Joseph Hunter, an antiquarian whose scholarship is still admired. In his youth Greenwood had been Sterne's personal servant and frequently accompanied his master to York. He talked to Hunter primarily about personal recollections from that period (1742–1745). Some of his stories can be corroborated from other sources. We must respect this man's description of Sterne as a preacher: "When he preached the audience were quite delighted with him, & he never preached at Sutton but half the congregation were in tears—the Minster was crowded whenever it was known that he was to preach."[10]

The discrepancy in the two accounts can be explained: Greenwood was describing Sterne at the zenith of his success as a preacher, Croft at the nadir, probably in 1766. In short, my hypothesis is this. Despite the hemorrhages of the lungs which had recurred periodically since his college days, Sterne as a young man had a strong, sonorous voice. He was a very successful preacher, perhaps the best in the York area. But during the period of his novel writing, his tubercular throat and lungs were attacked by other diseases which left him only a weak, cracked voice. The sermons he preached thereafter were failures.

Sterne's success in the pulpit during his younger years is indicated most obviously by the very number of sermons he preached at York Minster. As Prebendary of North Newbald, he was responsible for only two of the eighty-eight sermons preached annually at the Minster,[11] but he seems to have done as many as a fifth or even a quarter during some of these years. In 1750 he wrote to Archdeacon Francis Blackburne, "my Daughter will be Twenty Pounds a Better Fortune by the Favors I've rec^d of this kind from the Dean & Residentiaries this Year" (*Letters*, 31)—in other words, twenty substitute sermons: the fee was one pound.[12] He may have exaggerated some, but not much, not to so knowledgeable a man as Blackburne. Certainly he got these opportunities in part because the two deans under whom he served, Richard Osbaldeston and John Fountayne, were friends. But that cannot explain everything. Other powerful churchmen were his enemies, notably his uncle, Dr. Jaques Sterne, precentor, residentiary, and archdeacon of the East Riding, who strongly objected to Sterne's appearing so often in that high pulpit. Sterne's friends could help him only because he was a good, popular preacher—as Greenwood said.

Even more significant are Sterne's invitations to preach for special occasions. We know about three of these during the early years, but I suspect there were more. We note that Parson Yorick in *Tristram Shandy* preached a visitation sermon, though we have no record of Sterne's preaching on such an occasion. The invitations Sterne received after he turned author—his sermon of 1760 "before the Judges" in London (*Letters*, p. 110) or the charity sermon of 1761 for the London Foundling Hospital (*Letters*, p. 134)—tell us little about his skill as a preacher. They indicate, rather, his fame. But why in 1747 should Sterne have been invited to preach on behalf of the Blue Coat School for poor boys and the Grey Coat School for girls, the most important annual charity sermon at York? He had no influence which might serve to pry open the pocketbooks of the gentry. Archbishop Thomas Herring had been asked to preach the sermon the year before, in part because he was famous and popular, but also in part because many of the wealthy people who attended were obliged to him or ambitious for his favor. Laurence Sterne was poor and without patronage or influence. He would have been asked for one reason only—his ability to deliver "a theologic flap upon the heart" (*Letters*, p. 134) which would open those purses.

The most important of these invitations amounted to the very highest compliment which could be paid to a preacher at York. In 1743 he was asked to do the sermon at the Minster for the enthronement of Archbishop Herring.[13] At that time, when he was less than thirty years old, Sterne must have had a strong voice. The dean and chapter would have anticipated a large gathering for such an important occasion and would have expected many people to sit or stand in the nave of the great cathedral.

The enthronement sermon was not well received—or so one surmises from the fact that it was not published. But the failure lay in Sterne's choice of a text, not in the writing or the delivery. As Kenneth Monkman has recently discovered, Sterne could not suppress his sense of comedy and chose a text which made a flippant allusion to the notorious late Archbishop Lancelot Blackburn and an audacious admonition to the new prelate: Genesis 4:7, "If thou doest well, shalt thou not be accepted? and if thou doest not well, sin lieth at the door."[14] That history may lie behind Sterne's description of Parson Yorick in *Tristram Shandy*, who was blown along by "life and whim, and *gaité de cœur*."

> With all this sail, poor *Yorick* carried not one ounce of
> ballast; he was utterly unpractised in the world; and, at

the age of twenty-six, knew just about as well how to steer
his course in it, as a romping, unsuspicious girl of thirteen:
So that upon his first setting out, the brisk gale of his spirits,
as you will imagine, ran him foul ten times in a day of some
body's tackling; and as the grave and more slow-paced
were oftenest in his way——you may likewise imagine,
'twas with such he had generally the ill luck to get the most
entangled. (pp. 25–26)

Four years later, when he did the charity sermon for the Blue
Coat and Grey Coat Schools, he kept his hilarity in check and
met with some success. The sermon was published—*The Case of
Elijah and the Widow of Zerephath, Consider'd* (1747). The considerable contribution which Sterne raised, £64, was noted as
far away as London. True, the archbishop had extracted a larger
amount the year before, but Herring was then at the height of
his popularity because of his leadership during the Jacobite rebellion. At least Sterne brought in more money than did the
archbishop's cousin the following year even though William
Herring had become chancellor of the diocese with influence
and power very nearly as great as that of the dean.[15]

In 1750 Sterne was invited to preach the sermon for the
summer assizes. From a social and polticial standpoint this was
the most important annual sermon at York, for it brought to
a close that period of judicial and political activity which engaged
so many gentry and nobility and ushered in the festivities of Race
Week. The judges, high sheriff, and gentlemen of the grand jury
requested Mr. Sterne to send this sermon to the press, which he
did. *The Abuses of Conscience*, 1750, is now famous for its re-
appearance, whole, in *Tristram Shandy*, read by Corporal Trim.

Sterne's delivery on these occasions may not have been so
theatrical as that of the Abbé Clément, but it must have been
dramatic. We have no comment about his preaching style in the
Minster from these early years, but there is a suggestive remark
made by John Wilkes in 1764. Wilkes may have heard Sterne
preach in London in 1760 or 1761. "His *action* will divert you,"
he wrote, trying to entice a friend to come hear Sterne, "and
you know that *action* is the first, second, third, &c parts of a great
orator."[16]

The sermons which survive seem to be those which Sterne
preached before genteel audiences, probably because he took the
time to write them out and tended to save them. He certainly
did not save all. It appears that he destroyed those which seemed

overly intellectualized. "Is it that we are like iron, and must first be heated before we can be wrought upon?" (*Sermons*, I, 319). He was proud that his published sermons came "more from the heart than the head" (*Sermons*, I, xlviii), and he had Parson Yorick in the novel destroy the visitation sermon because "it came from my head instead of my heart" (p. 317). Nevertheless, the surviving sermons, written for reasonably educated audiences, were probably among the most subdued that Sterne preached.

His most dramatic sermons were preached to rural congregations and never committed to paper except as notes. Few university-trained clerics other than Methodists could muster much enthusiasm for preaching to illiterate country folk. Sterne loved it. Sterne the clergyman was at his best among his rural flocks. His exceptional devotion to the religious education of the servants and children of Sutton is well known.[17] Scholars are less aware of that Sunday service at Stillington on 28 May 1749, during the black days of the cattle plague, when Sterne permitted his parish clerk to sing "a Psalm of my Own Making." Two stanzas will demonstrate its tenor:

> No Christian Bull or Cow they say
> But take it soon or sine,
> And it is Ten to one I lay,
> Good God take Care of Mine.

> For Lord thou know'st we are full poor
> So help us for thou can,
> And we will put our Trust no more
> In any Other Man.[18]

That service could have been performed only in a church where there was some understanding and sympathy between the parson and the people.

To the farmers and laborers of Sutton and Stillington, Sterne preached extempore, probably with spontaneous inflections and gestures. The effect was electric: "he never preached at Sutton but half the congregation were in tears [said Greenwood]. . . . He used often to preach nearly extempore—He had engaged to preach at Fa[r]lington a few miles from Sutton, & when there found he had forgot his sermon—he only asked for a bible, & composed a most excellent sermon which he delivered from a scrap of paper no bigger than his hand." Perhaps it was after a sermon such as this that an amusing thought popped into his head, a thought he later converted for use in his novel: Tristram protests that his is the most religious way of writing because "I begin with writing the first sentence——and trusting to Almighty God for the second" (p. 540). Certainly Sterne projected his delight in haranguing the country folk into Corporal Trim's spontaneous, ad-libbed declamation to the servants in the kitchen.

Sterne continued to enjoy rural preaching even after the first volumes of *Tristram Shandy* had appeared. In 1760 he moved to Coxwold to take charge of a third parish, to which he had been preferred by Lord Fauconberg. A letter, heretofore unknown, from Fauconberg's steward, Richard Chapman, describes Sterne's success among his new parishioners. Chapman wrote to his master in London on 20 July 1760: "I gave Your Lordship's Service to Mr Sterne, whose Doctrine, (tho Chiefly Extempory) takes so well amongs the Congregation that the Church can Scarce Contain the Number of People that appear every Sunday."[19] Sterne's rural eloquence was bringing to church virtually the entire parish.[20]

But Sterne was growing weaker, and the summer of 1760 may have been the last period in which he preached well. The one witness who left a comment about the Foundling Hospital sermon of May 1761 was not impressed.[21] The next month, back in Coxwold, he wrote to John Hall-Stevenson about his "miseries": "if God, for my consolation under them, had not poured forth the spirit of Shandeism into me, which will not suffer me to think two moments upon any grave subject, I would else, just now lay down and die——die——" (*Letters*, p. 139). His summer of 1761 is summed up in his letter to Lady Dacre: "Hard writing in the summer, together with preaching, which I have not the strength for, is ever fatal to me—but I cannot avoid the latter yet, and the former is too pleasurable to be given up—" (*Letters*, p. 150). When he went to London in November to publish the fifth and sixth volumes of his novel, he may have carried with him the virus disease which took many lives in the North Riding.[22] He managed to see the volumes through the press, and then he collapsed. "Indeed I am very ill, having broke a vessel in my lungs" (*Letters*, p. 150). Nursed back to life by his friend, the Rev. Dr. Henry Egerton, he wrote a memorandum to his wife, "In Case I should die abroad," and fled Death across the English Channel.

> Pray captain, quoth I, as I was going down into the cabin, is a man never overtaken by *Death* in this passage?

> Why, there is not time for a man to be sick in it, replied
> he——What a cursed lyar! for I am sick as a horse, quoth
> I, already. . . .
> Sick! sick! sick! sick!——. (*Tristram Shandy*, p. 481)

But Sterne would not give in, and as he traveled along he coaxed himself into believing he was better. He was furious with his companion for saying anything about his "mortified looks": "Phelps is a son of a Bitch for saying I was worse than when I left you," he scribbled to Henry Egerton, "for I am ten, nay 15 per Cent better."[23]

Sterne lost his voice that spring. He later told John Hall-Stevenson how in Paris he was struck down again: "I had the same accident I had at Cambridge, of breaking a vessel in my lungs. It happen'd in the night, and I bled the bed full. . . . I sent immediately for a surgeon to bleed me at both arms—this saved me, and with lying speechless three days I recovered" (*Letters*, p. 180). To his new Archbishop, Robert Hay Drummond, he wrote about his loss of voice: "I was unhappily myself attack'd with a fever, which has ended the worst way it could for me, in a *defluxion Poitrine* as the french Physicians call it—it is generally fatal to weak Lungs, so that I have lost in ten days all I have gain'd since I came here—& from a relaxation of my lungs have lost my voice entirely, that twill be much if I ever quite recover it—" (*Letters*, p. 164). He alluded to his voicelessness in Tristram's conversation with Eugenius about that "son of a whore," Death: "I have forty volumes to write, and forty thousand things to say and do . . . and as thou seest he has got me by the throat (for *Eugenius* could scarce hear me speak across the table)" (p. 480).

Although his sojourn in the south of France that winter put Sterne back on his feet, he still found himself unable to preach. He wrote the Archbishop again on 7 May 1763:

> in spring I shall return home, never, I fear, to be of service,
> at least as a preacher. I have preached too much, my Lord,
> already; and was my age to be computed either by the
> number of sermons I have preached, or the infirmities they
> have brought upon me, I might be truly said to have the
> claim of a *Miles emeritus*, and was there a Hotel des Invalides
> for the reception of such established upon any salutary
> plain betwixt here and Arabia Felix, I w^d beg your Grace's
> interest to help me into it—. (*Letters*, pp. 195–196)

It was not Sterne's nature to retire. He spent the rest of his years in feverish activity. He preached, however, only twice that we know of.

Returning toward England in the spring of 1764, he stopped off at Paris where he enjoyed some weeks with John Wilkes and other gay blades. One day, while playing at whist, he was surprised with an invitation from the newly appointed English ambassador, the Earl of Hertford, to preach the first sermon in his new Anglican chapel. The earl had recently taken over and refurbished the Hôtel de Lauraguais. Excessively proud of his new establishment, he delighted to show visitors about it. Sterne did preach at his chapel, and again the clerical jester showed, as he had years before when Sterne had preached at the enthronement of Archbishop Herring. Officially the text was II Kings 20:15 (*Sermons*, I, 269), but Sterne may have announced the spurious text which he recited in a letter, actually a paraphrase of verses 13, 15, and 17: "And Hezekiah said unto the Prophet, I have shewn them my vessels of gold, and my vessels of silver, and my wives and my concubines, and my boxes of ointment, and whatever I have in my house, have I shewn unto them: and the Prophet said unto Hezekiah, thou hast done very foolishly" (*Letters*, p. 219). But this time, surely, Sterne's joke succeeded. The chapel was full of rakes like Wilkes and freethinkers like David Hume, Diderot, and the Baron d'Holbach—"a concourse of all nations, and religions too," said Sterne (*Letters*, p. 212).

The chapel may have been small enough that Sterne could be heard, but he was still having difficulties with his weak voice. Wilkes was worried about it the day before the sermon, for in that letter I have already quoted in which he described Sterne's diverting "action," he also warned about Sterne's voice. He was writing to Jean-Baptiste Suard, the writer and student of English letters who later became a good friend of Sterne's: "If, for dear variety, you chuse a slice of the Church of England and of Tristram Shandy, I will carry you this morning to the Embassador's Chapel—Tho' you may not catch every word of Tristram." One suspects that Sterne was sorry later he had made the attempt. "The last sermon that I shall ever preach," he wrote that summer, "was preach'd at Paris" (*Letters*, p. 222).

Unfortunately Sterne did not persist in his resolution. He may have been in a particularly gay mood in August of 1766 when Race Week was in full swing. More people came that year than ever before. The gaming tables, entertainments, concerts, and balls at the Assembly Rooms were bright with the "splendid retinues" of the nobility, present in large numbers to attend the principal guest, Edward Augustus, Duke of York. Men usually found an easy companion in this younger brother of George III. Women found his coarse addresses troublesome. Sterne had known him for some years, and he may have enjoyed his company; it is hard to know. The duke was half Sterne's age, his wit was somewhat dull, but he was not devoid of sympathy. It is more likely that the duke enjoyed Sterne. It was he, probably, who requested a sermon from Mr. Sterne at the Minster service which would close the festivities. In any event, "On Sunday his Royal Highness went to the Minster, where he was received at the West Door by the Residentiary and Choir, the Lord Mayor, Recorder, and Aldermen, who usher'd him up to the Archbishop's Throne, where he heard an excellent Discourse from the Rev. Mr. Sterne." [24]

The duke did hear the discourse, I am sure, because he and Sterne faced each other from airy perches only about twenty-five feet apart. The archepiscopal throne and the pulpit both rose high above the benches and prebendal stalls in the choir. The officials, dignitaries, and honored guests who were seated in the choir may have strained to catch the weak, sick voice, but they heard most of the sermon.

The gentry of lower rank, the country squires with their ladies, the merchants and lesser clergy, as well as the *canaille* who had trailed in after them, had to content themselves with listening from the transept or the great nave. Among them, I suspect, was a gentleman recently returned from Portugal. Most could not see the preacher. Many would have been annoyed by the barely audible voice coming intermittently from beyond the screen. I am sure a good many left.

Who would have guessed that the spectral parson would outlive the plump and lusty young duke? His Royal Highness died at Monaco a year later. Laurence Sterne, though he survived him by only six months, managed to finish the final volume of *Tristram Shandy*, to fall wildly in love with Eliza Draper, and to write *A Sentimental Journey*. A quarter of a century later, the author of *A Dissertation on the Nature and Use of Wines*, the editor of *A Select Collection of the Beauties of Shakespeare*, and the compiler of a joke book called *Scrapeana* sat down to write some anecdotes for Caleb Whiteford—"am sorry to venture to pronounce, and dissent from the old Quodlibet de mortuis nil nisi bonum, that he was far from being a good man."

Notes

1. References to *Tristram Shandy* are to the James Aiken Work edition (New York, 1940).   2. *Laurence Sterne's "Sermons of Mr. Yorick"* (New Haven, 1948), p. 64.   3. *Tristram Shandy's World* (Berkeley, 1954), p. 106.   4. "Sterne's 'Theological Flap,'" *The Eighteenth-Century Pulpit* (Oxford, 1969). 5. "Sterne's Conversational Style," *The Winged Skull: Papers from the Laurence Sterne Bicentenary Conference*, ed. Arthur H. Cash and John M. Stedmond (Kent, Ohio, 1971), pp. 229–236.   6. *York Courant*, 4 March 1760.   7. References to *Letters* are to the edition of Lewis Perry Curtis (Oxford, 1935).   8. References to the *Sermons* are to the two volumes bound together and numbered vol. v in *Complete Works*, introduction by Wilbur L. Cross (New York, 1904).   9. *Whitefoord Papers*, ed. W. A. S. Hewins (1898), p. 231. The best account of John Croft is that of Robert Davies, *A Memoir of the York Press* (1868), pp. 307–310.

10. British Museum, Add. MSS. 24, 446ff., 26–27. James Kuist, who discovered the document, published it entire in "New Light on Sterne: An Old Man's Recollections of the Young Vicar," *PMLA*, LXXX (1965), 549–553.   11. Thomas Ellway, *Anthems: For Two, Three, Four, Five, Six, Seven, and Eight Voices* (1753).   12. Chapter Acts, York Minster Library, 1 March 1760.   13. *York Courant*, 14 June 1743.   14. Kenneth Monkman and J. C. T. Oates, "Towards a Sterne Bibliography," *The Winged Skull*, pp. 279–310.   15. *General Advertiser*, 25 April 1747, quoted by Cross, *Sermons*, I, xviii; *York Courant*, 1 April 1746 and 12 April 1748.   16. Quoted by Joel J. Gold, "Tristram Shandy at the Ambassador's Chapel," *PQ*, XLVIII (1969), 421–424.   17. S. L. Ollard, "Sterne as a Young Parish Priest," *TLS*, 18 March 1926, p. 217.   18. Thomas Beckwith Commonplace Book, York Minster Library, MS. Add. 40, f. 3ᵛ, discovered by Lewis P. Curtis and published by him in "Forged Letters of Laurence Sterne," *PMLA*, L (1935), 1076–1105.   19. I wish to thank Capt. and Mrs. V. M. Wombwell of Newburgh Priory for their kind permission to read and use the Chapman-Fauconberg correspondence.

20. There were 158 families in the parish (Archbishop Drummond's Visitation Papers, Borthwick Institute for Historical Research) and the Church of St. Michael will hold about 300 people. Not many of this congregation would have traveled from York or other towns to remote Coxwold only to hear the author of *Tristram Shandy* preach.   21. Charles Brietzcke, the Polish servant to the Duke of Grafton, wrote in his diary on 3 May, "At the Foundling to hear Dr. Sterne, the Author of Tristram Shandy, whose preaching, to me was as indifferent as his Writings are" (quoted by Emma Hailey, *N&Q*, cc, 1955, 443).   22. Chapman to Fauconberg, 1 November 1761, at Newburgh Priory.   23. Egerton MSS, AH 2237, Hertfordshire

County Record Office, reproduced by Arthur H. Cash, "Some New Sterne Letters," *TLS*, 8 April 1965, p. 284.   24. *York Courant*, 26 August 1766.

A STATE OF WARFARE
Some Aspects of Time and Chance in *Tristram Shandy*

Jean-Claude Sallé

IT is not surprising that the reader, entering Shandy Hall, should meet almost immediately that symbolic signpost, a "large house-clock." It stands there, on the back-stairs head, to warn the unwary that time in *Tristram Shandy* is a character in its own right. Anyone who attaches as much importance as Walter Shandy does to omens, signs, and influences, who dabbles as he does in astrology and takes steps to determine the future, must believe in the objective reality of time. Man's conflict with time and chance is dramatized both by Walter Shandy's attempts to make his son's life conform to a predetermined pattern and by the narrator's unavailing efforts to introduce order into his book. Inner duration and clock time are played off one against the other in a way which hypostatizes time into a malicious figure subjecting man to its whimsical rule. The defeats it inflicts on the human will seem to endow it with a will of its own.

Following a suggestion made by Addison in *Spectator* no. 94, Sterne believed in the relativity of duration, dependent on the individual consciousness: "I doubt not . . . but that by a *different conformation* of the Brain a Creature might be made to apprehend any given portion of time as longer or shorter in any proportion than it appears to us. Glasses can make an *inch* seem a *mile*. I leave it to future ages to invent a method for making a *minute* seem a *year*."[1] In fact, as we know, Sterne stole a march on future ages by using his newly invented temporal microscope in *Tristram Shandy*, deliberately stretching out time in order to examine phenomena which we usually fail to notice. As a naturalist might take a slow-motion picture of the growth of a plant, Sterne created a world moving slowly enough to enable the observer to study those intricate workings of cause and effect which escape detection in life by the very swiftness of their succession. He knew that human motives are as elusive as Locke's "cannon-bullet"[2] and can often be perceived only by the havoc they leave in their train. In the novel, at least, time loses its irreversibility, and the author can move backward to investigate at leisure the complex clusters of causes which combine to determine each moment of our lives. "This will not be explained the worse, for setting off, as I generally do, at a little distance from the subject."[3] It may be argued that, in doing so, the novelist is asserting his independence from the most frustrating of life's limitations: "The liberty that counts . . . is that of shifting oneself as one wishes in the world of the memory and the imagination."[4] Paradoxically the outcome of the narrator's investigations is that the human will, caught in a mesh of causes and accidents, is left with hardly any free play. The assumption which underlies *Tristram Shandy* is that no moment of experience can be understood properly if it is not related to the trains of causation whose convergence has brought it about. And thus the narrator's ambition is no less than to arrive at that perfect intelligibility which would result from a thorough knowledge of the sequence of cause and effect; Tristram's mind moves from the event to its causes, reaching far back into the past "to come at the first springs of the events [he] tells" (I, 21, 66). The undertaking is of course Quixotic, since the first cause fades in the distance as the explorer advances. No doubt Sterne satirizes here the complacent assurance of his fellow novelists; but he also moves beyond satire to the grim seriousness of great comedy. Human motives, brought under the temporal microscope, fade into a blur of indefinable accidents. Man's beliefs owe little to reason and much to chance associations and casual mixtures of emotions. Walter Shandy's behavior is never what could reasonably be expected, since it is subordinated to the minute chances of the moment (V, 24, 382). Man's fickle mind is but the picture of a rapidly changing and unpredictable world. "REASON is, half of it, SENSE" (VII, 13, 494). Microscopic scrutiny, far from eliminating chance, reveals a stubborn residue of uncertainty. The world of *Tristram Shandy*, in B. H. Lehman's phrase, is "contingency incarnate."[5]

It may be that the narrator's futile attempts to grasp the original cause are a dramatization of Locke's skeptical view of the mind. By pushing the principle of causality to an extreme, Sterne works it to death, and uses the tool of rationalism to show up the deficiencies of human reason. In the comic atmosphere of Shandy Hall, Locke's reasonable critique of reason turns into the humorous complaint of a disappointed rationalist, a disappointment

which occasionally flares up in outbursts of romantic impatience
at human finitude. The narrator's efforts to circumscribe contingency are constantly defeated and, though dismissed with a
shrug, his conclusions on the subject are consistently pessimistic.
Circumstances which, in a rational universe, should remain
inconsequential, in fact play a prominent part in the process of
causation. "But need I tell you, Sir, that the circumstances with
which every thing in this world is begirt, give every thing in this
world its size and shape;——and by tightening it, or relaxing it,
this way or that, make the thing to be, what it is——great——
little——good——bad——indifferent or not indifferent, just as
the case happens" (III, 2, 158). Life mischievously runs "opposite
to the natural workings of causes and effects," which "shews the
weakness and imbecility of human reason" (VIII, 5, 543). The
relation of cause and effect, which we lazily assume to be simple
and amenable to rational explanation, eludes the grasp of the
reflecting writer's mind because of its complexity; in actual life,
the pace of existence is so quick that it leaves us no leisure to reflect
upon its flight: "Melancholy account of the life of man! which
generally runs on in such a manner, as scarce to allow time to make
reflections which way it has gone."[6] Sterne the preacher and
Sterne the novelist are of a mind on this point. The characters in
Tristram Shandy find experience generally opaque.

Time plays them false by flowing too fast, and, in league with
chance and causation, by submitting them to the past whose
determining influence is a further cause of unreason. The past
contains the seeds of events, which, after a period of obscure
gestation, will burst into actuality. Like time-bombs, misfortunes
lie waiting patiently to have their effect: this affliction, says
Tristram, "might lye waiting till apt times and circumstances
should give it an opportunity to discharge its office" (I, 21, 66).
Thus events which, at the time when they occurred, seemed
rather trifling, turn out later to have caused lasting damage. For
time has the power to snatch events out of man's reach, and drop
them into the past where they become inaccessible, though they
still continue to exert an influence on the present. The ill effects of
the past can rarely be undone, and are mitigated only at the cost
of great effort. Sterne's awareness of the irreversibility of time is
expressed on the very first page of the book; man's destiny is cast
from the outset in an inflexible mold: the animal spirits "once
set a-going, whether right or wrong, 'tis not a halfpenny matter,
——away they go cluttering like hey-go-mad; and by treading

the same steps over and over again, they presently make a road
of it, as plain and as smooth as a garden-walk, which, when they
are once used to, the Devil himself sometimes shall not be able to
drive them off it" (I, 1, 5). A parallel passage, as every reader
knows, may be found in Locke's *Essay* (II, 33, 6), but the verbal
similarity merely serves to emphasize the difference in tone:
despite the superficial playfulness, Tristram takes the matter to
heart far more than the philosopher does. Hence the nightmarish
feeling of the importance of the first moment, the original cause;
from it, from the circumstances surrounding it, will spring an
endless chain of effects whose course defies man's desire to control
or correct it. Hence the importance of procreation and of birth.
"*Quanto id diligentius in liberis procreandis cavendum*" (VI, 33, 463).
For procreation is the moment when man first falls under the
dominion of time; not only is birth the origin of being-in-time,
but its importance for the "curious psychologist" is primordial:
within the bounds of the logic of Shandy Hall, much of the hero's
"fortune" could be explained if all the circumstances surrounding
his birth were known. Here again can be found Sterne's reductio
ad absurdum of the principle of causality; in this perspective,
man's origin becomes as mysterious as man's end; both escape
investigation, both fall outside the realm of logical reasoning—a
baffling circumstance for Mr. Shandy and Tristram, who are
constantly trying to apply logic to situations that lie outside its
jurisdiction. "Consider the beginnings and ends of things, the
greatest and the smallest, how they all conspire to baffle thee;—
and which way ever thou prosecutest thy enquiries,—what fresh
subjects of amazement, and what fresh reasons to believe there are
more yet behind which thou canst never comprehend."[7] The
conclusion we are invited to draw is bound to shake the assurance
of the staunchest rationalist.

Since the past has the upper hand over the present, time itself
is an element of irrationality, for chronological priority invests
occurrences and beliefs with an unjustifiable superiority (IV, 27,
322). The past's unfair advantage is that it *is* past, hence irrever-
sible, which inevitably curtails human freedom. Crushed between
the determining past and the deceptive, alluring future, the
present is so thin that an action can hardly be inserted in it side-
ways. Given to procrastination, the Shandean man is singularly
deficient in presence of mind, postponing endlessly the decisions
by which he could exercise some control over his destiny; for him
the present moment is never opportune. Thus he never regains

the advantage time has over him; the outside world always keeps the initiative; time's start enables it to dictate to man the whole course of his life. The Shandean hero never knows what he is doing at the present moment; the present eludes him in his ineffective efforts to grasp the meaning of the past. This helplessness is indeed that of a dreamer in a nightmarish world, conscious of the imminence of impending accidents, and yet unable to act in order to ward them off, since the rate at which his mind calculates is slower than the time in which they occur. For the sympathetic reader, Mr. Shandy's reckless disregard for clock time is a source of impatient concern. Sometimes, like children at a play, we want to warn him that, while he is fondly cherishing his hopes, the villain is near.

The enemy, of course, is already within the gates. In the minds of the Shandy brothers, memory and habit are a built-in mechanism of unreason, the breach through which time enters the psyche and conquers it from within. My uncle Toby is the first full-length study of a man whose life has lost its meaning, and who merely survives in order to recapture the excitement of his past. Originally Toby found in "Corporal *Trim's* project" (II, 5, 97) an answer to his desire to reconstitute the past in exact detail; for Toby is endowed with one of the tyrannical memories which run in the Shandy family. As he tries to communicate his past to others, more and more implements become necessary, since Toby assumes that by pinpointing every circumstance of the past he will cause it to rise and live again with its full original meaning— the closer the reproduction, the more meaningful the image of his own experience. The difficulties which assail him, as he tries to break down the barriers which their different pasts have erected between him and his listeners, seem to represent the tragic incommunicability of experience—a theme which runs through the parallel soliloquies which serve the Shandy brothers for conversation.

The triumph of Toby's past is revealed by his "associations," substituting automatic responses for intelligent reactions in the mind of this mild monomaniac. Indeed the past has become so compelling that reminiscence no longer suffices, and actual mimicking of his former life becomes indispensable to him; as soon as Trim's make-believe gives him the means—and the illusion—of transporting himself into his past at will, Toby's existence regains its intensity of feeling. Thus the insipid present is annihilated. Toby's "large map of the fortifications of . . . Namur," "pasted down upon a board" (II, 1, 83), which he carries about with him, might almost be regarded as a symbol of the burden of the past, just as its irrecoverable character is brought out by Toby's need of a cumbersome apparatus of mechanical aids. Seen in this light, Toby's campaigns might appear as a derisive comment on the futility of remembrance; they illustrate the paradoxical nature of past time, both irremediably vanished and able to tyrannize over the present.

Turning to Walter Shandy, we find the same obsessive dominance of the past, but (of course) with a greater self-consciousness. He suffers even more acutely from the family disease, a hypertrophy of memory. This faculty in him has precedence over all others. Since he spends most of his time in his study, his memory preys upon words and rhetorical notions, and especially on those whose quaintness makes them more attractive. In accordance with Locke's psychology, the jumble of heterogeneous ideas in Mr. Shandy's mind is linked together by chance associations; though irrational, these links are so strong that Mr. Shandy cannot pull at one of the threads without bringing out a whole tangled skein. When something happens to move him deeply, a set of these stored-up ideas is suddenly released, with such violence that the mind loses all control over them. "Philosophy has a fine saying for every thing.——For *Death* it has an entire set; the misery was, they all at once rushed into my father's head, that 'twas difficult to string them together, so as to make any thing of a consistent show out of them" (V, 3, 353). The past prevents Mr. Shandy from reacting naturally to present emotions. Indeed his mind has lost all freedom, paralyzed as it is by the cancerous growth of ingrained "notions," swallowing up mercilessly all other elements of the psyche. "It is the nature of an hypothesis, when once a man has conceived it, that it assimilates every thing to itself as proper nourishment; and, from the first moment of your begetting it, it generally grows the stronger by every thing you see, hear, read, or understand" (II, 19, 151). Not only does Mr. Shandy's learning warp his emotional life, but it bears with all its accumulated weight upon his mind, and leads him to misinterpret the present: "Dr. *Slop*'s presence, at that time, was no less problematical than the mode of it; tho', it is certain, one moment's reflection in my father might have solved it; . . . But my father's mind took unfortunately a wrong turn in the investigation" (II, 10, 108). His perverse bent of mind leads Mr.

Shandy to investigate the past in detail before reaching any conclusion, a peculiar necessity of his own nature, shared, as we have seen, by the narrator. These "investigations," like the writing of the *Tristra-poedia*, last so long that the conclusion is reached too late, when change has partly or wholly invalidated it. An obvious instance is Walter's dilemma over Aunt Dinah's legacy (IV, 31, 332). Unable to decide which of two equally ancient family traditions has had the longer claim upon him, Mr. Shandy finds himself in a quandary, out of which even the computation of future profits could not lead him. Never does he think of evaluating which of the two choices would be more expedient at the present moment. As usual, clock time interrupts the philosopher rudely, solving his dilemma for him by removing one of the possible choices. The Sternian hero is here seen in his characteristic attitude, one of abstract speculation which inhibits the will, and leads the mind away from action by involving it in an endless consideration of causes and effects; thus Mr. Shandy is constantly left behind by life, which recklessly ruins whole systems by its swift changes. Through the satire of learning appears the comic exposure of the limitations of human freedom.

Seen against the background of the temporal necessity reigning over Shandy Hall, the narrator's frequent boast that he acts on impulse (IV, 10, 281), that he disregards all "rules" (I, 4, 8), sounds like a vindication of the claims of free will. Whether intentional or not, a contrast is established between Tristram's spontaneity and Walter's "extreme exactness," "to which he was in truth a slave" (I, 4, 8). Impulse at least *seems* to initiate a train of events independently of antecedent causes; but this, as we know, is just another instance of self-deception, since impulse is largely conditioned by the circumstances of the moment. Walter's behavior is both mechanical and unpredictable ("There was that infinitude of oddities in him, and of chances along with it, by which handle he would take a thing,——it baffled, Sir, all calculations" (V, 24, 382) but even this unpredictability does not make him a free agent, since there exists, besides the iron rule of causation, a milder necessity of contingent circumstances. Sterne's intention, of course, is to remind us that the simple rules of causation do not apply in the mysterious realm of human motives, that we often misconstrue other people's behavior when we over-confidently attempt to trace the unknown causes of some ascertained effect. In this respect Sterne is the ancestor of Proust who wrote what sounds like a commentary on the incident of *"Phutatorius's*

chestnut": "la réalité, même si elle est nécessaire, n'est pas com-
plètement prévisible; ceux qui apprennent sur la vie d'un autre
quelque détail exact en tirent aussitôt des conséquences' qui ne le
sont pas et voient dans le fait nouvellement découvert l'explication
de choses qui précisément n'ont aucun rapport avec lui."[8]

In the time-dominated world of *Tristram Shandy* floats the
paralyzing sense of the futility of human intentions. Yorick falls
a victim to his noble neglect of small enmities and misunder-
standings which, accumulating in time, will eventually strike him
with their combined force. Nothing in the world happens as
Mr. Shandy desires it. The inmates of Shandy Hall, manipulated
by obscure forces, strive blindly for futile aims, finding satisfaction
in puerile entertainments; they discourse with downright seriousness on issues devoid of all practical foundation. In this parody of
philosophical inquiry, they betray their infinite capacity for self-
deception through their misuse of language. Reason is defeated
by reasonings which deceitfully claim kinship with it, clothed in
the absurdly rigorous logic of a misleading verbalism. But their
misfortunes are momentous only if considered in the light of
Walter Shandy's own system; his theories are so fantastic that his
worries seem trifles to the reader, and, thus transposed, the image
of man's condition presented by Sterne is essentially humorous.
Mr. Shandy's subjection to time is translated into the ludicrous
race he runs in Susannah's tracks, his inability to catch up with
time into the comic misadventure of the *Tristra-poedia*. But were
it not for Sterne's forgiving sympathy, *Tristram Shandy* would be
a pessimistic universe.

Presented in a humorous mode in Mr. Shandy's misfortunes,
the sadness of man's temporal condition appears in its fundamental
tragic tone in the narrator's own words. Though restrained, and
often shrugged off with a jest, Tristram's sense of the flight of time
is almost romantic in its acuteness. It is overtly expressed in the
last book when the narrator, wondering whether his work will
live after him, exclaims: "I will not argue the matter: Time wastes
too fast: every letter I trace tells me with what rapidity Life
follows my pen; the days and hours of it, more precious, my dear
Jenny! than the rubies about thy neck, are flying over our heads
like light clouds of a windy day, never to return more——"
(IX, 8, 610). This antedates Rousseau's musings by slightly more
than ten years: "Tout est dans un flux continuel sur la terre: rien

n'y garde une forme constante et arrêtée, et nos affections qui s'attachent aux choses extérieures passent et changent nécessairement comme elles."[9] But over against Tristram's open admission of dismay should be placed this exchange between Toby and Trim, "moralising" upon the Corporal's *Montero*-cap : " '*Nothing in this world, Trim, is made to last for ever.*'——But when tokens, dear *Tom*, of thy love and remembrance wear out, said *Trim*, what shall we say? There is no occasion, *Trim*, quoth my uncle *Toby*, to say any thing else" (VIII, 19, 560). This passage can serve to show how close Sterne was to romantic sensibility, at the same time as it makes the difference unmistakably clear: romantic feeling tempered by skeptical irony—a convenient definition, though perhaps over-neat.

Even if it is but an undertone, the theme of mutability can be heard throughout *Tristram Shandy*; it grows more insistent in the last five books. Man carries "the principles of change within [his] frame" (VII, 9, 490), and "eternally forego [es] [his] purposes, in the temperate act of pursuing them" (V, 16, 375). Notice that Sterne's pranks at time's expense are less elaborate in the final books; nor does he play with time in *A Sentimental Journey*; as if the joke had lost some of its fun as time's threat became more urgent. "La farcissure [des] exemples" betrays a courageously muted preoccupation with death, as Montaigne admits in his *Essais.*[10] To the same secret obsession may be attributed the narrator's insistence that he writes about dead characters, his wilful pricking of the bubbles of illusion which he so convincingly invests with the colors of life (VI, 25, 451).

Sterne's presentation of time in *Tristram Shandy* is thus twofold: the idea of the fragility of human existence is usually transposed into a humorous register, but the underlying pathetic note is also sounded by the narrator; in his shifts from self-pity to self-mockery appears the first stage of the attempt to turn an object of anxiety into one of laughter. The culmination of this process flashes forth in such triumphs of wit as the close of the *Tristra-poedia* episode: "drawing a sun-dial, for no better purpose than to be buried under ground" (V, 16, 375). Death may be the ultimate cause of futility, but words can keep it in its place.

Sterne was no doubt obsessed with mortality but found in writing a means of liberation. For him, as for John de la Casse, fencing off all the devils in hell, "the life of a writer . . . was not so

much a state of *composition*, as a state of *warfare*" (v, 16, 374). The
idea of transiency was what Sterne fought against, lifting it from
the plane of experience to the plane of contemplation. Hence
Sterne's voluntary confusion of life and art. "I perceive I shall lead
a fine life of it out of this self-same life of mine; or, in other words,
shall lead a couple of fine lives together" (IV, 13, 286). "I——I who
must be cut short in the midst of my days, and taste no more of
'em than what I borrow from my imagination" (VII, 14, 495). The
idea, if not the tone, is definitely romantic. The writer's creation
making up, by its intensity, for the brevity of life; the successful
completion of an artistic purpose restoring to significance a life
made meaningless by the "great catastrophe" (VII, 12, 492) of its
necessary end; the awful responsibility that this instrument of
salvation places upon the individual, whose efforts alone "can
save / Imagination from the sable charm / And dumb enchant-
ment";[11] the feverish anxiety taking hold of a mind who has
grasped only too vividly the meaning of *ars longa, vita brevis;* all
these are Keatsian themes. A striking parallel appears in the
Letters: "if I live but even three or four years, I will acquit myself
with honour," wrote Sterne to Hall-Stevenson.[12] And Keats to
Fanny Brawne: "if I had had time I would have made myself
remember'd."[13]

It is the successful transmutation of personal anguish into
comedy that distinguishes Sterne so sharply, not from Keats
whose courage matched his, but from our own age. If we turn to
Tristram Shandy with such relish, after two centuries, it is not so
much perhaps because of our fondness for ambiguity as because
the delicate balancing of pathos and comedy seems to be a lost art.
Hume confesses that, after demolishing the idea of substance, he
was able to go down to dinner with unimpaired appetite.[14] The
same moral elegance, or skepticism perhaps, enabled Sterne
"brilliantly [to maintain] his comic equilibrium."[15] And it may
be that the most valuable aspect of his work for our time is his
refusal to take himself seriously. Just as Sterne's technical in-
novations anticipate most modern experiments with the novel
form, many of his perplexities with time invite comparison with
the attitudes of Joyce or Beckett. Sterne's superiority over these
writers is that his insights into the mechanics of fiction are not
elaborated into a ponderous rationale, and that his acute ques-
tionings, when they lead him into a metaphysical impasse, are
met by my uncle Toby's quiet rejoinder: "There is no occasion
to say anything else."

Notes

1. Paul Stapfer, "Unpublished Fragment," *Laurence Sterne* (1870), p. xvii.   2. Locke, *An Essay concerning Human Understanding*, Bk. II, chap. 14, sec. 10.   3. Laurence Sterne, *The Life and Opinions of Tristram Shandy, Gentleman*, ed. James A. Work (New York, 1940), VI, 23, 449. All subsequent references to *Tristram Shandy* will appear in the text, noted by book, chapter, and page in this edition.   4. Jean-Jacques Mayoux, "Laurence Sterne," *Laurence Sterne: A Collection of Critical Essays*, ed. John Traugott (Englewood Cliffs, N.J., 1968), p. 119.   5. Benjamin H. Lehman, "Of Time, Personality, and the Author," *Laurence Sterne*, ed. Traugott, p. 24.   6. Sterne, *The Sermons of Mr. Yorick* (1775), pp. 155–156.   7. Sterne, *Sermons* (1769), III, 294–295, quoted by Alan D. McKillop, *The Early Masters of English Fiction* (Lawrence, Kans., 1956), p. 193.   8. Proust, *A la Recherche du Temps Perdu*, Bibliothèque de la Pléiade (Paris, 1954), III, 9–10.   9. Rousseau, "Cinquième Promenade," *Les Rêveries du Promeneur Solitaire, Oeuvres Complètes*, Bibliothèque de la Pléiade (Paris, 1959), I, 1046.

10. Montaigne, *Essais*, I, xx.   11. Keats, "The Fall of Hyperion," I, 9–11.   12. Sterne, *Letters*, ed. L. P. Curtis (Oxford, 1965), p. 390.   13. Keats, *Letters*, II, 263.   14. Hume, *A Treatise of Human Nature*, ed. L. A. Selby-Bigge (1888), Bk. I, pt. iv, sec. 7, p. 269.   15. McKillop, p. 218.

DISENCHANTING THE MAN
OF FEELING: Smollett's
Ferdinand Count Fathom

Thomas R. Preston

THE dominant critical view of *Ferdinand Count Fathom* is fairly well summarized in George Saintsbury's assertion that it "may be considered Smollett's least good novel."[1] This low opinion of *Fathom* derives, in part, from the assumption that it seeks to imitate Fielding's *Jonathan Wild*.[2] If such is the case, the novel is indeed a miserable failure, and only the patriotic Sir Walter Scott could prefer it to *Wild*.[3] Smollett, however, nowhere suggests he intended to follow Fielding's precedent of an ironically admirable anti-hero. As Saintsbury himself observes, Smollett's presentation of Fathom completely lacks the sustained ironical admiration that so characterizes *Wild*.[4] To the contrary, Smollett rather self-consciously represents his novel as the biography of a rogue treated as a rogue. In the preface, Smollett almost overemphasizes Fathom's villainy, and in the opening chapter the narrator goes out of his way to disagree with Cardinal de Retz's theory that histories should be autobiographical on the very grounds that autobiographers "are naturally partial to their own causes" (VIII, 6). Fathom would certainly not project himself in the lurid and true light the objective narrator will. Indeed, the narrator is so sensitive to Fathom's villainy that he often comments on it, even breaking into the narrative once, with great rhetorical flourish, to repent his writing the biography of such a miscreant (IX, 87).

Except for using the villain as hero, which practice Smollett carefully traces in the preface to the English stage villains of the Renaissance and not to Fielding, Smollett's presentation of Fathom contrasts with Fielding's presentation of Wild, and the repeated assertions of Fathom's villainy constitute direct rather than ironic satiric attacks. Smollett's overt insistence on this villainy suggests that the novel will come into clearer focus if

approached with its other main character in view, the benevolent
Renaldo. On the surface, as Saintsbury argues, Smollett uses
Renaldo as "a virtuous character in opposition to the adventurer."[5] Renaldo is doubtless opposed to Fathom, as Heartfree
is to Wild, and his benevolence receives high praise from the
narrator. But the purpose of this opposition is not to demonstrate
that virtue ultimately triumphs, as it does in the allegorical terms
of *Wild*,[6] but that to survive in the world virtue needs protection
against the wiles of the Fathoms and of society, which both
tolerates and encourages the Fathoms.[7] *Fathom* is, in fact, an
educational novel in which the virtuous man learns from the
villain that the world is a place of fraud and deceit calculated to
destroy virtuous men. The novel's structure derives less from the
tradition of rogue biography than from the eighteenth-century
tradition of the man of feeling.

The man of feeling emerged from the benevolist philosophy
of human nature that, arising during the Restoration, came to
dominate moral and literary thought during the second half of
the eighteenth century. Whether enunciated by Latitudinarian
divines or by secular moralists like Shaftesbury and Hutcheson,
Benevolism maintained that virtue consists in benevolence, that
the feelings of man are so constituted that he is "naturally"
inclined to act benevolently, and that acting benevolently is rewarded with pleasure.[8] In the words of Hutcheson, "Benevolence is our greatest Happiness."[9] Benevolism projected the man
of feeling as an ideal all men could supposedly realize with ease,
for the man of feeling was simply natural man. Benevolism also
prompted the sentimental idea that because man is "naturally"
good, he can be converted back to his "natural" state by intensive
exposure to benevolence in action. Moral discourses and literature informed by Benevolism often give way to such sentimentalism and depict the man of feeling as an exemplary character
to allure misguided men to the pleasures of virtue. Shaftesbury,
for example, in the *Characteristics*, urged the use of exemplary
characters, and Richardson, perhaps his most famous supporter,
argued for exemplary characters both in the practice of his novels
and in his preachments.[10] According to Richardson, "Lessons of
morality and disinterestedness, given by Example are far more
efficacious than those endeavoured to be inculcated by Precept,"
and again, "The Example of a beneficent spirit, gracefully exerted,
will awaken in others a capacity to enjoy the true pleasure that
arises from benevolent action." Contrary to Smollett's attitude

in *Fathom*, Richardson cries, "How happy are they who are set up for Examples, rather than Warnings!"[11]

Ironically, however, if Benevolism's claim that the man of feeling was natural man could lead to sentimentalism, it simultaneously made urgent the problem of how the man of feeling, exemplary though he may be, could survive without imposition in society, where, it was almost universally admitted, the majority of men seemed to live contrary to their nature. "It can serve no good Purpose," argues Bishop Sherlock, "to give Men a great Opinion of themselves and of the considerable Figure they make in the Universe; nor can it be done with Truth and Justice. Experience, which shews us daily our own and the Follies of those about us, will be too hard for Reasonings upon this Foot; and the Mind of Man, Conscious of its own Defects, will see through the Flattery, which ascribes to it Perfections and Excellences with which it feels itself to be unacquainted."[12] Shaftesbury himself asserted the paradox that society, though the natural state for expressing benevolent feelings, also works against their development. The moral "sense of right and wrong . . . being a first principle in our constitution and make," he argues, "there is no speculative opinion, persuasion, or belief, which is capable immediately or directly to exclude or destroy it. That which is of original and pure nature, nothing besides contrary habit and custom (a second nature) is able to displace."[13] This contrary "second nature" is acquired from society, "from the force of custom and education in opposition to Nature." In society "marks are set on men; distinctions formed; opinions decreed under the severest penalties; antipathies instilled, and aversions raised in men against the generality of their own species. So that 'tis hard to find in any region a human society which has human laws. No wonder if in such societies 'tis hard to find a man who lives naturally and as a man."[14]

Concern for the problem of the man of feeling living in an unfeeling world appears with almost monotonous regularity in nearly every form of mid and late eighteenth-century discourse, often emerging in the very midst of arguments that benevolence is natural to man. William Richardson's analysis of Hamlet's character symbolizes the ambivalent attitude the man of feeling generated. The virtuous man of feeling may represent natural man and he should attain happiness, but, Richardson argues, he is paradoxically unfit for the world as it is; his feeling will be rather "a fountain of bitter suffering, than of immediate pleasure."

Hamlet clearly exemplifies this thesis: "We love, we almost revere the character of Hamlet; and grieve for his sufferings. But we must at the same time confess, that his weaknesses, amiable weaknesses! are the cause of his disappointments and early death." Richardson, therefore, concludes that "the instruction to be gathered from this delineation is that persons like Hamlet should retire, or keep aloof, from situations of difficulty and contention: or endeavour, if they are forced to contend, to brace their minds, and acquire such vigour and determination of spirits as shall arm them against malignity."[15]

Being armed "against malignity" meant, in moral terms, that the man of feeling should acquire the virtue of prudence—not expediency or calculated self-interest, what the schoolmen called "carnal prudence,"[16] but the ability to perceive the evil designs of others and to exercise benevolence with discrimination. Even the early eighteenth-century benevolist Francis Hutcheson, whose works are primarily intended to promote the man of feeling, pauses nervously to note the need for prudence: "Our Reason can indeed discover certain Bounds, within which we may not only act from *Self-Love*, consistently with the *Good* of the *Whole*, but every Mortal's acting thus within these Bounds for his own *Good*, is absolutely necessary for the *Good* of the *Whole;* and the want of such *Self-Love* would be *universally pernicious.*"[17] As early as 1694, however, Francis Atterbury, the non-juring Bishop of Rochester, evidently disturbed at the rapid spread of Benevolism, pointed out the grave dangers surrounding the man of feeling.

> Charity is grafted always on Good-Nature, and a Sweetness of Disposition: which though it be a Temper of Mind very lovely and desirable; yet is it such as, in the Circumstances of our present Imperfect State, hath its Inconveniencies; and is what makes Conversation dangerous in a World, where we are surrounded with Temptations. . . . It makes us easy and yielding to Common Customs, and receiv'd Opinions; Ready to comply with a thousand things (of which we are not exactly well satisfied) upon the pure score of good Nature, and because we cannot allow ourselves to be troublesome. And being found and known to be of this easy and complying Temper; this very thing will invite Ill Spirits, and Ill men, to make their attempts upon us.[18]

During the mid century Fielding became one of the major expounders of prudent benevolence. Prudent benevolence is the theme of *Tom Jones*, for example, and is discursively defended in the *Enquiry into the Causes of the Late Increase of Robbers*, written three years after Fielding became a court magistrate:

> As it hath pleased God to permit human societies to be con-
> stituted in a different manner [from Plato's Utopia], and
> knaves to form a great part (a very considerable one, I am
> afraid) of every community, who are ever lying in wait to
> destroy and ensnare the honest part of mankind, and to
> betray them by means of their own goodness, it becomes
> the good-natured and tenderhearted man to be watchful
> over his own temper; to restrain the impetuosity of his
> benevolence, carefully to select objects of his passion, and
> not by too unbounded and indiscriminate an indulgence to
> give the reins to a courser which will infallibly carry him
> into the ambuscade of the enemy.

Fielding concludes his admonition to the man of feeling on a Christian note by alluding to Christ's warning that his disciples be as wise as serpents and as innocent as doves.[19]

Ferdinand Count Fathom dramatizes the man of feeling in need of disenchantment with the pleasing appearances of the world, in need of acquiring the wisdom of the serpent. It, indeed, sets forth one of the eighteenth-century's most comprehensive fictional cases for arming the man of feeling "against malignity." In the preface Smollett totally inverts the sentimental exemplary formula by appealing not to the alluring powers of virtue to deter vice, but to fear: "The impulses of fear, which is the most violent and interesting of all the passions, remain longer than any upon the memory; and for one that is allured to virtue, by the con-templation of that peace and happiness which it bestows, a hundred are deterred from the practice of vice, by that infamy and punishment to which it is liable, from the laws and regula-tions of mankind" (VIII, 3–4). The villain thus replaces the man of feeling as an exemplary character—and in Smollett's new formula he is exemplary for the man of feeling as well. "I de-clare," Smollett claims, "my purpose is to set him [Fathom] up as a beacon for the benefit of the unexperienced and unwary, who, from the perusal of these memoirs, may learn to avoid the manifold snares with which they are continually surrounded in the paths of life" (VIII, 4). Ironically, Smollett's inversion of the exemplary formula to include the man of feeling reintroduces Fielding again, for in carrying out this formula Smollett seems to have borrowed his structural pattern, some dominant imagery, and the various modes of deception Fathom employs from Fielding's most important nonfictional contribution to the prudent benevolence theme, *An Essay on the Knowledge of the Characters of Men.*[20]

Smollett's intended use of Fathom as a warning to men of feeling echoes Fielding's claim that in the *Essay* he seeks to expose hypocrisy and to "arm as well as I can, the honest, undesigning, open-hearted man, who is generally the prey of this monster, against it" (XII, 238). In the first paragraph of the *Essay* he reiterates this intention, lamenting the fact that many writers have expended their talents on works that assist the hypocrite while few or none have helped to arm the innocent (XIV, 281). Smollett's first allusion to Fielding's *Essay*, however, probably occurs in his title-page epigram:

> _____ Materiam risus, invenit ad omnes
> Occursus hominum. _____
> Ridebat curas, nec non et gaudia vulgi;
> Interdum et lachrymas fundebat. _____

Lewis Knapp translates the epigram as "Food for laughter he found in all his meetings with men. He laughed at the worries and even at the joy of the rabble; at the same time he shed tears." The first part of the epigram comes from the tenth satire of Juvenal, but Knapp can find no source for the concluding line.[21] That source is probably the *Essay*: "For admitting, that laughing at the vices and follies of mankind is entirely innocent (which is more, perhaps, than we ought to admit), yet, surely, their miseries and misfortunes are no subject of mirth; . . . the world is so full of them, that scarce a day passes without inclining a truly good-natured man rather to tears than merriment" (XIV, 286).

Borrowing Fielding's major comments on the evils and frauds of the world, Smollett translates them into dramatic action. Fielding claims that a determining principle for good or evil exists in everyone from childhood, even "in persons, who from the same education, etc., might be thought to have directed nature in the same way" (XIV, 282). Fielding, of course, displayed this belief in his contrasting portraits of Blifil and Tom Jones, and it turns up significantly in the early chapters of *Fathom* as the basic distinction between Ferdinand and Renaldo. While Renaldo was fated from infancy to benevolence, Ferdinand was "determined, ere he was yet twelve days old" to villainy (VIII, 10). This natural villainy is enhanced by the fact that before Fathom was thirteen months old, he had been taught to "suck brandy impregnated with gunpowder, through the touch-hole of a pistol" (VIII, 12).

Fielding warns that "while the crafty and designing part of mankind, consulting only their own separate advantage, endeavour to maintain one constant imposition on others, the whole world becomes a vast masquerade, where the greatest part appear disguised under false vizors and habits" (XIV, 283). Smollett seizes the masquerade metaphor for Ratchcali's rhapsody of England. London, Ratchcali exclaims to Ferdinand, "is a vast masquerade, in which a man of stratagem may wear a thousand different disguises, without danger of detection" (VIII, 203). Ratchcali's confidence that the two villains can impose upon the town without danger of detection probably alludes to Fielding's efforts to form an efficient police force. Ratchcali comes to his conclusion, based on an earlier statement that England is a paradise for frauds, because "so jealous are the natives of their liberties, that they will not bear the restraint of necessary *police*, and an able artist may enrich himself with their spoils, without running any risk of attracting the magistrate" (VIII, 202–203). Fielding had been appointed justice of the peace for Westminster in 1748 and was diligently organizing the London police force. The outbreak of crime in 1750 produced his essay, *An Enquiry into the Causes of the Late Increase of Robbers*, which appeared in 1751, two years before the publication of *Fathom*.

In Don Diego's first encounter with Fathom, Smollett dramatizes Fielding's comment on physiognomy as a revealer of character. Fielding believes that "the passions of men do commonly imprint sufficient marks on the countenance" to discern character, and "it is owing chiefly to want of skill in the observer that physiognomy is of so little use and credit in the world" (XIV, 284). Echoing the first part of Fielding's statement, Don Diego tells Fathom: "Indeed, I was at first sight prepossessed in your favour, for, notwithstanding the mistakes which men daily commit in judging from appearances, there is something in the physiognomy of a stranger from which one cannot help forming an opinion of his character and disposition" (VIII, 174–175). Don Diego confides to Fathom that "We live in such a world of wickedness and fraud, that a man cannot be too vigilant in his own defence" (VIII, 166), and then illustrates a "want of skill in the observer" by concluding, "For once, my penetration hath not failed me; your behaviour justifies my decision; you have treated me with that sympathy and respect which none but the generous will pay to the unfortunate" (VIII, 175). Don Diego is betrayed by Fathom precisely because of a failure of penetration, just as earlier he had failed to penetrate Renaldo beneath the disguise of a tutor.

Since "a more subtile hypocrisy will sometimes escape undiscovered from the highest discernment," Fielding offers a more "infallible guide" (XIV, 289), which is the judgment of men's actions instead of their words or their public reputation. Smollett capitalizes on Fielding's advice, for Fathom deceives the benevolent and innocent precisely because they accept either his word or his public reputation. Mademoiselle de Melvil's maid, Teresa, for example, enters into a collusion with Fathom to steal from her mistress, but she allows Fathom to seduce her only after he has made several pious oaths that he will be true to her (VIII, 39–40). Wilhelmina surrenders to Fathom, in the narrator's ironical words, "Without any other assurance, than his solemn profession of sincerity and truth" (VIII, 66). And since Fathom's public character is one of virtue, he goes unscathed most of the time, even when he is clearly guilty, as when Renaldo is blamed by his teacher and his father for Fathom's cheating (VIII, 25ff.). Renaldo, however, finds it difficult to learn from experience, for his benevolence overcomes his reason; he accepts the blame for cheating and then puts more confidence in Fathom than ever. Even late in the story, when Renaldo finds Fathom in prison, he "implicitly believed the story and protestations of Fathom" (IX, 23). Smollett underscores the irony of this naive faith when we learn that Fathom himself expected a violent rebuke (IX, 22), and a few pages later we discover that Renaldo had been summoned to the prison by a trick—once again the victim of "fraud and imposition" (IX, 25).

Fielding next lists the various characters whom the man of feeling should consider as potential hypocrites (XIV, 292ff.). A summary of the list with references to *Fathom* should sufficiently demonstrate Smollett's borrowings. The flatterer appears first, followed by the professor of friendship, the promiser, the pryer into secrets, the slanderer, and the saint. Fathom's use of the art of flattery needs little comment, for it is the basis of his ability, to use Fielding's words, of "obtaining our good opinion" (XIV, 291). Fathom is, of course, adept at professing friendship and promising his help, as illustrated in his "sincere" determination to help Renaldo obtain money to return to Hungary (IX, 61–70). As a slanderer, Fathom successfully separates Renaldo and Monimia (IX, 42ff.), and as a "saint" he is constantly offered to Renaldo "as a pattern and reproach" (VIII, 25). Count de Melvil sends Fathom with Renaldo into the world both as a companion and as a "preceptor and pattern" (VIII, 53). In effect, with this gallery of deceptive portraits, both Fielding and Smollett seek to disenchant the man of feeling with the world's false appearances and instill in him the perceptiveness that comes from prudence. Perhaps the most recurring words in the *Essay* are *perceive*, *discern*, and other synonyms for perceptiveness, and the pattern is repeated in *Fathom*. So pervasive is it that the faculty of perception is raised, on both the physical and spiritual levels, to symbolic status.[22]

Ironically, however, in *Fathom* all the men of feeling—Monimia, Don Diego, Count de Melvil, and Renaldo—are conspicuous for their lack of perception. Only the villains see the significance of perception, for it is they who "always keep the faculty of discerning in full exertion" (VIII, 56). Fathom takes Fielding's advice and studies the characters of men: "He dived into the characters of mankind, with a penetration peculiar to himself" (VIII, 36). Fathom "seldom or never erred in his observations on the human heart" (VIII, 125), for "He had studied mankind with incredible diligence, and knew perfectly well how far he could depend on the passions and foibles of human nature" (VIII, 180). Smollett never implies that completely accurate perception is always possible; Fathom, after all, "was calculated by nature to dupe even the most cautious" (VIII, 25). The narrator comments on the seduction of Elenor to this same point: "Had she been well seasoned with knowledge and experience, and completely armed with caution against the artifice and villainy of man, her virtue might not have been able to withstand the engines of such an assailant" (VIII, 194). At the same time, however, men of feeling have an inherent tendency to blind themselves with appearances of virtue.

Count Melvil, Renaldo's father, establishes the pattern of blindness Smollett sees in the man of feeling. He is completely deceived by the young Fathom's professions of filial devotion, for "being himself a man of extraordinary benevolence, [he] looked upon the boy as a prodigy of natural affection" (VIII, 21). The blindness, however, is communicated from one man of feeling to another. The Count advises Renaldo "to encourage every sentiment of candour and benevolence, and to behave with moderation and affability to all his fellow-creatures" (VIII, 28). Renaldo's benevolence needs little encouragement, but, ironically, his good deeds are soon misinterpreted. As the narrator shrewdly comments, "Nothing is more liable to misconstruction than an act of uncommon generosity; one half the world mistake the motive . . . and the rest suspect it of something sinister or selfish" (VIII, 29). Not only is the man of feeling's vision blind, it often fails to gain sight even from experience, as the scenes with Don Diego and Renaldo cited above suggest. Of all the men of feeling in the novel, only Madam Clement is enlightened, for she perceives Fathom's duplicity and saves Monimia from his clutches.

Against the background of Fielding's *Essay, Ferdinand Count Fathom* becomes, in effect, a problem or thesis novel, and the extremely black and white characters, the overcharged scenes of sensibility, and the elaborately formal, even stilted, style—all points usually held against it—suggest that Smollett is imposing something like a morality play structure on his familiar fictional world. His vision of the man of feeling's need for disenchantment seems to be cast in a quasi-allegorical and symbolic mold that instantiates character and sometimes action. Highly stylized, anaglyphic characters enact, in terms of the man of feeling, an almost archetypal struggle between good and evil against the grim background of a satirically heightened and intensified world.

Much of this symbolic intellectual drama arises from the religious imagery describing the principal characters and several of the notorious sentimental scenes. Renaldo, the man of feeling, for example, possesses "more than mortal goodness" (IX, 255), and Monimia, whose real name is significantly Serafina, stands out as an essentially redemptive figure; she is continually described as divine, celestial, and angelic. When separated from her, Renaldo, considering her a heavenly vision, trembles with "the infirmity of human nature, oppressed by the presence of a superior being" (IX, 203). The chapter relating Fathom's frustrated attempt to ravish Monimia is pointedly titled "Monimia's Honour Protected by the Interposition of Heaven" (IX, 77). Faced with her drawn sword, Fathom "was not so much affected by his bodily danger, as awe-struck at the manner of her address, and the appearance of her aspect, which seemed to shine with something supernatural" (IX, 79). Fathom himself is usually depicted by both the narrator and the other characters in satanic imagery. His birth is even somewhat diabolic, for his mother, a camp-follower, was thought to have "some supernatural quality inherent in her person" (VIII, 17), and, "though he first saw the light in Holland, he was not born till after the carriage arrived in Flanders" (VIII, 7). Wilhelmina, one of the first women he seduces, once mistakes him for Satan "in *propria persona*" (VIII, 71). He is continually described as the "devil incarnate" (VIII, 218), a serpent nourished in Renaldo's bosom (IX, 165), a "fiend in reality" (IX, 171), and a "venomous serpent" (IX, 199). The religious imagery and instantial representation carries over to the secondary characters also, particularly to the benevolent ones. Madam Clement, as her name indicates, personifies "clemency," while the Jew's benevolence is "more than human" (IX, 68).

The characters are instantial throughout the novel, but the scenes are not instantiated until roughly the last quarter of the narration, which traces the progression of Renaldo's disenchantment. The preceding action is no less symbolic, but the symbolism is rendered primarily through the more usual Smollettean form of satiric intensification. Smollett again frames his novel with the familiar travels, and in the first sections they serve to reveal a world that is little more than a Hobbesian battlefield. The celebrated opening battlefield scene, in which Fathom's mother robs the dead and wounded, may be cynical, but it also serves as a brilliant symbolic introduction to the Hobbesian world presented in most of the novel. In the time sequence of the novel, it precedes the idyllic paradise of Count de Melvil's home, where Fathom, the snake in the garden, grows up with Renaldo. Fathom's entrance into society immediately follows this pastoral interlude. Smollett's society is a metaphoric battlefield that is just as real as the battlefield of a literal war.

Fathom's "aim was to dwell among the tents of civil life, undisturbed by quarrels and the din of war" (VIII, 105). As Smollett's image suggests, Fathom wishes to exchange one kind of war for another. All his activities are described in military terms: he "reconnoitres" the ground, sets up "operations," "takes to" or "retreats from" the field. Even his seductions are viewed as military operations. Elenor, for example, "submitted to his desire; not with the reluctance of a vanquished people, but with the transports of a joyful city, that opens its gates to receive a darling prince returned from conquest" (VIII, 198). Moreover, society justifies Fathom's satiric view that it is a civil battlefield: "He had formerly imagined, but was now fully persuaded, that the sons of men preyed upon one another, and such was the end and condition of their being. Among the principal figures of life, he observed few or no characters that did not bear a strong analogy to the savage tyrants of the wood" (VIII, 54). This Swiftian vision is not limited to Fathom, who often functions as a satirist even while being satirized,[23] for the narrator editorializes often enough to indicate that he shares it. When, for example, Fathom achieves fame as a doctor through malpractice instead of ability, the narrator intrudes:

> Success raised upon such a foundation would, by a disciple of Plato, and some modern moralists, be ascribed to the innate virtue and generosity of the human heart, which naturally espouses the cause that needs protection. But I, whose notions of human excellence are not quite so sublime, am apt to believe it is owing to that spirit of self-conceit and contradiction, which is, at least, as universal, if not as natural, as the moral sense so warmly contended for by those ideal philosophers. (IX, 116–117)

This very Christian society, which exalts benevolence and admires men of feeling, refuses to aid the "benevolent" Renaldo, forcing him to resort to a Jew (IX, 62ff.), while it adds plumes to Fathom's character when he is brought to court by the Trapwells; it even receives him back as an equal member, consciously pretending he had been abroad, when he procures more money (VIII, 239–240; IX, 88).

The remarkable "Gothic" scenes in the storm-lashed forest and at the hut of the murderous peasant woman structurally reinforce the Hobbesian world in which Fathom thrives. The gloomy forest and the midnight terrors of the storm may foreshadow the trappings of the Gothic novel, but, for Smollett, they are more than mere decoration or intensification of the *surnaturel expliqué*. First of all, the scenes occur just after Ratchcali's robbery and desertion of Fathom and immediately precede Fathom's entrance into Hobbesian society. They thus unite the evil of Fathom's personal world to the evil of the larger world of man. Secondly, the terrors of the forest and of the old woman's hut are accurate foreshadowings of future evils, not merely the exploitations of emotional situations for their own sake; nor is there any question of the supernatural involved, for the old woman is not a witch or ethereal being, but a real murderess in collusion with a real band of robbers who plan to murder and rob Fathom. These two scenes, then, symbolize in miniature the

world Fathom will encounter and simultaneously recall the opening battlefield scene.

The last quarter of the novel drops Fathom and the satiric
scenes into the background and focuses on Renaldo's progressive
disenchantment with the world. The process of disenchantment
occurs in a rapid succession of what can best be described as
symbolic tableaux in which religious imagery rises to almost
unparalleled heights in Smollett. The disenchantment begins
when Renaldo's sister "removes the Film which had long ob-
structed his Penetration, with regard to Count Fathom" (IX,
158). Immediately following this revelation, Renaldo receives
the letter informing him of Monimia's supposed death, and,
like her, he falls into a fever, dies, and then revives—climaxing
a pattern of deaths and resurrections initiated by Monimia (who
does not "arise" until the last pages of the book), continued by
Renaldo's stepfather Count Trebasi, reechoed in Don Diego's
flashback relation of his supposed murder of his wife, daughter,
and Orlando (Renaldo in disguise), and concluded by Fathom
himself. Renaldo, however, is "reborn" with a hatred of Fathom
as excessive as his former love. But finally alerted to the reality
of evil, he gradually learns to transfer his hatred from the individual to mankind. After hearing Ratchcali's tale, he is "inspired . . . with great contempt for human nature. And next day
he proceeded on his journey with a heavy heart, ruminating on
the perfidy of mankind" (IX, 182). Almost immediately this
hatred is countered by Don Diego's reference to the honest
individual: " 'Praised be God,' said he, 'that virtue and generosity
are still to be found among the sons of men' " (IX, 184).

Monimia's "resurrection" in the tomb scene marks the re-
demption of the man of feeling from blindness. Renaldo's return
to England was originally conceived as "a pilgrimage to the dear
hallowed" tomb of Monimia and as an opportunity to take
"vengeance on the perfidious Fathom" (IX, 177), to sacrifice
him, in Major Farrel's words, "to the manes of the beauteous
Monimia" (IX, 175–176). But it is the "reborn" Monimia, the
"divine" Serafina, who completes Renaldo's enlightenment by
teaching him to transform vengeance into justice and then to
temper justice with mercy: always to keep the individual in
view. In Monimia's eyes, Fathom has already received both the
vengeance and justice of Heaven: "His fraud, ingratitude, and
villainy are, I believe, unrivalled; yet his base designs have been
defeated; and heaven perhaps hath made him the involuntary

instrument for bringing our constancy and virtue to the test. . . .
The doctor, who has traced him in all his conduct and vicissitudes
of fortune, will draw a picture of his present wretchedness, which,
I doubt not, will move your compassion" (IX, 227–228). Renaldo
finally agrees to see Fathom who, suddenly revived from a feverish delirium, thinks that he is "now arrived at the land of departed
souls, and that the shades of those whom he had so grievously
injured were come to see him tormented according to his de-
merits" (IX, 252). The whole scene in which Fathom repents and
converts, like that in Monimia's tomb, is obviously theatrical
and probably based on current theatrical practice.[24] But Fathom's
plea for mercy, set speech that it is, completes the imagery of
fear of divine justice: "Is there no mercy then for penitence? Is
there no pity due to the miseries I suffered upon earth? Save me,
O bountiful Heaven! from the terrors of everlasting woe; hide
me from these dreadful executioners, whose looks are torture"
(IX, 252). Fathom's Pauline decision to "work out . . . [his] salvation with fear and trembling" (IX, 256) seems valid in Smollett's
world for villain and man of feeling alike—but for different
reasons.

Fathom's conversion and repentance conclude the death-
rebirth symbolism and clarify Smollett's attitude towards the
man of feeling's uselessness as an exemplary character. In Smollett's world virtue, with perception, can and must combat and
restrain evil, but rarely will it deter those hesitating on "the brink
of iniquity" (VIII, 4) or convert those who have already made
the plunge. As Smollet argued in the preface, fear of secular and
ultimately of divine justice is a more assured moral persuader
than an exemplary character. Moreover, as the narrator observes,
Fathom might never have repented had he successfully evaded
the law and "remained without the verge of misfortune" (IX,
156). At the same time, the man of feeling's blindness makes him
unfit for the struggle with evil. Indeed, benevolent feeling can
be one of the principal causes for the success of hypocrisy in the
world. As Renaldo's sister finally tells him, "Nothing is more
easy . . . than to impose upon a person, who, being himself unconscious of guile, suspects no deceit. You have been a dupe,
dear brother, not to the finesse of Fathom, but to the sincerity
of your own heart" (IX, 162). In the narrator's terms, "All that
can be done by virtue, unassisted with experience, is to avoid
every trial with such a formidable foe, by declining and dis-
couraging the first advances towards a particular correspondence

with perfidious man, however agreeable it may seem to be. For there is no security but in conscious weakness" (VIII, 228).

Renaldo's triumph in the final section of the novel stands in ironic contrast to the opening scene of the battlefield and constitutes a "tonal bifurcation," as M. A. Goldberg contends, [25] only if Renaldo is accepted as a serious combatant against evil. Renaldo becomes disenchanted with Fathom and the pleasing appearances of the world, but it is too late to defeat Fathom. Nor are any of the other men of feeling ever responsible for Fathom's various downfalls. Fathom is often gulled, as Ronald Paulson notes, [26] and he certainly ends miserably, but it is extremely important to observe that he is always gulled and finally defeated by other sharpers—criminals whose faculty of discerning is keener than his own. He falls a victim to the machinations of the jeweller's wife (VIII, 95), Ratchcali (VIII, 114), Sir Stentor Stiles and Sir Giles (VIII, 149–150), Trapwell (VIII, 236ff.), Maurice and the lawyer (VIII, 248ff.), and finally Dr. Buffalo (IX, 138ff.). Fathom is usually superior to his fellow criminals "in point of genius and invention," but, as the narrator comments when Ratchcali deceives Fathom, they have "the advantage of him in the articles of age and experience" (VIII, 114). The irony of Fathom's various downfalls and of his final defeat, however, does not reside merely in the complete ineffectuality of the men of feeling; much of its pungency arises from the paradoxical legal injustice of his imprisonments. Fathom's crimes undoubtedly deserve legal action, but strikingly enough, whenever he is brought to trial or imprisoned, he is being punished for crimes he never committed. He is usually imprisoned for debt or because of the false accusations of people like the Muddys and Dr. Buffalo (IX, 128ff.). Fathom suffers for his crimes, but he suffers at the hands of villains greater than himself, not at the hands of justice. Indeed, in Smollett's Hobbesian world justice seems always to be at the mercy of fraud and deceit, although with grim irony it is served.

The novel, in a sense, ends where it began—on the battlefield. Renaldo and his friends have been disenchanted and Fathom has repented, but Smollett's Hobbesian society remains intact. Renaldo must even suspect Fathom's repentance, as Fielding advises in his *Essay*:

> I shall not here dispute the doctrine of repentance, any more than its tendency to the good of society; but as the actions

of men are the best index to their thoughts, as they do, if well attended to and understood, with the utmost certainty demonstrate the character; and as we are not so certain of the sincerity of repentance, I think we may with justice suspect, at least so far as to deny him our confidence, that a man whom we once knew to be a villain, remains a villain still. (XIV, 302)

Renaldo and the other men of feeling retain their benevolence, even for Fathom: "Though not one of them would say that such a miscreant ought to live, yet all concurred in approving the offices of humanity which had been performed" (IX, 253). At the same time, however, the now disenchanted Renaldo refuses Fathom any "office requiring integrity" and a resumption of personal friendship until there is "undoubted proof of amendment" (IX, 256). In the society Smollett depicts it is almost certain that a villain remains a villain still, and men of feeling enter that society at their peril if they lack the security of "conscious weakness."

Notes

1. *The Works of Tobias Smollett*, ed. George Saintsbury (Philadelphia, 1895–1903), VIII, xviii. All quotations from the novels are from this edition.   2. Even from the time of its first publication *Fathom* has been viewed as an imitation of *Wild*. See Lewis Knapp, *Tobias Smollett: Doctor of Men and Manners* (Princeton, 1949), pp. 318ff.; and M. A. Goldberg, *Smollett and the Scottish School* (Albuquerque, 1959), pp. 194ff.   3. *Lives of Eminent Novelists and Dramatists* (1887), p. 465.   4. *Works*, VIII, xiii.   5. Ibid.   6. See Alan Wendt, "The Moral Allegory of *Jonathan Wild*," *ELH*, XXIV (1957), 306–320.   7. Robert Spector discusses *Fathom* in terms of Iago. See *Tobias Smollett* (New York, 1968), pp. 87–106.   8. Classic treatment of Benevolism and the man of feeling will be found in R. S. Crane, "Suggestions towards a Genealogy of the 'Man of Feeling,'" *ELH*, I (1934), 205–230; Cecil A. Moore, "Shaftesbury and the Ethical Poets," in *Backgrounds of English Literature, 1700–1760* (Minneapolis, 1953); Ernest Tuveson, "The Importance of Shaftesbury," *ELH*, XX (1953), 267–299.   9. *An Inquiry into the Original of Our Ideas of Beauty and Virtue*, rev. ed. (1726), p. 196.

10. *An Inquiry Concerning Virtue or Merit*, in the *Characteristics*, ed. John M. Robertson (New York, 1964), I, 272. Fielding, of course, satirizes the exemplary character in the opening chapter of *Joseph Andrews*.   11. *A Collection of Moral and Instructive Sentiments, Maxims, Cautions, and Reflextions Contained in the Histories of Pamela, Clarissa, and Sir Charles Grandison* (1755),

p. 259.   12. *Several Discourses Preached at the Temple Church* (1764), Discourses XI, III, 312.   13. *Inquiry*, in the *Characteristics*, I, 260.   14. Ibid., pp. 261, 292.   15. *Essays on Shakespeare's Dramatic Characters*, 6th ed. (1818), pp. 76, 119–120.   16. See St. Thomas Aquinas, *Summa Theologica*, trans. Fathers of the Dominican Province, First Complete American Edition, 3 vols. (New York, 1947), II–II, Q. 55, A. 1–2. On the virtue of prudence itself, see II–II, Q. 47–52.   17. *Inquiry*, pp. 174–175.   18. "The Power of Charity to Cover Sin," in *Sermons and Discourses on Several Subjects and Occasions*, 5th ed. (1740), I, 61–62.   19. *Works of Henry Fielding*, ed. W. E. Henley (London, 1903), XIII, 110. For the use of the prudent benevolence theme by Fielding generally, see Henry Knight Miller, *Essays on Fielding's Miscellanies* (Princeton, 1961). For its use in the novels especially, see Eleanor Hutchens, "'Prudence' in *Tom Jones:* A Study of Connotative Irony," *PQ*, XXXIX (1960), 486–570; Glenn W. Hatfield, "The Serpent and the Dove: Fielding's Irony and the Prudence Theme of *Tom Jones*," *MP*, LXV (1967), 17–32; Martin Battestin, "Fielding's Definition of Wisdom: Some Functions of Ambiguity and Emblem in *Tom Jones*," *ELH*, XXXV (1968), 188–217.

20. All quotations are from the Henley edition.   21. Knapp, p. 304.   22. See, for example, VIII, 20–22, 26–27, 31, 35–39, 54, 56, 58, 63, 91, 97, 113, 119, 125, 150–151, 175, 178–179, 214, 218; IX, 29–31, 41–42, 46, 51, 64, 66, 76, 89, 109, 162.   23. On Fathom's use as both a satirist and an object of satire, see Ronald Paulson, *Satire and the Novel in Eighteenth-Century England* (New Haven, 1967), pp. 187–188, and his earlier essay, "Satire and the Early Novels of Smollett," *JEGP*, LIX (1960), 399–400.   24. For Smollett's use of theatrical conventions, see George M. Kahrl, "The Influence of Shakespeare on Smollett," *Parrott Presentation Volume*, ed. Hardin Craig (Princeton, 1935), pp. 399–420.   25. Goldberg, pp. 99ff.   26. *Satire and the Novel*, p. 188.

Notes on Contributors

JOHN ADEN is professor of English at Vanderbilt University. Educated at the University of Tennessee, Cornell, and the University of North Carolina at Chapel Hill, he is widely known as a teacher and scholar. Among his most recent publications are *The Critical Opinions of John Dryden* and *Something Like Horace*.

BENJAMIN BOYCE is professor emeritus of English at Duke University. He was educated at the University of Michigan and at Harvard; and he has taught at Northwestern University, the University of Omaha, and the University of Nebraska. In addition to numerous articles in scholarly journals, his publications include *Theophrastan Character in England to 1642*, *The Polemic Character, 1640–1661*, and *Character Sketches in Pope's Poems*.

ARTHUR H. CASH, with degrees from Chicago, Wisconsin, and Columbia, has been prominent in Sternean scholarship for over a decade. He was one of the organizers of the Bicentenary Conference on Laurence Sterne at the University of York in 1968, is a director of the Sterne Trust, and is now engaged in writing a biography of the novelist. He is professor of English at the State University College in New Paltz, New York.

LARRY S. CHAMPION is professor of English and chairman of the department at North Carolina State University. He has studied at Davidson College, the University of Virginia, and the University of North Carolina at Chapel Hill. Among his numerous articles are studies of Swift, Milton, Jonson, Shakespeare, Brontë, and Herbert. In addition he has published *The Evolution of Shakespeare's Comedy: A Study in Dramatic Perspective* and *Ben Jonson's "Dotages": A Reconsideration of the Late Plays*.

JAMES L. CLIFFORD, William Peterfield Trent professor emeritus of English at Columbia University and coeditor of the *Johnsonian Newsletter*, is one of the best-known figures in the field of eighteenth-century literature. Trained originally as an engineer, he left a manufacturing business to take a doctorate in English at Columbia University. His biography of Mrs. Thrale-Piozzi, his continuing publication of a definitive biography of Johnson, his bibliography of Johnsonian studies, and his editions of eighteenth-century studies have won for him a high reputation in this country and a fellowship in the Royal Society of Literature in England.

OLIVER FERGUSON, educated at Vanderbilt and the University of Illinois, is professor of English and chairman of the department at Duke University. He has held an international Rotary fellowship at the University of London, a Guggenheim fellowship, and a Huntington Library fellowship. His publications on Swift and Goldsmith are widely known.

J. PAUL HUNTER, who received his doctorate at Rice University and who has taught both on the east and west coasts, is professor of English at Emory University and is one of the most active of the younger scholars in the field of eighteenth-century fiction. His publications include numerous articles, an edition of *Moll Flanders*, and *The Reluctant Pilgrim: Defoe's Emblematic Method and Quest for Form in Robinson Crusoe.*

A. S. KNOWLES, JR., who has studied at the University of Virginia and the University of North Carolina at Chapel Hill, is associate professor of English at North Carolina State University. In 1967 Knowles was selected as alumni distinguished professor in recognition for excellence in teaching. In addition to his work as associate editor of *Southern Poetry Review*, he has published several articles on twentieth-century literature.

J. C. T. OATES, a graduate of Trinity College, Cambridge, is under-librarian in the Cambridge University Library, a fellow of Darwin College, president of the Bibliographical Society, and a former editor of *Library*. In addition to numerous articles in scholarly journals, he has published *A Catalogue of the Fifteenth-Century Printed Books in the University Library, Cambridge* and *Shandyism and Sentiment, 1760–1800.*

THOMAS R. PRESTON, educated at the University of Detroit and Rice University, has taught at Duquesne University, the University of Florida, and Loyola University at New Orleans.

Presently chairman of the Department of English at the University of Tennessee at Chattanooga, Preston has published *Christabel and the Mystical Tradition* and numerous articles on eighteenth-century literature in scholarly journals.

CLAUDE J. RAWSON, a graduate of Magdalen College, Oxford, and a former lecturer at the University of Hull, is now senior lecturer in English at the University of Warwick. He has published articles on Swift, Pope, and Fielding, and a critical volume on Fielding. He has lectured widely at universities in Malaysia, Australia, and the United States.

B. L. REID, who holds degrees from the University of Louisville, Columbia University, and the University of Virginia, has taught at Iowa State College, Smith, and Sweetbriar. Currently he is professor of English at Mount Holyoke College. In 1969 he was awarded the Pulitzer Prize for *The Man from New York: John Quinn and his Friends*. His essays have appeared in *Hudson Review*, *Sewanee Review*, and the *Virginia Quarterly*. The University of Georgia Press in 1969 published his *The Long Boy and Other Essays*. *Tragic Occasions* is his most recent book.

H. K. RUSSELL is professor emeritus of English at the University of North Carolina and a recipient of the Tanner Award for excellence in teaching at that university. In 1967 Russell was awarded an honorary D.Litt. degree from Davidson College. In addition to coediting *Literature in English*, he has published articles in *Studies in Philology* and *Modern Fiction Studies*.

JEAN-CLAUDE SALLÉ, a graduate of the Sorbonne, is senior lecturer in the Faculty of Letters at the University of Dijon and is a regular reviewer for the *Review of English Studies*. He was Fulbright fellow at the University of Pennsylvania in 1952. His articles on Sterne and Hazlitt have appeared in England.

ROBERT B. WHITE, JR., who received his doctorate from the University of North Carolina, is associate professor of English at North Carolina State University. He has previously published on the *Tatler* in *Philological Quarterly* and elsewhere, on Chaucer in the *Journal of English and Germanic Philology*, and on Milton in *Modern Philology*.

CALHOUN WINTON is best known as the author of the definitive biography of Sir Richard Steele in two volumes. Educated at the University of the South, Vanderbilt, and Princeton, he taught at Dartmouth, the University of Virginia, and the University of of Delaware before going to the University of South Carolina as professor of English and chairman of the English Department.

Index